The EVERYTHING®
Casino Gambling Book
SECOND EDITION

Dear Reader:

Casinos are theme parks for adults. Everything about them is designed to transport you far away from everyday life, for a few hours anyway. You can't be a slave to the clock in a casino; there aren't any clocks. You don't have to worry about the weather; there are no windows to show you what nature is up to on the outside. From the moment you arrive to the moment you leave, you are a Very Important Person, and everyone from the doorman to the beverage server to the casino host to the dealer focuses on your comfort and enjoyment.

I am but a casual gambler myself. When I go to the casino, I spend as much time watching the other players and taking in the grand, celebratory atmosphere as I do placing wagers. But I admit to feeling a sort of smug satisfaction at being "in the know" about the various games, and this knowledge adds to my enjoyment when I watch others play.

It is my hope that this book will allow you, too, to savor the feeling of being "in the know" the next time you find yourself on the gaming floor.

Meg Elaine Schneider

The EVERYTHING® Series

Editorial

Publishing Director	Gary M. Krebs
Managing Editor	Kate McBride
Copy Chief	Laura MacLaughlin
Acquisitions Editor	Kate Burgo
Development Editor	Karen Johnson Jacot
Production Editor	Jamie Wielgus

Production

Production Director	Susan Beale
Production Manager	Michelle Roy Kelly
Series Designers	Daria Perreault
	Colleen Cunningham
Cover Design	Paul Beatrice
	Frank Rivera
Layout and Graphics	Colleen Cunningham
	Rachael Eiben
	Michelle Roy Kelly
	John Paulhus
	Daria Perreault
	Erin Ring
Series Cover Artist	Barry Littmann
Interior Illustrations	Argosy

Visit the entire Everything® Series at www.everything.com

THE
EVERYTHING®
CASINO GAMBLING
BOOK

SECOND EDITION

Feel confident, have fun, and win big!

Meg Elaine Schneider

Adams Media
Avon, Massachusetts

To Bear
Someday I'll beat you at poker

Copyright ©2004, F+W Publications, Inc. All rights reserved.
This book, or parts thereof, may not be reproduced
in any form without permission from the publisher; exceptions
are made for brief excerpts used in published reviews.

An Everything® Series Book.
Everything® and everything.com® are registered trademarks of F+W Publications, Inc.

Published by Adams Media, an F+W Publications Company
57 Littlefield Street, Avon, MA 02322 U.S.A.
www.adamsmedia.com

ISBN: 1-59337-125-X
Printed in the United States of America.

J I H G F E D C

Library of Congress Cataloging-in-Publication Data
Schneider, Meg Elaine.
The everything casino gambling book / Meg Elaine Schneider.
p.   cm.
(An everything series book)
ISBN 1-59337-125-X
1. Gambling. 2. Gambling systems. 3. Casinos. I. Title. II. Series.
GV1301.S382   2004
795–dc22   2004008222

This book is available at quantity discounts for bulk purchases.
For information, call 1-800-872-5627.

Contents

Acknowledgments

This book never could have been completed without the help and support of Bud Schmunk, David Hollis, and the countless people who taught me both the rules and the nuances of various games; my agent, Barb Doyen; and my editor at Adams Media, Kate Burgo. Many thanks for your faith, encouragement, and practical advice.

Top Ten Ways
to Get the Most Out of Your Gambling Experience

1. Know the difference between games of chance and games of skill.

2. Understand the house edge on each game you play.

3. Study strategies for improving your chances of winning.

4. Practice to improve your skills.

5. Set a reasonable gambling budget and stick with it.

6. Establish goals for your winnings and limits for your losses.

7. Avoid sucker bets.

8. Don't let alcohol, fatigue, or other factors impair your judgment.

9. Know where to get help if you think you have a gambling problem.

10. Treat gambling as a recreational pastime and have fun with it.

Foreword

▶AS A WRITER, EDITOR, AND PUBLISHER in the gambling field for some thirty-five years, I have often been asked, "What is the secret to winning at gambling?" The answer is really quite simple, and, if you think about it, you will realize it is the same answer to any question regarding succeeding in life: available and usable information. The secret of this little book, which covers so many topics, is that the author presents the right kind of information. Of course, there is another way to profit from gambling not covered here, and that is to go to the biggest casino of all, the New York Stock Exchange, and invest in some of the many public companies that own and operate casinos.

This book provides not only the essential information for winning at those games that can be beaten, but also offers solid advice for those games that cannot be beaten, except by Lady Luck herself. Along with nuggets of valuable information, this book gives essential guidance for developing the proper attitude on handling yourself in the tempting and somewhat terrifying atmosphere of a public gambling establishment.

For those who develop a problem with gambling, there are references in this book to places where you can seek help. If you have difficulties with anyone in a public gaming hall, you will find guidance for lodging a complaint, if that is necessary.

When you have thoroughly digested this primer for beginners, there are reference sources listed for books, periodicals, and even Web sites where you can find much more detail as you find those games that grab your interest the most.

This book covers all of the classic games and gaming activities that you can participate in, in a public facility. A few of the games are relatively new and some are not played in every casino. Some of the new games, and many that are still seeking their public, will not be around in the distant future. Even the venerable slot machines of the past end up in collector's hands, as casinos seek out new and innovative games to attract a wider audience and improve their bottom line. At this moment in time, poker has captured the fancy of the public through the wide reach of television, and learning how to play correctly can result in life-changing winnings, like hitting the lottery or a megabucks slots jackpot.

Few activities in life provide the kinds of thrills that gaming does. Few moments are more exciting than playing a hot craps table, the homestretch run at the track, or the final minutes of a big football or basketball game—when you have some money on the result. Public gaming provides safe environments in a dangerous world, where you can escape the problems of ordinary living. There is only one danger in a casino . . . losing your money. This book will give you the best start on protecting your money and betting it wisely. Avoid the bets with a large house edge, ration your daily risk amounts, and don't let alcohol or other distractions keep you from playing your best game. If you stay within your own limits for acceptable losses and play the games that give you the best chance of winning, you will always find your gambling experiences fun and sometimes rewarding.

—Stanley Roberts

Introduction

▶ALTHOUGH WIDESPREAD LEGALIZED GAMBLING is a relatively recent phenomenon in the United States, humans have been gambling in one form or another for thousands of years. Ancient Egyptians played games with dice. The Hun Dynasty in China is credited with devising keno and using the proceeds to build the Great Wall. The earliest European explorers observed American Indians playing games of chance or betting on the outcome of games of skill.

But until just a few decades ago, Americans' gambling options were limited to the bright lights of Las Vegas, horse tracks, or the seamy underground of illegal betting. A handful of states had lotteries, and sometimes you could get hold of an Irish Sweepstakes ticket, but for the most part gambling was the milieu of only two kinds of people: wealthy Vegas high rollers and street hustlers who lured the naive into three-card monte or fixed craps games in dark alleys.

Today, legalized gambling is a $54 billion a year industry, employing about 1 million people and pumping hundreds of millions of dollars into the economy through payroll, vendor spending, and taxes. Americans today have more gambling options than our parents ever dreamed of, from instant scratch-off tickets at the corner convenience store to Vegas-style casinos that sprang up seemingly overnight in what used to be cornfields. No longer does the average American have to plan a trip to Las Vegas or Atlantic City to put his or her luck to the test. Gambling in one form or another is legal and available in every state except Hawaii and Utah.

Thirty-nine states and the District of Columbia have lotteries. Some states offer video lottery games in bars and restaurants, and others have added video lottery terminals—sometimes called "virtual slots"—to horse and dog racetracks, creating so-called "racinos." Several states have riverboat casinos, off-track betting parlors, high-stakes bingo halls, or full-fledged casinos owned by American Indian tribes.

Attitudes toward gambling have undergone a major shift as well. The occasional flutter at the slots, the blackjack table, or the racetrack is no longer widely considered even slightly wicked. Commercial casinos alone drew more than 51 million visitors in 2002, and according to a recent survey commissioned by the American Gaming Association, 85 percent of American adults think gambling is an acceptable activity for themselves and/or others. In fact, four of every five respondents view casino gambling as "a fun night out," the equivalent of going out to dinner or to the movies.

All the new gambling venues and the cornucopia of games they offer can make gambling in the twenty-first century a bewildering proposition for the novice. But armed with an understanding of how the games work, even the rawest gambler can be confident of enjoying the thrill of playing—and occasionally beating—the odds. Ⓔ

Chapter 1

What Are the Odds?

Gambling is a numbers game, whether you're playing with dice or cards or spinning a roulette wheel. The savvy player bases his or her wagers on knowledge of the game and an understanding of the odds for that game. Armed with this information, you can make better choices at the gaming table, bump up your win rate, and perhaps even turn an enjoyable pastime into a profitable hobby.

What the Odds Mean

Odds are a mathematical calculation of the likelihood of a given outcome. For example, when you toss a fair coin, there are two possible outcomes: the coin will land either heads up or tails up. The likelihood of it landing heads up is 1 in 2. If you wager that a coin will land heads up, you have a fifty-fifty chance of winning the bet.

Figuring out odds is a relatively simple proposition. All you need to know is the total number of possible outcomes. When you toss one coin, there are two possible outcomes. When you toss two coins, there are four possible outcomes: both will land heads up, both will land tails up, the first coin will land heads up and the second coin will land tails up, or the first coin will land tails up and the second coin will land heads up.

Calculating the Odds

The easiest way to calculate this when more than one item is involved is to figure out the possible outcomes for one item—the coin—and multiply the outcomes for each item. So, in our two-coin example, multiply the possible outcomes of one coin (2) by the total number of outcomes for the second coin (2) to get the total possible number of outcomes (4).

Consider rolling a pair of dice, for instance. Each die has six faces, so there are six possible outcomes when you roll one die. If you roll two dice, the number of possible outcomes grows to thirty-six ($6 \times 6 = 36$). If you roll three dice, you suddenly have 216 possible outcomes ($6 \times 6 = 36 \times 6 = 216$).

Outcomes and Probability

Once you figure out the possible outcomes, you can determine the probability of any one outcome or series of outcomes occurring. For example, in craps, you can bet that the dice will come up "any craps," which is a 2, a 3, or a 12. There is only one way to roll a 2 with a pair of dice, and there is only one way to roll a 12. But there are two ways to roll a 3: the first die comes up 1 and the second die comes up 2, or the first die comes up 2 and the second die comes up 1. Thus, there are four possible ways to roll a craps out of thirty-six possible combinations, and the probability of rolling a craps is expressed as a percentage: 4 (the number of possible craps combinations)/36 (the total possible combinations) = 1/9, or 11 percent.

FACT

In mathematics, probability is often expressed as a value between zero and one—0.42, for example. But most of us think of probability as a percentage, with an outcome more likely as its probability approaches 100 percent. To convert mathematical probability values to percentages, move the decimal point two places to the right. Thus, 0.42 becomes 42 percent.

You can use this formula to figure out the probability of virtually any outcome in virtually any game, and to figure out changes in probability. In a single-deck blackjack game, for example, the probability of drawing a given card changes according to how many cards have already been dealt and what those cards are. Suppose there are three players, plus the dealer, at the blackjack table. There are fifty-two cards in the deck, including four aces and sixteen cards that have a value of ten—the 10, jack, queen, and king of hearts, diamonds, spades, and clubs. Assuming you're the first player to receive a card, the odds of you getting an ace as your first card are 4 in 52, or about 7.5 percent (4/52 = .076 = 7.6 percent). The odds of you getting a 10-value card first are 16 in 52, or about 31 percent (16/52 = .307 = 30.7 percent).

The odds change after the first round of cards is dealt. We've got three players plus the dealer in our example, so the first round consists of four cards. Let's say those four cards are a 10, a king, an ace, and another king. Now, let's figure the odds for the second round. The deck now consists of forty-eight cards, including three aces and thirteen 10-value cards. The odds of getting an ace as your second card are now 3 in 48, or 6.25 percent (3/48 = .0625 = 6.25 percent). The odds of getting a 10-value card as your second card are 13 in 48, or 27 percent (13/48 = .270 = 27 percent).

Games of Chance

Games of chance are those where the outcome of each event is independent, like the flip of a coin. In casinos, roulette, craps, bingo, keno, and slots are games of chance; the result of a spin of the roulette wheel, a toss of the dice, the drawing of bingo or keno numbers, or one pull of a slot arm is not affected by anything that happened before, nor does it influence anything in the future. The odds of any given outcome in a game of chance are exactly the same every time.

That means, of course, that there's nothing you can do as a player to improve the odds of a specific outcome. In these games, the only way to "bet smart" is to place your bets based on the probability of a given outcome. In craps, for example, you know that the probability of the roller throwing a 2, 3, or 12 is about 11 percent; the probability of the roller tossing a 7, however, is about 17 percent.

ESSENTIAL

In games of chance, there will inevitably be streaks. Just as you can flip a coin ten times and end up with ten straight heads, you might encounter streaks of the same outcome in craps, roulette, keno, or bingo, where the same numbers seem to come up time after time. Don't be fooled into seeing a pattern in these streaks; they are just as random as the outcomes themselves.

Some casino card games also are games of chance, if they don't allow players to make any decisions that can improve their odds of winning. Casino war is a game of chance—you win or lose solely depending on how the cards turn up. Some experts consider three-card poker a game of skill, but chance plays a bigger role than skill; your odds of winning depend on the draw of the cards, and the only choice you can make is whether to fold or to play your hand against the dealer's hand. There's no skill involved beyond knowing how the hands are ranked in three-card poker.

The games of chance at most casinos are:

Money wheel (Big 6, Wheel of Fortune)
Baccarat
Craps
Roulette
Sic bo
Slots
Keno
Bingo
Casino war
Three-card poker

ALERT!

Don't be taken in by "sure-fire" systems to win at games of chance. Games of chance are random, independent events, and there is no such thing as a system to beat these games. The people hawking such schemes are making their money from naive gamblers, not from using their own "sure-fire" methods.

Games of Skill

In games of skill, your knowledge of and proficiency at the game can greatly influence your odds of winning. Blackjack and most variations of poker fall into this category, and the better you are at these games, the more likely you are to win in the long run. In blackjack, for example, understanding and following what is known as basic strategy can significantly improve your chances of leaving the table a winner. Likewise, your win rate at the poker table should improve as you gain experience, if you make wise choices when it comes to betting and deciding which hands to play and which to throw away.

Games of skill at the typical casino are:

Blackjack
Caribbean Stud poker
Pai Gow poker
Red Dog or Acey Deucy poker

Let It Ride poker
Video poker
Video blackjack
Horseracing
Sports betting

It should be noted that Caribbean Stud, Pai Gow, Red Dog, and Let It Ride poker involve less skill than the other games listed here. Knowledge of these games, your choices as a player, and the odds accompanying those choices can make you a better player and slightly improve your chances of winning. However, these games have house edges that most experts consider unbeatable over the long haul.

Horseracing and sports betting are games of skill because your level of knowledge and understanding directly influence your choices. The more you know about racing or sports, the more often you will make winning selections. If you rely on hunches and gut feelings, you're more likely to lose when you wager.

Classes of Gaming

In 1988, to clarify the rights of state governments and federally recognized American Indian tribal governments when it comes to gambling activities, Congress passed the Indian Gaming Regulatory Act, or IGRA. Among other things, IGRA divides gambling into three classes of games and sets out regulatory responsibilities for the tribal, state, and federal governments.

Class I Games

Class I games are described in IGRA as social or charitable games, such as bingo nights sponsored by churches or fire departments, where prizes have minimal value, and social, traditional; or ceremonial games conducted by tribes as part of their cultural activities. Many states have laws that limit charitable casino gaming in terms of admission fees, total prize pools, frequency, and other factors. Tribal Class I games are regulated by the tribes themselves; the states have no authority to restrict or regulate Class I tribal gaming.

Class II Games

Class II games are those in which you play against other players instead of against the house. Generally, there are no government-imposed limits on entry fees or prize pools. High-stakes bingo, poker clubs, and card rooms where the operator does not "bank" the games are all Class II operations. Pull-tabs and scratch-off tickets—especially these types of games offered at tribal gaming facilities or retail outlets—also are considered Class II games. At tribal gaming facilities, such as bingo halls and card rooms, the tribal government and the federal government are responsible for regulating and ensuring regulatory compliance of the games.

Class III Games

Class III games are all games that don't fit the definitions of Class I or Class II games. Typically, Class III games pit the player against the house, or casino operator. Blackjack is a Class III game because your opponent is the dealer, or the house. Poker is not Class III because your opponents are the other players; the dealer is simply an employee who facilitates the game.

Virtually all table games and slot machines in both bricks-and-mortar establishments and online casinos are Class III games and are subject to extensive regulation and oversight by various levels of government. Some electronic bingo games, which look like their slot machine cousins, are designated as Class II games because of the way the game is structured. But in most cases, slot machines—whether they're the traditional one-armed bandits or the new-fangled cashless gaming machines—are considered Class III games.

Tribal casinos are governed by legally binding agreements, called "compacts," between the state and tribal governments, with approval of the federal government. These compacts spell out everything from background checks and licensing requirements for employees to the way games are run, minimum payouts, and other minute details. As of this writing, there are 178 tribal-state gaming compacts in force in the United States, involving twenty-three states and 160 tribes.

Playing Against the House

Casinos and other gambling establishments are in business to make money. They do this by altering their payouts from true odds to casino odds, guaranteeing them a percentage of every wager. The difference between true odds and casino odds is called "the house edge" or "the house advantage"; it's also known as a "vigorish" or "vig." The house edge varies from game to game. It can be as low as 1.1 percent or as high as 40 percent, depending on the game and the type of bet.

Casino Odds Versus True Odds

Roulette offers a prime example of the difference between true odds and casino odds. On an American roulette wheel, there are thirty-eight pockets. The odds of any given number coming up on any given spin are 37 to 1. But when you bet on a given number, the casino only pays out 35 to 1 if you win.

Say you bet $1 on each number, for a total wager of $38. For the winning number, you'll be paid $35, plus you'll get your $1 back on that particular number, for a total of $36. So, even when you bet on every available number, you lose $2. That's the house edge: 2/38, or 5.26 percent—the difference between true odds and casino odds.

If this seems too abstract, imagine wagering on the flip of a coin. As discussed already, there are two possible outcomes—heads or tails—in a coin toss, so the probability for either one occurring is 50 percent. Let's say you bet $10 that the coin will land heads up. But instead of receiving even money—$10 in addition to your original $10 wager—you get only $9 for winning. The $1 difference is the house edge, in this case a healthy 10 percent for the house.

The chart on page 9 illustrates some typical house edges on common casino games.

Games of chance usually have the highest house edges. In land-based bingo games, for example, the prizes awarded usually total around 75 percent of the total money taken in; the house keeps the remaining 25 percent

Game	Type of Bet	House Edge
Baccarat	Banker	1.17 percent
Baccarat	Player	1.36 percent
Big 6	$1	11.11 percent
Big 6	$5 or $20	22.22 percent
Blackjack	Playing basic strategy	0.6 percent or lower(in a 6-deck game)
Caribbean Stud	—	5.22 percent
Casino war	Bet on ties	18.65 percent
Casino war	Surrender on ties	3.7 percent
Craps	Pass/Come	1.41 percent
Craps	Any craps	11.11 percent
Craps	Proposition bets	11.11 percent to 16.67 percent
Let It Ride	—	3.51 percent
Pai Gow	—	2.5 percent
Acey Deucy/Red Dog	—	2.69 percent
Roulette	Double-zero wheel	5.26 percent
Sic bo	—	2.78 percent to 47.22 percent
Slots	Nickels	15 percent*
Slots	Quarters	10 percent*
Slots	$1	8 percent*
Slots	$5	5 percent*
Three-card poker	Pair plus	2.32 percent
Three-card poker	Ante plus play	1.46 percent

* These are approximations only. Odds for slots may vary greatly according to the individual casino, the type of machine, and payout tables.
— Indicates that house edge is the same for any bet.

to cover expenses and profits. Keno also has a high house edge, typically paying out only 50 percent to 78 percent of what it takes in. In games of chance, you don't have much control over the house edge. The best you can do is try to shave the edge by learning which bets are most advantageous for you and avoiding the "sucker bets"—the wagers with overwhelmingly high house advantages.

Games of skill, like blackjack and many variations of poker, have lower house edges, usually around 5 percent, and savvy gamblers have more opportunities to trim that edge. Players who follow recommended playing strategies and money management techniques can reduce the house edge on these games to less than 1 percent or even turn the odds in their favor. Knowledge, skill, and discipline are every player's best weapons in fighting the house edge, whatever your game of choice may be.

ESSENTIAL

Payout odds are expressed as either "to" or "for." When the ratio is 3 *to* 1, that means you get your original wager back, plus triple that amount in winnings. When the ratio is 3 *for* 1, it means you get triple the amount you wagered, but you do not get your original wager back. In this case, your actual winnings are only two-thirds what they would be on a 3-to-1 bet.

House Edge Versus Hold

The house edge is not the same as the "hold." The hold is the percentage of money won from players by the casino, and this can vary wildly from day to day, and even from shift to shift. For illustration, suppose the casino sells $10,000 in chips during a twenty-four-hour period. At the end of that period, the casino has $5,000 in chips; the rest of the chips have been cashed in by players. In this case, the casino's hold is 50 percent.

The built-in house advantage on all types of wagers is designed to ensure that the casino always takes in more money than it pays out in winnings. No matter how well you play most games (blackjack and poker are exceptions), if you play long enough, the house edge will catch up with you, and the casino's hold is virtually assured. Fortunately for the casinos, relatively few players either follow recommended strategy or bother to understand the effects of the house edge. As a result, the casinos' real return—the amount players actually lose—can be ten times or more the expected return from the house edge.

Add-on Bets

Lots of popular casino games offer additional bets, ostensibly to add a little extra excitement to the action. In blackjack, the add-on is the insurance bet; in craps, it's the "crapless craps" bet; in American roulette, it's the five-number bet. The house edge for almost all add-on bets is high, sometimes absurdly so. The insurance bet in blackjack carries a house edge of about 6 percent. The tie bet in baccarat has a 14 percent house edge, and the side bet in Caribbean Stud poker has a house edge of more than 25 percent. Though these offerings seem to add some spice, experts recommend ignoring the gimmicks and concentrating on the game. The add-on bets are almost always sucker bets and should be avoided.

There seems to be a direct correlation between luck and skill, or knowledge, on the gaming floor. According to many experts, a large percentage of gambling losses can be attributed to poor playing decisions, poor execution of strategies, and failure to have a money management plan. The more you know about the games you play, the better prepared you are to "bet smart," and the more likely you are to go home a winner.

Playing Against Other Players

In games like poker, your money is matched against money from other players instead of against the casino's money. The casino or card room makes its profit by taking a percentage of the pot, called the "rake." Pari-mutuel systems, like those used in horse and dog racing, also pool the wagers of all bettors; the track or betting parlor takes a cut from the pooled bets to cover its expenses and profit, and divides the remainder among the winners. Other games in which you compete against other gamblers rather than the house include bingo, keno, and state lotteries.

There is no house edge to consider when your opponents are other players. Instead, your level of skill and experience—as well as some luck—determine your win rate. Because the house takes the rake from the total pot, in which all the players' money is pooled, you can think of it as a service fee for the house. The house is hosting the game, providing space, equipment, and personnel, and you and the other players are paying the house for that service.

Chapter 2

Keno

Some serious gamblers turn up their noses at keno, disdainful of its high house edge, the lack of skill involved, and its relatively slow pace. But for those who are looking for a relaxing game of chance that requires little study, no practice, and a small wager, while offering the potential for a large payout, keno is just the ticket. Like playing the lottery or buying scratch-off tickets, keno can provide a good hour or two of entertainment without breaking your budget.

History of Keno

Keno is one of the oldest documented games of chance in human history. According to ancient writings, the game was invented around 200 B.C. by a Chinese warlord named Cheung Leung. His city had been at war for many years; his army was running out of supplies and armament, and the city treasury was virtually empty. Residents of the city, weary of the long years of violent conflict, refused to contribute any more to the war effort. Desperate to raise money, Cheung Leung created a game of chance wherein people could select characters from the Chinese alphabet and win money if their character was pulled in a random drawing. This new game was so popular that Cheung Leung was able to raise more than enough money to supply his army, and the city was saved from financial and military ruin.

FACT

Cheung Leung's game became known as the "white pigeon game" because carrier pigeons were used to communicate the results of the drawings among far-flung cities and villages. The game gained such widespread popularity that its proceeds paid for the construction of the Great Wall of China.

In the mid-1800s, Chinese immigrants who flocked to the United States to help build railroads in the West brought their age-old game with them, and it became known as "Chinese lottery." For years, though it was illegal under U.S. antigambling laws, the Chinese-American community kept the game alive. At some point, probably to make the game more enticing to non-Chinese, the field of Chinese characters was replaced with a field of numbers, and people chose which numbers they thought would be pulled in the drawing.

When Nevada legalized gambling in 1931, the law still barred lotteries. But the new gambling halls recognized the potentially huge profitability of Chinese lottery, so to get around the prohibition, they changed the name of the game to "horserace keno." Under this new name, the numbers ostensibly represented horses, and gamblers bet on which horse would win the "race"—that is, which number or numbers would be pulled. Eventually, when lotteries were legalized, the game's name was shortened to "keno." But the "horserace" association persists even today. Most casinos refer to individual drawings as "races," and if you play more than one game with the same numbers, you are said to be playing a "multirace" ticket.

The Object of Keno

Keno may be the most familiar game in the casino because it so closely resembles the state lotteries that many people play. The object of keno is to choose one or more numbers out of a field of 1 to 80 that match the numbers drawn during a race or a series of races. Payouts are determined by a number of factors, including how many of your numbers match the drawn numbers, how much you wagered, and whether you wagered for the regular rate or a special rate. Keno is strictly a game of chance, which means there is no particular strategy or method of play that will affect the odds of winning.

How to Play Keno

If you've ever played a state lottery, you know how to play keno. In fact, the numbers game known as "lottery" is based on keno, although there are some differences between the modern versions of these two games. In lottery, you choose a fixed set of numbers to play—five numbers plus a bonus number, for example—and that fixed set must be the same as the set of numbers pulled in the drawing. To win the jackpot, you have to match every number in the drawing.

In keno, you can choose how many numbers you want to play in a given game, usually between one and fifteen numbers. Each keno race pulls twenty numbers, and you only have to match fifteen of the twenty numbers drawn to win the jackpot. As with the lottery, the thrill of keno lies in the possibility of winning a huge, life-changing sum of money in exchange for a nominal wager. It's not uncommon for keno jackpots to be in the tens of thousands of dollars.

The Internal Revenue Service requires casinos to file a W2-G form—the form on which gambling winnings are reported—on all net keno winnings of $1,500 or more. You'll have to provide two forms of identification to the casino, usually a driver's license and social security card. If you don't have identification with you, the casino will probably withhold federal income taxes from your winnings.

You also can win smaller amounts by matching fewer of the numbers drawn. Payout schedules vary from casino to casino, but at some places you can even win your wager back by matching none of the drawn numbers. These are called "special pay rates," and they may not be available at all keno lounges. Check your casino's keno brochure or ask keno personnel.

The Keno Ticket

The keno ticket is a piece of paper with two blocks of forty numbers each—1 through 40 on the top half of the ticket, and 41 through 80 on the bottom half. To select your numbers, simply mark them with an "X" on the ticket.

At the top or along the side of the ticket are areas for you to indicate your wager per game, how many games you want to play, and the total wager for the ticket. If you want to play the same numbers for five games and you want to bet $1 per game, for instance, the total wager for the ticket will be $5.

Also at the top or side of the ticket is a box to indicate how many numbers, or "spots," you want to play. If you play four numbers, it's called a "four-spot ticket"; if you play ten numbers, it's called a "ten-spot ticket." You also indicate here whether you want to play combinations of numbers (explained in the following section) or special rates, if these are available at your casino.

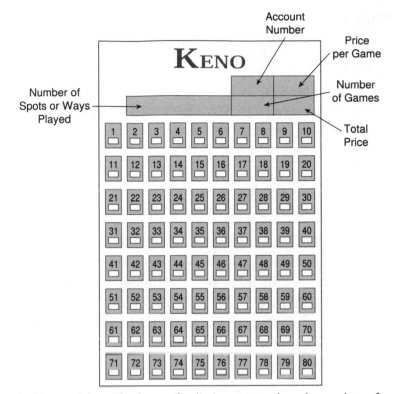

▲ A typical keno ticket. The boxes for listing spots played, number of games, etc., may be on the top of the ticket as shown here or down one side, usually to the right. Some tickets don't label the area but simply provide a blank area for you to note your choices.

Keno Lounges

Keno lounges provide supplies of tickets, black crayons for marking, and brochures explaining rules, payouts and special rates, or betting options. These lounges usually have rows of seats facing the keno counter, with small desktops on the arms with the supplies you'll need and a place to set a drink. A large LED board behind or to the side of the keno counter displays the current game number and lights up the numbers as they are drawn. The last number drawn in a given game will usually flash several times to alert players that the game is over.

Keno Runners

Virtually every casino has keno runners who roam the property to collect tickets and wagers from patrons who are playing other games or sitting in the restaurant or coffee shop. You fill out your ticket the same way you would at the keno lounge. The keno runner takes the ticket and your money to a keno writer to place your bet, then returns to you with a computer-generated ticket that shows which numbers you have selected and which games your numbers are good for. Monitors around the casino—either smaller versions of the board in the keno lounge or television screens—let you track which game is being played and which numbers have been drawn.

Always check the ticket you receive from the keno operator for the correct wager, game or series of games, and numbers selected. Most casinos have a policy absolving them of responsibility for incorrectly entered tickets, so it's up to you to make sure you're getting what you asked for.

The Catch

Any number you match is called a "catch." Rules vary on how many catches you need to win any money, and the number of catches is usually tied to how many numbers you select. For example, if you play fifteen numbers, you usually have to catch six to win any money. If you play six numbers, you have to catch three to win your wager back. Sometimes on special games, you can win your money back even if you don't catch any numbers. Check the keno brochure or ask keno personnel for the house's payout rules.

Selecting Your Numbers

Keno, like the lottery, is a game of pure chance. Any given number in any given race has the same chance of being drawn, no matter what happened in the drawing before. The odds of, for example, the number 5 being drawn in this game are 79 to 1, and theoretically those are the odds of the number 5 being drawn in the next game.

However, mathematical purists will note that computer programs to generate random numbers—which is how most keno games are operated—sometimes have flaws that skew the actual results. But the average bettor should assume each number is indeed randomly drawn. Operate from this assumption, and you can view keno as an entertaining way to pass the time without succumbing to wild (and baseless) theories of probability.

FACT

Some keno experts advise you to play fewer numbers because the likelihood of catching two numbers out of twenty is better than that of catching four numbers out of twenty. While this is true, keep in mind that payouts are proportionally smaller the fewer numbers you play.

When you play keno, you should play whatever numbers you like, based on whatever rationale you like. For example, you might want to play the birthdays of everyone in your family, or the number of pets you have, or the number of letters in your first and last names.

Some people like to play the numbers that came up in the last game, because sometimes it seems as though one or two numbers keep turning up in consecutive games. Others like to play back-to-back numbers, such as 4 and 5 or 42 and 43, because it seems that consecutive pairs are drawn fairly regularly. Choose whatever pattern appeals to you, but remember that the probability of any given number being drawn in any given game is exactly the same each and every time.

Single Games and Multirace Games

At most casinos, you must claim your winnings on an individual game before the next game begins. Usually you have about five minutes between the end of one game and the beginning of the next. If you don't turn your winning ticket in on time, you forfeit any winnings you might have had.

Because many casino patrons don't want to spend their time standing in line for individual keno race tickets, most casinos offer multirace tickets. You have to play the same numbers for a series of consecutive games, usually between two and twenty races, and usually you can't claim any winnings until the last race in your series is finished. You also pay at least the minimum for each race. On a $1 game, you'll pay $20 for a twenty-race ticket; on a $5 game, you'll pay $100 for a twenty-race ticket. As with the individual games, you may have to claim your winnings immediately after the last race in your series ends. Check with keno personnel to find out what the casino's policy is.

ESSENTIAL

If you don't want to sit in the keno lounge to keep track of the game and claim your winnings immediately, play a multirace ticket instead. This gives you time to explore other areas of the casino before returning to the keno lounge to see whether you've won.

Most casinos also offer something called "walk away keno," "play and stray keno," or "keno to go." With this option, you play the same numbers on twenty-one games or more—up to as many as 999 games—and you usually have up to a year to claim any winnings. So, for example, you could go to the casino in March, buy a ticket for fifty keno races, go home, return to the casino at Thanksgiving, then turn in your ticket at the keno counter and collect any winnings you might have earned from the March races. Check with keno personnel for your casino's rules on this option.

How to Bet Keno

Casinos have developed different ways to place wagers on keno to add variety and interest to the game. These variations have virtually no effect on your odds of winning any given race, but they do give you more bang for your buck, because there are several ways to win at least *some* money. Also, many of the variations allow you to bet less than the straight minimum, so they can be a good way to stretch your gambling dollar.

Straight Bets

A straight keno ticket is just like a lottery ticket. You pick the individual numbers you want to play and wait to see whether you catch any in the drawing. You can play as many numbers as you like, up to the casino's maximum, usually fifteen. You might be able to play more numbers at some casinos or on special games, but no matter what the player's limit is, only twenty numbers are drawn in a keno race.

On straight tickets, you must place at least the minimum wager for each race. The minimum bet can range from seventy cents to $2, depending on the casino. The keno brochure will tell you what the minimum and maximum wagers are.

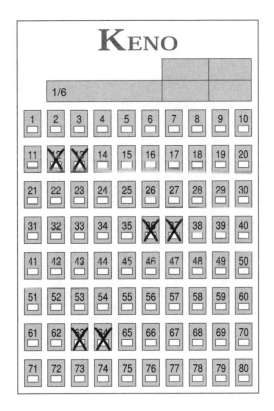

◀ This is a one-way, six-spot ticket, written 1/6.

Way Bets

Way tickets group the numbers you've selected into sets, which gives you more ways to win—hence the name. If you select six numbers, you can separate those six numbers into three groups of two numbers each. This gives you four different ways to win: a straight bet, plus the three groups. It's the equivalent of playing four separate tickets.

For example, say you decide to play 7, 15, 27, 39, 56, and 68. If you only catch two numbers, you probably won't win anything, since most casinos require a catch of three on a six-spot ticket. But if you pair these numbers—7 and 15; 27 and 39; and 56 and 68—and one of these pairs is a catch, you will win something.

To mark your ticket for way bets, circle the numbers you want to pair. Note that the numbers don't have to be consecutive in order for you to group them together; all you have to do is draw a circle that includes the numbers you have marked with an *X,* and the keno writer will ignore any numbers that aren't marked. At the top or side of the ticket, indicate the "ways" you want to bet. For our example, we have a one-way, six-spot bet, written 1/6, and three two-spot bets, written 3/2. You must mark both of these on your ticket in order to get paid. Always check your ticket carefully to make sure keno personnel have recorded the bet you intended to make.

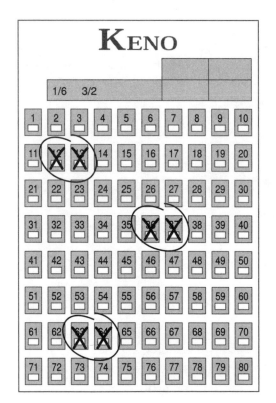

◀ By grouping the six numbers into three sets, you create a one-way, six-spot ticket (written 1/6), and a three-way, two-spot ticket (written 3/2).

The advantage of way betting is that, at most casinos, you can play way tickets for half or less of the regular minimum bet. So, if the minimum is $1 on a straight ticket, a five-way ticket will cost only $2.50 instead of $5. Alternatively, some casinos will let you pay the straight minimum on a way ticket, effectively reducing the cost of betting on each way. If you pay $1 on a five-way ticket, you are wagering only twenty cents on each way.

FACT

Most casinos require that way bets be divided into equal sets of numbers. If you want to play fifteen numbers, you could divide your numbers into three groups of five, five groups of three, or seven groups of two; you can have one leftover number, but you can't have six groups of two and one group of three.

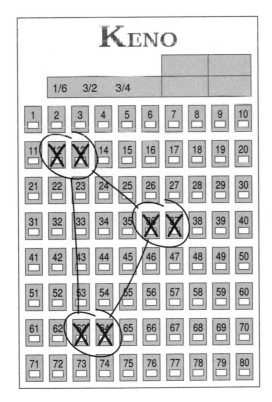

◄ Out of the three groups of two spots, we can create three groups of four spots: 12-13-36-37, 12-13-63-64, and 36-37-63-64. Now we have a one-way six-spot, three-way two-spot, and three-way four-spot ticket, written 1/6, 3/2, 3/4.

Combination Way Bets

Combination way bets give you even more ways to win on the same ticket, by combining the ways you already selected. It may sound complicated, but it's really just another method of grouping your numbers.

In our previous example, you chose six numbers to play, and then separated those numbers into three groups of two. In a combination way bet, you link those three groups together. Let's call the original pair group A, group B, and group C. You're going to combine those couples into three sets of four numbers each: A and B, A and C, B and C. Now we have a three-way, four-spot ticket, written 3/4, to add to our one-way, six-spot wager, and our three-way, two-spot wager. And there are now seven possible ways to win on this ticket.

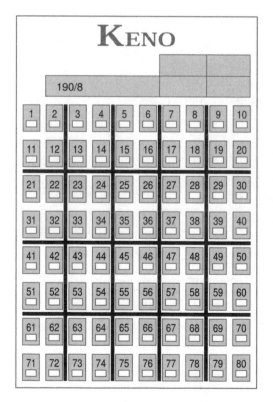

◀ This is a 190-way 8-spot ticket. Each group of four numbers works with every other set, and you use all eighty numbers.

Casino rules on way tickets and combination way tickets vary, but many places let you play up to a 190-way, eight-spot ticket. On this ticket, you divide all eighty numbers into groups of four, either vertically or in two-by-two squares, and each group of numbers can be combined with any other group of numbers to produce a winning ticket. You'll get a steep per-way discount on this type of bet; if you were required to pay $1 per way on this ticket, one race would cost you $190, and most keno players wouldn't pay that much for a single race. So the casino will charge perhaps ten cents per way on a 190-way ticket, making the single-race cost a much more affordable $19.

Variations and Special Games

Most keno operators offer a menu of special options, again to infuse the basic game with more variety and interest. Some of the more common options include betting catch-alls, top/bottom or left/right, or edges. Most of these options have special payout rates, and they may have different minimum bets.

A catch-all ticket allows you to select a small set of numbers, say three to six numbers, and offers bigger-than-normal payouts if you catch all the numbers you selected. For example, on a $3 bet, a six-spot catch-all might pay you as much as $16,000. Such a huge payoff on such a small investment naturally appeals to the gambler, but remember that the house edge on keno—and especially on high-payout options—is incredibly high, so your odds of actually winning are quite slim.

As always, you have to mark your ticket, usually with "CA," if you want this betting option. Catch-all bets usually cannot be made on the same ticket as a way or combination bet.

Most casinos allow you to play top/bottom or left/right tickets. In these options, the ticket is divided into two groups of forty numbers each; you bet whether most of the numbers drawn will fall on the top or bottom, or on the left or right. Generally, you have to catch thirteen of the twenty drawn numbers on the half you selected to win.

Some casinos also allow you to place an "edges" bet. This is when you mark all thirty-two numbers along the top, bottom, and side edges. House rules determine how many you need to catch on this ticket to win. Ask keno personnel or look for it in the casino's keno brochure.

FACT

Some casinos offer a variation called "stud keno." This is a progressive jackpot game, where the top prize keeps growing until someone wins it. The jackpot contribution may be a percentage of total wagers on each individual game, a flat amount per hour or day, or any of a number of methods decided by the house. Keno personnel can tell you whether they offer this game and any special rules, such as minimum bets, attached to it.

General Odds

Keno has the highest house edge—and therefore the worst odds for the gambler—of virtually any game at the casino. At a minimum, the house will keep 22 percent of every keno dollar wagered. Sometimes the house edge is as much as 50 percent, making it a very poor wager for the player.

Various mathematicians have calculated the odds of matching the numbers you play against the numbers drawn in a given keno race, and the odds grow exponentially with the amount of numbers you select. For example, if you play one number, the odds of that number being among the twenty drawn are about 3 to 1. If you play two numbers, the odds of matching one number are a little more than 1.5 to 1, but the odds of matching both numbers are nearly 16 to 1. Play five numbers, and the odds of matching all five leap to 1,550 to 1; play ten numbers, and the odds of matching all ten explode to 8.9 million to 1. Your odds of matching 15 numbers—the amount required at most casinos to win really big money—are less than 400 million to 1.

These almost insurmountable odds are why experts advise keno players to look on the game as nothing more than amusement, a low-cost way to see some action or a restful break from the blackjack, craps, or poker tables. That way, if you aren't lucky enough to hit it big, at least you have enjoyed yourself.

Chapter 3

Bingo

For many, bingo evokes images of elderly ladies sitting in a church basement, earnestly scanning a series of cardboard sheets in search of the one number that will earn them a meager jackpot. Bingo on this scale remains a staple fund-raiser for charitable and civic organizations. But, increasingly, today's commercial bingo halls are becoming full-service, high-stakes operations, offering a much faster pace, a much wider variety of games, and, of course, enormous jackpots for their loyal players.

History of Bingo

Bingo is a first cousin of the lottery—a game of chance in which players try to match randomly drawn numbers to win. Most historians agree that modern bingo is based on the Italian National Lottery, or Lo Giuoco del Lotto d'Italia, that began in the early 1500s and is still played weekly. The game is believed to have migrated to France, Great Britain, and other parts of Europe in the 1700s. Players were issued special cards marked with rows and columns of numbers; to win, the numbers called had to form a complete row or column on the card.

In 1929, on the verge of the Great Depression, a toy company owner named Ed Lowe saw a version of this game in Georgia, in which players used beans to cover the numbers on their "cards," as they were called. Upon his return to New York, Lowe introduced the game, with a few refinements, under the name "beano." According to the story, one woman who played Lowe's game got so excited when she won that she stuttered out, "Bingo!" instead of "Beano!" The new moniker stuck, and the game grew so popular that Lowe was able to charge his game-hall competitors $1 a year for the right to use the bingo name.

FACT

In the 1930s, John Harrah, father of Harrah's Casinos founder William Fisk Harrah, operated a $100-a-week bingo hall in California. He sold the business to his son, who moved it to Reno, Nevada, and built it into a $50,000-a-year operation. When the first Harrah's Casino opened, it was known as "the house that bingo built."

In the United States, commercial bingo is considered a Class II game and is legal even in most states that prohibit other forms of gambling. The American version of the game uses a field of seventy-five numbers, while European versions use ninety numbers. Bingo is allowed for charitable purposes in Ireland and is highly regulated in Great Britain; it is the only form of gambling allowed in the British military, where it is known as "tombola," "house," or "housy-housy."

Truly high-stakes bingo really came into its own in the 1970s on American Indian reservations. Because tribes are recognized as governments, they are able to offer games that far exceed the prize limits imposed on non-Indian bingo operations. In a very short time, high-stakes bingo palaces became economic engines for impoverished tribes across the United States, bringing in much-needed revenue and providing steady jobs for thousands of people. Today, it isn't uncommon to see tribal bingo operations advertising payouts of $50,000 or $100,000 or even more.

The Object of Bingo

Though many variations have been introduced as bingo has grown into a multimillion-dollar segment of the gambling industry, the basic premise of the game remains the same: to match randomly drawn numbers to corresponding numbers on a bingo card in a specific pattern, traditionally a straight line across, up and down, or diagonally. Most bingo halls rotate a broad range of patterns during any given bingo session. Those patterns can be as simple as a "corners" game, where you have to match the numbers in the four corners of your card to win, or as creative as a "butterfly" game, where winning numbers create that pattern on the bingo card.

Use your dauber gently when marking your cards. Banging or slamming the dauber can cause the dauber to leak, and it may annoy your neighbors. Most daubers work best with a light touch.

Numbers are marked with flat-ended ink bottles called "daubers" that work much like highlighters—bright enough to make matched numbers easily identifiable, but light enough so as not to obscure the numbers printed on the card. Recently, bingo halls also have begun offering electronic daubers, especially to assist the visually impaired.

How to Play Bingo

The bingo card consists of a 25-by-25-square field. Five vertical columns are headed B, I, N, G, and O; except for the N column, each has five numbered squares. The center square in the N column traditionally is an unnumbered "free" space, which can be used to complete a bingo up and down, across, or diagonally. Getting a bingo without using the free space is called a "hard-way bingo."

There are permanent and disposable bingo cards. Permanent cards are thick and have small sliding "windows" that you pull out to cover your numbers; at the end of the game, you simply slide the windows back and play the same card again. Disposable cards, which are more common, are thin pieces of paper, often with more than one card on a sheet, and they are thrown away when the game is over.

B	I	N	G	O
2	17	31	48	63
6	20	38	51	68
7	22	FREE	54	69
12	23	39	57	72
15	27	44	60	75

◀ A standard bingo card. At many bingo halls, the top of the card carries the establishment's logo. The "free" square also may bear a logo or other symbol.

In the United States, bingo uses a field of numbers from 1 to 75. The numbers 1 through 15 are always found in the B column, 16 through 30 are in the I column, and 31 through 45 are in the N column. The numbers 46 through 60 are in the G column, and 61 through 75 are in the O column.

Although some bingo halls use a computerized program to generate the numbers, most still use actual bingo balls. Balls labeled with the letter-and-number combinations are kept moving in a large wire cage or kettle-like container, and forced air pops out one ball at a time. The bingo caller announces the number on the ball. Once drawn, the ball is set aside until the end of the game so it won't be called twice. In most bingo palaces, large electronic boards around the room light up the numbers as they're drawn. These boards also often display the pattern being played for a given game.

When you complete the pattern on your card, you yell out, "Bingo!" and wait for a clerk to come and verify your win. Play is halted until the win is confirmed. Prizes are divided evenly among multiple winners.

ALERT!

It's crucial that you pay attention during your bingo session and make sure you mark the numbers on your cards as they are called. Most bingo halls require that "bingo" be made on the last number called; they won't pay on so-called sleepers, or cards where a previous number created a winner but wasn't called by the player.

At most bingo halls, you can play as many cards as you like, or as many as you can handle. It isn't uncommon for veteran players to follow a dozen or more cards in a given game. If you're just starting out, you might want to restrict yourself to three or four cards at a time until you become more adept at finding the numbers.

The Bingo Atmosphere

Today's commercial bingo halls are huge, buzzing caverns of almost ceaseless activity. Many bingo halls allow smoking, although some have separate rooms—and even separate games—for smokers and nonsmokers. When the games are separated like this, the payouts typically are smaller for each game. Several state and local governments have enacted laws prohibiting smoking in public places; American Indian bingo halls usually are exempt from these laws, but many of them have built separate smoking areas in response to player demand.

Even when a bingo hall is part of a casino, it will be separated from the main gaming floor. The reason for this is twofold. First, bingo halls make their money by charging admission fees, rather than encouraging players to just walk up to a table and place a wager. Second, the noise of the gaming floor would interfere seriously with players' ability to hear the bingo numbers being called. In some cases, usually at tribal casinos, the bingo hall may be located in a different building from the casino.

Bingo Etiquette

Perhaps more than any other casino game, bingo is a social activity. It isn't uncommon for players to form lasting friendships with the floor clerks and other personnel at their favorite bingo hall. Nor is it unusual for players to bond with each other, at least for a given session. Many bingo palaces encourage this friendly, family-like atmosphere, offering, for example, "birthday bingo" once a month to celebrate players' birthdays or specials where everyone at the game winner's table shares the wealth.

In this kind of atmosphere, novices are welcomed into the fold and are likely to find a seasoned veteran offering (solicited or unsolicited) tips and advice. On the other hand, unfamiliarity with bingo etiquette can lead to some hard feelings or harsh words from the regulars. The following are among the most important etiquette rules:

- Buy a card for one of your neighbors at least once a session.
- When you win, "share the wealth" by tossing a lucky dollar or two to the people at your table.
- Don't be standoffish, but try to keep your conversations brief and your voice low so the people around you can hear the caller.
- If you get up to get a drink or a snack, ask your neighbors if you can bring anything back for them so they don't have to miss a game.

How to Bet Bingo

Bingo is different from other casino games in that you don't make bets on individual games. In most cases, you purchase an admission pack, which includes a set of game cards and entitles you to play during a specific session. Usually, you can buy additional cards or packs of cards for a relatively small fee. For example, a standard admission pack might include two cards each for four regular games, two special games, and the jackpot game. You can then purchase extra cards for each of the games in the session for an additional charge.

Admission rates and prize payouts vary from operator to operator. Each bingo hall will have a brochure or flier describing its admission packages and prices, as well as the prizes for each type of game and a disclosure of the "hold," or the amount the house keeps back to cover operating expenses and profits. On average, high-stakes bingo halls pay out in prizes about 75 percent of what they take in from admissions and other sales.

Strategic and Dead Squares

There are twenty-four numbered spaces on a bingo card. Of these, sixteen are considered "strategic squares" because they can be used with the free space in the middle to create a traditional bingo. The other eight squares are considered "dead squares." The strategic squares for traditional bingo—a straight line up and down, across or diagonally—are the first, third, and fifth squares on the top and bottom rows, the middle three on the second and fourth rows, and all four numbered squares on the third row.

The dead squares come into play when you fill a "hard-way" bingo, or one that doesn't include the free space. They also are used in special patterns such as coverall or blackout, where you have to cover every square, and postage stamp, where you cover a two-by-two area to win.

B	I	N	G	O
2	17	31	●	●
6	20	38	●	●
7	22	FREE	54	69
12	23	39	57	72
15	27	44	60	75

◀ A "postage stamp" pattern

◀ A "butterfly" bingo pattern

Identifying Patterns

Some experts recommend looking for certain number groups within the columns—numbers 1 through 10 in the B column, for example, or 29 through 39 in the N column. These recommendations are usually based on the expert's observation of which numbers in a given column tend to come up most often. The fact is that the odds of any given number coming up during any given bingo game are always the same. For the first number drawn, the odds are 1 in 75; for the second number drawn, the odds are 1 in 74; for the third number, the odds are 1 in 73; and so on until a bingo is called. As with a coin toss, what happens in one game has no effect on the next, and any clusters of repeat numbers in consecutive bingo games are like clusters of "heads" in consecutive coin tosses.

Most bingo card printers create series of 6,000 to 9,000 cards with distinct number combinations. By selecting as many unique combinations as you can and avoiding repeat numbers on two or more cards, you increase your chances of winning because your cards cover more possible combinations.

Likewise, don't be fooled into thinking that so-called lucky numbers, like 7 or 11, increase your odds of winning. In fact, 7 and 11, both in the B column, show up on about 20 percent of all winning bingo cards, so they are no "luckier" than any other numbers in the field.

Variations

To keep players coming back, bingo halls continually introduce new variations to their regular games. Many of them offer early-bird specials or mini-games, which are played before a regular session starts. Sometimes a bingo winner also will get a chance to spin a money wheel, enter a "cash cage" to grab money as it is being blown by powerful air currents, or play a version of *Let's Make a Deal,* where the player has to decide whether to keep the bingo winnings or risk it for a potentially larger prize.

Most bingo halls also offer monthly specials with bigger jackpots or slashed admission prices. For example, many halls offer "birthday bingo" once a month, where anyone whose birthday falls in that month gets a free admission pack for the regular session. Other variations include mystery bingo, where the prize is determined by the last number called. In a regular game, for example, if the last number called is N-42, the prize would be 42 times, say, $25, or $1,050.

Virtually every bingo hall offers a free newsletter to alert players of upcoming specials and promotions. Signing up for such a newsletter is usually free; ask at the admission desk to get your name added to the mailing list.

General Odds

On average, bingo operations pay out about 75 percent of the revenue they take in. That makes the house edge on bingo one of the highest in the casino, but it's still less than half the house edge on a typical state lottery, which averages a 45 percent payout rate.

The number of possible unique bingo cards—those where no two numbers are the same—is in the millions. But the odds of winning depend not on the number of possible cards, but on the number of cards in play at any given time. That's because in every bingo game, no matter what the pattern, numbers are drawn until someone wins.

Like every business, bingo has its busy days and times and its slow days and times. The fewer people there are participating in a game, the fewer cards there are in play, and the better the odds of winning are for each of those people. If there are 100 people playing bingo, and each of these 100 people is playing four cards, each person has 4 opportunities out of 400—or a 1 in 100 chance—to produce the winning card. Now let's say there are 1,000 people playing, still playing four cards each. That means there are 4,000 cards in play, and each player's odds of having the winning card are reduced to 4 chances in 4,000, or 1 in 1,000. (These figures assume there are no duplicate cards and the numbers drawn do not create more than one winning bingo pattern.) Simply put, your odds of winning are better if you can play when the bingo hall is not crowded. On the other hand, the prize money will probably be less.

The number of cards you play also affects your odds of winning, but not necessarily in the way you might think. Most of us would assume that we increase our chances of winning automatically by playing as many cards at a time as possible. Theoretically, this is true. But remember that bingo numbers are called at a fairly fast pace, and if you can't keep up because you have too many cards in front of you, you're more likely to miss a potential winning pattern than to claim a big prize. (E)

Chapter 4

Blackjack

Blackjack may be the most familiar table game in the world. In the United States, it certainly is the most popular, outnumbering other table games by an average of two to one at most gaming halls. Blackjack offers everything most gamblers want in their games: easy-to-follow rules, fairly generous odds for the player, a variety of betting levels, and fast action.

History of Blackjack

No one seems to know exactly how blackjack came to be. The most common theory is that it evolved from French games such as *chemin de fer* or baccarat. At any rate, the modern version of the game is believed to have originated in the 1700s in France, where it was known as "twenty-one," and it has been played in the United States since the 1800s.

Blackjack got its first boost as a winnable "everyman's game" in the 1950s, when a team of mathematicians led by Roger Baldwin published a paper in the *Journal of the American Statistical Association* showing how the house's advantage in the game could be reduced by using probability and statistics formulas. A few years later, a professor named Edward O. Thorp expanded on Baldwin's work and published his findings in the 1962 bestseller *Beat the Dealer*. So many players used Thorp's system to win at the blackjack tables that casino managers became alarmed and changed the rules to regain the house advantage. Other players who were disadvantaged by the changes rebelled by refusing to play under the new rules, and the resulting loss of revenue forced the casinos to reinstate the original blackjack game.

FACT

Blackjack derives its name from an early rule, which is no longer widely used, that paid a player up to 10 to 1 if his or her first two cards were the ace of spades ("black") and the jack of spades ("jack").

Julian Braun, an IBM employee who ran hours of simulated blackjack games through the corporate giant's mainframe computers in the 1960s and 1970s, is credited with devising today's "basic strategy"—the rules of thumb that most experts strongly recommend for every blackjack player, regardless of experience. By following basic strategy, even the novice can narrow the house's edge to a slim 1 percent or less (depending upon the house rules and the number of decks in play).

The Object of Blackjack

The object of blackjack is simple: to get cards totaling 21, or as close to 21 as possible without going over, and to get a better total than your opponent (the dealer). The cards 2 through 10 count at their face value. Face cards—jack, queen, and king—count as 10, and aces can be counted as 1 or 11. Suits don't matter in blackjack.

Because aces can be counted two ways, hands that contain an ace are called "soft" hands. An ace and a 7, for instance, is a soft 18; if the next card is a 6, you would count the ace as 1 to avoid going over 21. Hands without aces are called "hard" hands; a hard 18 could be a 10 and an 8.

At a casino, your opponent is the dealer. There may be other players at your table, but each of them is playing against the dealer as well. Therefore, unlike poker and many other table games, it's possible for every player at a blackjack table to win the same round. Of course, it's also possible for the dealer to beat every player at the table at once.

Some casinos in Las Vegas still offer single-deck blackjack games, but most casinos today use a minimum of two decks. More common are six- and eight-deck games, which give the house a stronger edge without having to discourage card-counting. Generally, a deck with a high proportion of low cards is considered favorable to the house because the chances of the dealer going bust, or going over 21, are lower. A deck with a high proportion of 10s, face cards, and aces is considered more favorable to the player, in this case because there's a better chance of the dealer drawing a high card and going bust and of the player getting an ace and a 10, for a "natural" blackjack (which pays a bonus).

When a player and a dealer have the same total, it is a "push" or "standoff." The player doesn't win any money, but she doesn't lose any either. At most tables, a win pays 1:1; so a win on a $5 bet will earn you $5. Although you won't find 10:1 payouts on a natural blackjack these days, most casinos do pay higher for an ace-10 or ace–face card combination.

A true blackjack—an ace paired with a 10, jack, queen, or king—is the highest hand in the game and beats all other combinations of 21. For example, if you have an ace and a 10 and the dealer has three cards that are each a 7, you win. A natural also pays slightly more, usually 3:2. On a $5 bet, that means $7.50 instead of the usual even money.

How to Play Blackjack

A typical blackjack table has six or seven seats for players. The seat closest to the dealer's left is sometimes known as "first base," while the seat closest to the dealer's right is called the "anchor seat" or "third base." The anchor seat often gets a lot of attention—and pressure—from other players, because it is the last position to get cards before the dealer works on his or her own hand.

ALERT!

The "anchor" seat, or "third base," is considered by many gamblers to be critical to the outcome of a game, because the last player's decision to hit or stand affects the dealer's hand. If you don't follow basic strategy in this position, other players may blame you for the outcome of a game. Avoid this seat unless you intend to follow basic strategy strictly.

Getting Started

Bets are placed before the cards are dealt. Most blackjack tables have a minimum bet of $5 to $100 per hand. Once in a great while you might find a $2 table. Minimum bets are posted on or near the table; if the table has a maximum bet per hand, that will be posted, too.

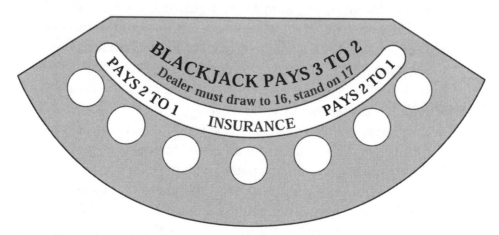

▲ A typical blackjack table layout. Most will indicate dealer rules, blackjack payout, and insurance payout.

Each player, beginning with the one on the dealer's left, is dealt one card, face-up; the dealer's first card also is dealt face-up. Each player is dealt a second card, also face-up, and the dealer's second card, called the "hole card," is face-down. Then, beginning with the player on the dealer's left, each player either taps the table to indicate he wants a hit (an additional card), or holds his hand palm-down over his cards to indicate that he wants to stand. Each player can take as many cards as he wants until the total is close to or equals 21, or until the player "busts" by going over 21. When all players have either indicated they wish to stand or have busted, the dealer reveals his hole card and plays out his hand.

Dealer Options

The dealer's choices are controlled by the house rules. At virtually all casinos, dealers must draw on any total of 16 or lower and stand on totals of 17 or higher. So, for example, if the dealer's up-card is a 2 and his hole card is a 10, he must take cards until his total hand is at least 17. If his third card is a 3, he has to take at least one more card, because his total now is only 15.

On the other hand, if the dealer's up-card is a 7 and his hole card is a 10, he must stand. A player whose hand is more than 17 (but not more than 21) wins; a player whose hand also is 17 is in a standoff, where no money is exchanged.

Some casinos require dealers to stand on a soft 17 (an ace and a 6), and others require them to hit in that situation. Generally speaking, the house has more of an edge when a dealer is required to hit on a soft 17.

Player Options

The player has many more options than the dealer. You can request a hit or stand. If your first two cards are a pair, you can split them, place an additional bet, and play each half of the pair as a separate hand, hitting and standing as warranted. You can "double-down," where you increase your bet—usually by no more than a total of double your original bet—but agree to accept only one more card.

If the dealer has an ace showing, you can make an insurance bet before the hole card is revealed. You put up half of your original bet on the assumption that the dealer has blackjack; if you're right, insurance pays 2:1, which means you win twice the amount you bet. If you're wrong and the dealer doesn't have blackjack, you lose your insurance bet, and the rest of the hand is played out as usual.

FACT

Insurance is considered a "sucker bet" by most experts. Unless you've been counting cards, it's hard to know whether the dealer has a 10 in the hole. In general, the house advantage on insurance bets is around 6 percent. If you follow basic strategy, the house's edge can be as low as a fraction of 1 percent, so you're better off pretending there's no such thing as insurance.

Finally, some casinos allow bettors to surrender. Rules on surrender vary; some casinos allow early surrenders (before the dealer looks at the hole card) only if the dealer's up-card is a 9, 10, face card, or ace, while others allow you to surrender no matter what the dealer is showing. If you choose to surrender, you lose only half of your original bet. Some casinos also allow "late" surrenders, after the dealer looks at the hole card. According to some experts, you'll lose the hand three times out of four when the dealer has an ace or 10 showing, so a surrender bet can help you cut your losses. On multiple-deck games, basic strategy recommends surrendering when you hold a hard 15 and the dealer shows a 10, or when you have a hard 16 and the dealer shows a 9, 10, or ace.

The Magic Number

Experts in blackjack theory have determined that the average winning hand in blackjack is 18.3. Since you can't get fractions in blackjack, and since most casinos require their dealers to stand on 17, the true "magic number" in the game is a hard 17, both for the player and for the house. There's a very good reason for this: the chances of going bust on a hand of 17 are high, because only an ace, 2, 3, or 4 can improve this hand. Anything higher than a 4—and there are many more of the higher cards in the deck—means losing the hand. This is why most casinos require the dealer to stand on 17.

It makes sense if you think about how the cards' values are spread throughout a deck. In a single fifty-two-card deck, there are only four aces, four 2s, four 3s, and so on, right up to the 9 cards. But there are four cards that count as 10—the 10, jack, queen, and king—and there are four of each of these cards in a single deck. So, there are sixteen cards whose value in blackjack is 10, or more than 30 percent of the total cards in a single deck. By contrast, only about 7 percent of the cards in a single deck are 3s. This ratio remains the same no matter how many decks are being used.

At best, when you hold a hard 17, only 31 percent of the cards can help your hand (ace, 2, 3, or 4, each representing a little over 7 percent of the total cards). That leaves 69 percent of the cards as hand-busters, and that figure only goes up if your hand is an 18, 19, or 20. The odds are against you every time.

There are a number of card-counting methods that, theoretically, allow the player to determine the ratio of high and low cards left to be played and to adjust the betting accordingly. Though technically this is not cheating, most casinos dislike the practice and, if they catch you, will ask you to stop playing, limit the amount you can bet, or change the shuffle to remove the advantage card-counting can give you.

If you have an ace and a 6 for a soft 17, you have more options. You might double-down, increasing your bet and hoping you draw a 3 or 4, which would give you 20 or 21, or a 10, which would give you a solid 17. Or you might opt for a hit, anticipating a series of smaller cards. In this situation, as always in this game, your best choice depends on what the dealer is showing. The dealer's up-card is the only clue you have in blackjack as to what your next move should be, and basic strategy differs according to the dealer's up-card.

How to Bet Blackjack

Some players go with their gut, and some try various card-counting schemes. Most experts recommend following basic strategy as the most consistent way to improve your odds of winning. Under this system, your decisions in blackjack always depend on what the dealer is showing.

Basic strategy varies, though sometimes only slightly, according to whether you're playing a single-deck or multiple-deck game. The surrender rule and other variations in house rules also can influence your best move under basic strategy. The following charts show basic strategy for single-deck and multiple-deck games, with notes on special rules.

Single-Deck Blackjack									
Your Hand				**Dealer's Up-Card**					
	2	3	4	5	6	7	8	9	10	A
8	H	H	H	D/H	D/H	H	H	H	H	H
9	D/H	D/H	D/H	D/H	D/H	H	H	H	H	H
10	D/H	D/H	D/H	D/H	D/H	D/H	D/H	D/H	H	H
11	D/H	D/H	D/H	D/H	D/H	D/H	D/H	D/H	D/H	D/H
12	H	H	S	S	S	H	H	H	H	H
13 (hard)	S	S	S	S	S	H	H	H	H	H
13 (soft)	H	H	D/H	D/H	D/H	H	H	H	H	H
14 (hard)	S	S	S	S	S	H	H	H	H	H
14 (soft)	H	H	D/H	D/H	D/H	H	H	H	H	H
15 (hard)	S	S	S	S	S	H	H	H	H	H
15 (soft)	H	H	D/H	D/H	D/H	H	H	H	H	H
16 (hard)	S	S	S	S	S	H	H	H	H	H
16 (soft)	H	H	D/H	D/H	D/H	H	H	H	H	H
17–20 (hard)	S	S	S	S	S	S	S	S	S	S
17 (soft)	D/H	D/H	D/H	D/H	D/H	H	H	H	H	H
18 (soft)	S	D/S	D/S	D/S	D/S	S	S	H	H	H

Single-Deck Blackjack (continued)

Your Hand	Dealer's Up-Card									
19 (soft)	S	S	S	S	D/S	S	S	S	S	S
20 (soft)	S	S	S	S	S	S	S	S	S	S

Key: H = Hit; S = Stand; D/H = Double if allowed, otherwise hit; D/S = Double if allowed, otherwise stand.

Multiple-Deck Blackjack

Your Hand	Dealer's Up-Card									
	2	3	4	5	6	7	8	9	10	A
8	H	H	H	H	H	H	H	H	H	H
9	H	D/H	D/H	D/H	D/H	H	H	H	H	H
10	D/H	D/H	D/H	D/H	D/H	D/H	D/H	D/H	H	H
11	D/H	D/H	D/H	D/H	D/H	D/H	D/H	D/H	D/H	H
12	H	H	S	S	S	H	H	H	H	H
13 (hard)	S	S	S	S	S	H	H	H	H	H
13 (soft)	H	H	H	D/H	D/H	H	H	H	H	H
14 (hard)	S	S	S	S	S	H	H	H	H	H
14 (soft)	H	H	H	D/H	D/H	H	H	H	H	H
15 (hard)	S	S	S	S	S	H	H	H	H*	H
15 (soft)	H	H	D/H	D/H	D/H	H	H	H	H	H
16 (hard)	S	S	S	S	S	H	H	H*	H*	H*
16 (soft)	H	H	D/H	D/H	D/H	H	H	H	H	H
17–20 (hard)	S	S	S	S	S	S	S	S	S	S
17 (soft)	H	D/H	D/H	D/H	D/H	H	H	H	H	H
18 (soft)	D	D/S	D/S	D/S	D/S	S	S	H	H	H
19 (soft)	S	S	S	S	S	S	S	S	S	S
20 (soft)	S	S	S	S	S	S	S	S	S	S

Key: H = Hit; S = Stand; D/H = Double if allowed, otherwise hit; D/S = Double if allowed, otherwise stand; H* = Surrender if allowed, otherwise hit.

Standing

For hard hands—that is, hands that do not include an ace in the first two cards—there are general rules for deciding when you should stand. As discussed previously, it is always wisest to stand if you have a hard 17 (or higher), no matter what the dealer is showing. Basic strategy also calls for you to stand if your hand totals 13 to 16 and the dealer's up-card is a 2 through a 6. The concentration of 10-value cards can easily cause you to bust with one draw card. The same can happen to the dealer if the hole card is a 10-value card, but even if the hole card is a lower value, house rules require the dealer to draw if her cards total 16 or lower, and that provides additional opportunities for the dealer to bust.

Basic strategy changes for soft hands. With a soft 18 (an ace and a 7)—and this is true for both single-deck and multiple-deck games—you should stand if the dealer is showing a 2, 7, or 8; double-down (or stand, if house rules don't allow doubling down) if the dealer shows a 3 through 6; and hit if the dealer shows 9, 10, or ace. Always stand on a soft 19 (ace and 8) unless the dealer shows a 6; stand on a soft 20 (ace and 9) no matter what the dealer's up-card is.

Taking a Hit

There are times when you must take a hit if you want a decent chance at beating the dealer. When you have a hard hand totaling 8 or less, always, always, always hit, regardless of what the dealer is showing. Likewise, you should always hit when your hand totals 9 and the dealer is showing a 2 or a 7 through an ace. You should hit or double-down when your hand totals 10; if you have 12, take a hit when the dealer's up-card is a 2, 3, or 7 through ace.

It may seem counterintuitive to hit when you're holding an ace and a 7. When the dealer is showing a 9, 10, or ace in this situation, you have to assume the hole card is a 10. Remember that the ace can be counted as 1 or 11, so even if you draw a 10 you won't bust, and you will improve your chances of beating the dealer.

For soft hands, always hit or double-down when you have an ace paired with a 2 through a 6, no matter what the dealer shows. If you have a soft 18 (ace and 7), hit only if the dealer is showing a 9, 10, or ace; otherwise stand or double-down.

Splitting a Pair

When your first two cards are a pair, it can be tempting to automatically split them into two separate hands. But splitting only works to your advantage on certain pairs. For example, under basic strategy, you should never split 5s or 10s, albeit for different reasons. Fives can be problematic if you draw, say, a 7 or 8; a 9 or 10 on the next hit will bust you. If you keep the 5s together, though, that 7 or 8 gives you a solid hand on which you can stand.

Splitting 10s presents a different problem. In this case, you're giving up a hard 20 for the possibility that you'll draw at least one ace. But remember that aces make up only 7 percent of the total cards, so the odds of drawing one on a split are pretty low.

FACT

At most casinos, if you split a pair of aces or 10s and get a blackjack on one of the splits, you'll only get even money—not the higher payout for blackjack. That's because a blackjack on a split doesn't occur in the first two cards and so is not considered a natural blackjack.

Basic strategy recommends that you always split 8s because together they create a troublesome 16 and apart they represent a decent opportunity for two solid 18s. In multiple-deck games, split 2s and 3s when the dealer's up-card is a 2 through a 7 (if doubling after splitting is allowed; otherwise only split 2s and 3s if the dealer is showing a 4 through a 7); you also should split 7s when the dealer shows 2 through 7. Split 4s only when the dealer's up-card is a 5 or a 6 in multiple-deck games (if doubling after a split is allowed, otherwise don't); in single-deck games, never split 4s (but if doubling after a split is allowed, then split 4s). Split 9s unless the dealer is showing a 7, 10, or ace, in either single- or multiple-deck games. Always split aces, regardless of what the dealer is showing; remember, there is a higher concentration of 10-value cards and your chances of drawing two 21s are pretty good.

The following charts show basic strategy for splitting pairs in single-deck and multiple-deck games.

Splitting Pairs—Single-Deck Blackjack										
Your Pair	**Dealer's Up-Card**									
	2	3	4	5	6	7	8	9	10	A
2s	N	Y	Y	Y	Y	Y	N	N	N	N
3s	N	N	Y	Y	Y	Y	N	N	N	N
4s	N	N	N	N	N	N	N	N	N	N
5s	N	N	N	N	N	N	N	N	N	N
6s	Y	Y	Y	Y	Y	N	N	N	N	N
7s	Y	Y	Y	Y	Y	Y	N	N	S	N
8s	Y	Y	Y	Y	Y	Y	Y	Y	Y	Y
9s	Y	Y	Y	Y	Y	N	Y	Y	N	N
10s	N	N	N	N	N	N	N	N	N	N
Aces	Y	Y	Y	Y	Y	Y	Y	Y	Y	Y

Key: Y = Yes, split; N = No, don't split; S = Stand.

QUESTION?

Why should I keep a pair of 9s together when the dealer is showing a 7?
Remember that most house rules require the dealer to stand on 17. If his hole card is a 10, he has to stand, and you will beat him with your pair of 9s (which total 18). If his hole card is an ace, he has a soft 18 and has to stand. In that case, the hand is a push and you don't lose your bet.

Splitting Pairs—Multiple-Deck Blackjack										
Your Pair					**Dealer's Up-Card**					
	2	3	4	5	6	7	8	9	10	A
2s	N	N	Y	Y	Y	Y	N	N	N	N
3s	N	N	Y	Y	Y	Y	N	N	N	N
4s	N	N	N	N	N	N	N	N	N	N
5s	N	N	N	N	N	N	N	N	N	N
6s	N	Y	Y	Y	Y	N	N	N	N	N
7s	Y	Y	Y	Y	Y	Y	N	N	N	N
8s	Y	Y	Y	Y	Y	Y	Y	Y	Y	Y
9s	Y	Y	Y	Y	Y	N	Y	Y	N	N
10s	N	N	N	N	N	N	N	N	N	N
Aces	Y	Y	Y	Y	Y	Y	Y	Y	Y	Y

Key: Y = Yes, split; N = No, don't split.

Many casinos will allow you to split until you end up with a total of four hands; you have to finish one hand before you can act on the next. Some casinos allow you to double-down after splitting and others don't. In some casinos, if you decide to split a pair of aces, you'll be limited to a one-card draw on each ace and you won't be allowed to split again.

Doubling Down

Doubling down means doubling your initial bet but taking only one additional card. Basic strategy calls for you to double whenever your hand totals 11. The logic behind this rule of thumb again rests on the preponderance of 10-value cards in the deck; your chances of drawing to 21 with one more card are pretty good. Any of the higher-value cards will give you a strong hand since the dealer has to stand at 17.

Basic strategy experts also recommend doubling when your hand is a hard 10, again because you have a good chance of drawing to 20 with one additional card. However, if the dealer is showing a 10 or an ace, it's better to hit than to double. Hitting gives you a better chance of beating the dealer, who might have a 20 or 21, because if your third card is small, say a 2 or 3, you can hit again.

In single-deck games, you should double on a hard 9 only when the dealer is showing a 2 through a 6; in multiple-deck games, double-down on a hard 9 when the dealer shows 3 through 6. Otherwise, you should hit. If your hand totals 12 through 16 with no aces, it's not worthwhile to double-down no matter what the dealer is showing.

FACT

Casino rules on doubling vary. Some houses allow doubling after a split, but many don't. The advantage of doubling, especially when you hold a hard 11, is that you have a good chance of drawing to 21 with just one card and doubling your winnings on that hand.

Doubling on soft hands is a little different. If you have an ace paired with a 2, 3, 4, or 5, you should consider doubling when the dealer shows a 4, 5, or 6 in single-deck games. In multiple-deck games, double-down when you have an ace-2 or ace-3 combination only when the dealer shows 5 or 6; if you have ace-4 or ace-5, double-down when the dealer shows a 4, 5, or 6. If you have an ace and a 6 in a single-deck game, you might want to double when the dealer's up-card is a 2 through a 6. For a multiple-deck game, double-down if the dealer shows 3 through 6. With an ace and a 7, you should double only when the dealer shows a 3, 4, 5, or 6.

The Dicey Deuce

Novice blackjack players sometimes get nervous when the dealer shows an ace, thinking that unbeatable blackjack is waiting to steal their money. More experienced players know that the true villain in the game is the tricky 2—small enough to appear innocuous, but capable of wreaking all kinds of havoc at the table.

Say you hold a 10 and a 9, and you're feeling pretty confident against the dealer's puny 2. But wait: The dealer reveals an 8 in the hole and then—you know what's coming—draws an ace. You were sitting so pretty a second ago, and now you're sunk.

This kind of thing happens more often than you might expect. In the dealer's hands, the tiny 2 can blend with almost anything to upset your carefully played round; in your hands, it can cause more headaches than that pesky pair of 8s.

According to basic strategy, when you have a hard 12 and the dealer is showing a 2, you should take a card. The risk is that you'll draw from that rich lode of 10-value cards, thus going bust. Take some comfort in the fact that, if the dealer's hole card is a 10, she faces the same risk that you do. Besides, you might draw an 8 or a 9 and eke out a winner.

When you're faced with a dealer's 2 and your cards total 13 to 20, it's best to stand because the chances of going bust are too high and you'd rather have the dealer draw that next 10 card. If your cards total 3 through 8, hit until you get past 13 and then stand. Again, you're hoping the dealer will be undone by the 10s. Double-down on a hand totaling 9, 10, or 11 in single-deck games; in multiple-deck games, double-down only if you hold cards totaling 10 or 11 against the dealer's 2 card. If you draw a 10-value card in this situation, you have a good chance of beating the dealer and doubling your winnings.

Variations

Blackjack rules are generally standardized from casino to casino, but there may be differences in specific rules such as when doubling is allowed and whether the dealer has to hit or stand on a soft 17. If you're not sure what the rules are, find a dealer at an empty or nearly empty table and ask him to explain the rules to you, or watch others play for a while. Most casinos also have brochures or rack cards that spell out the rules for each of their games.

In late 2003, four Las Vegas casinos introduced a variation of blackjack called "royal 20s," which allows players to make side bets on whether the dealer, the player, or both will be dealt 20. In this variation, suit makes a difference. Two 10-value cards of different suits pays 5:1, but a pair of face cards in the same suit pays 25:1. If this variation on the game takes off, you may see it spring up in casinos around the country.

General Odds

According to most experts, the house advantage on a typical blackjack game is about 5 percent. By following basic strategy, you can reduce that edge to as little as half of 1 percent, which is about as close to even as you can get. Even professional players who religiously follow basic strategy generally report long-term returns of only 1 percent to 2 percent, so blackjack is not the game to make you rich overnight. Your expectation, even in following basic strategy, still will be negative over the long haul.

Side bets on blackjack, such as insurance and the new royal 20s variation, offer much worse odds for the player. In general, the house has a 6 percent edge on insurance bets; analysts say the royal 20s side bet gives the house a 21 percent advantage on double-deck games and an 18 percent advantage on six-deck games.

If you're like most of us, you'll experience winning streaks and losing streaks. If you find a losing streak is affecting your concentration, take a break. Likewise, don't let winning streaks go to your head; if you double your bankroll, stand up and walk away. The longer you stay at the blackjack table or any other game, the more the scales tip in the casino's favor.

Chapter 5

Poker

Poker is arguably the best-known and most popular card game in the United States. It also can be the most intimidating card game. Though luck plays a role in the cards dealt, skill almost always determines who wins a hand. Fortunately, today there are more ways than ever for the beginning player to learn the game and hone his or her skills at free or low-stakes games before taking on the challenge of a live, higher-stakes session.

History of Poker

The origin of poker is a matter of speculation. The Chinese are believed to have played a game with cards and dominoes as early as the tenth century, and the Persian game *as nas,* played with five players and a deck of twenty-five cards in five suits, dates from the seventeenth century. French settlers around present-day New Orleans played a game called "poque," which involved both betting and a heavy emphasis on bluffing.

The Cheating Game

In the 1830s, a man named Jonathan H. Green wrote about what he called "the cheating game," a popular card game making the rounds of the Mississippi riverboats. The game was played with twenty cards—10s, jacks, queens, kings, and aces—and two to four players were dealt five cards each. At the time that Green wrote about it, "the cheating game" was perceived to be a more honest game than three-card monte, which most people recognized as a hustle.

FACT

The word "poker" may have derived from the French *poque,* but there are competing theories. Some argue that the word comes from a German card game called *pochspiel,* while others believe it's a variation of "poke," a slang term that card sharks and pickpockets used to describe a sucker's bankroll.

The game that Green observed eventually evolved to include thirty-two cards, and later a full fifty-two-card deck. Poker made its way up the Mississippi and Ohio rivers via steamboat, and spread east and west via railroad and wagon train from there. Variations like stud and draw poker became increasingly popular during the Civil War era, and around the 1870s, the joker was introduced as a wild card.

Luck Versus Skill

For decades, poker flourished, particularly in the West, where virtually every saloon had a regular game and professional gamblers traveled from town to town looking for action. But, as the game grew more common, so did the image of poker as a tool for hustlers and cheaters. Poker, like other gambling games, suffered from a backlash against wagering in general, and by the early twentieth century, several states had enacted tough antigambling laws that prohibited playing cards for money.

Then, amid the debates about what constituted illegal games of chance, the California attorney general ruled that, while stud poker was illegal, draw poker was a game of skill and therefore not subject to antigambling laws. That decision led to the widespread growth of draw poker and its many variations, and poker developed from "the cheating game" into an acceptable pastime where good players were rewarded for their skills. Saloon games gave way to more decorous card rooms and poker clubs, and today it is estimated that more people in the United States play poker—either in a friendly weekly game at someone's home, online, or at the numerous casinos and card rooms that dot the country— than any other sport or game of skill.

FACT

These days, there are all kinds of tools to help you learn how to play poker, ranging from home computer games and free or low-stakes online games, to lessons at your local card room, to television shows. The Travel Channel, ESPN, and Bravo all have or are planning poker shows, and a new cable channel devoted to poker and other casino games—called, appropriately, the Casino and Gaming Television Network—is expected to be up and running in 2004.

The Object of Poker

The object of poker is to win the pot, the pool of money in the middle of the table where bets are collected. You can do this either by having the best hand, or by bluffing to make other players think you have the best hand and thus getting them to drop out. Whether you're playing at home, online, or in a casino's poker room, your opponent in most games is the other player or players, not the house. Your chances of winning depend on the cards, your own level of skill, and the skills of the opposing players. (Chapter 7 covers variations of poker in which players are pitted against the house instead of each other.)

Ranks of Hands

Although there are variations of poker where the worst hand, rather than the best hand, wins, most versions use the same standard ranking of hands. In every version except three-card poker (see Chapter 7), a player's final hand consists of five cards. From lowest hand to highest, here's what you need to know about poker hands.

High Card

A high-card hand is one in which the five cards contain no pairs and the cards are of differing suits. If no other hand exists, the player with the highest card in her hand wins. For example, if one player holds 2-4-5-9-J, and another player holds 2-3-7-10-K, the player with the king wins the hand. If high cards are identical—two players have jacks high, for instance—the winner is determined by the next highest card. If those two cards are identical, the third highest card breaks the tie, and so on down the line.

Pair

A pair is any two cards of the same denomination. If two players have identical pairs, the winner is determined by the high card among the three nonpair cards (which is also called a "kicker"). When cards are shown, the hand is announced by the pair and high card—for example: "Pair of 3s, 7 high."

Two Pair

This hand consists of two cards of the same face value, plus two other cards of the same face value, and one singleton. If two players have the same high pair, the second pair determines the winner. If both pairs are identical, the hand with the highest singleton wins. When cards are shown, the hand is announced like this: "Two pair, 10s over 7s."

Three of a Kind

This hand is three cards of the same face value, plus two mismatched cards. Unless the game allows for wild cards, it's impossible to tie with this hand, since there are only four cards of any given value in a deck. If there is a tie in a wild-card game, the highest nonmatching card determines the winner.

Straight

A straight is five cards of mixed suits, consecutively numbered. The ace can be a high or low card to finish a straight: high in 10-J-Q-K-A, and low in A-2-3-4-5. When two players have straights, the sequence with the highest card is the winner.

Flush

A flush is any five cards of the same suit, not in numerical order. If two players have flushes, the highest-value card determines the winner.

Full House

A full house is a combined pair and three of a kind. Ties are determined first by the value of the three of a kind, then by the pair. For example, if one player has three 6s and two 4s, and another player has three 5s and two 3s, the player with the 6s wins. If the game includes wild cards and both players have three 6s, the player with the pair of 4s wins.

Four of a Kind

This hand consists of four cards of the same face value, plus a singleton. When two players each have four of a kind, the winner is determined by the highest face value of the matching cards. As with the three-of-a-kind hand, ties are impossible unless wild cards are used, but in that event, the kicker becomes the tie-breaker.

Straight Flush

A straight flush is five consecutively numbered cards of the same suit, with the highest card a king or lower. As with a straight, the sequence with the highest card breaks a tie. For example, a diamond straight flush of 6-7-8-9-10 beats a spade straight flush of 2-3-4-5-6.

Royal Flush

This is the highest standard poker hand, consisting of the five highest cards 10 J Q K A all in the same suit. This is also known as an ace-high straight flush. If two players have royal flushes, it's a tie; there is no tie-breaker.

Five of a Kind

Five of a kind is the highest poker hand in a wild-card game. It consists of four cards of the same rank, plus a wild card. When two players each have five of a kind, the winner is determined by the highest face value of the matching cards.

In general, poker hands are ranked according to the probability of each hand being dealt pat—without discards and redraws—from a standard deck. The exception is the ranking of flushes: An ace-high flush is actually more likely to be dealt pat than a 7-high flush.

As a rule, card rooms never use wild cards. The exception is draw poker, where the joker is wild. In games where the joker can be used only as an ace—to fill an ace-high straight, for example—the joker is called "the bug."

How to Bet Poker

Poker, perhaps more than any other casino game, requires you to have a solid knowledge of rules and strategies in order to leave the table a winner. Strong, disciplined players will consistently overpower weak players, so the more practice you have, either in live play or online, the better your chances of raking in the pot. You need to be able to not only identify the value of your own hand, but to decide whether it's worth your money to stay in or fold, and what the chances are of drawing to that inside straight.

At most card clubs and poker rooms, a dealer handles the cards, and a marker, called a "button," is passed around the table to the left to denote which player is acting as dealer for a given hand. Sometimes, the player-dealer is selected by dealing the cards face-up until a joker lands in front of a player; that player then becomes the first dealer, and the action begins to his or her left.

General Rules for Betting

In most versions of poker, you ante for the right to play before the cards are dealt; the amount you ante depends on the table limits. Some games call for a "forced bring-in," in which a player is required to bet to start the action; in seven-card stud, the player with the lowest up-card has to make the forced bring-in to get things started. Other games, like Texas Hold'em and Omaha, have blind bets, which are similar to the bring-in; blinds are paid by the player or players to the left of the dealer's button.

> When you sit down to a game with blinds, the dealer will ask if you want to "post." This means you pay a blind bet to see the cards before the regular betting starts. You are not required to post. Your best option is to say no, which means you will not be dealt any cards. Instead you will watch the game until the action comes around to you again.

After the antes, bring-ins, and blinds, betting rules vary according to the version of poker you're playing. In general, for each betting round, you have the option to check (stay in the game but not bet), call (match the previous player's bet), raise (match the previous player's bet and add another bet), or fold (withdraw from the game and forfeit any bets you've already made).

The rules for placing bets in public poker clubs and card rooms are more stringent than those you may be used to following at home. In a game with friends, you might be accustomed to making "string bets"—that is, bets that start out as calls but turn into raises, as in, "I see your dollar, and I raise you another dollar." This is a huge no-no at a card room. Unless you announce the size of your bet before you place your chips, you aren't allowed to double-dip from your stack; you can't call and then decide to raise. In the card room, once you declare your wager, either verbally or by the amount of chips you push forward, you can't change your mind.

Understanding Betting Limits

Betting limits usually are either "spread limit" or "structured-limit." Spread limits are expressed as a range, such as $1 to $5. This means that the minimum bet is $1, the maximum bet is $5, and players are free to bet or raise anything in between. Structured limits also look like a range, but are distinguishable from spreads because the higher number usually is double the lower number (e.g., $2–$4 or $3–$6). In structured-limit games, bets and raises are made at the lower limit in early rounds and at the higher limit in later rounds; players decide whether to bet or raise, but the amount of the bet or raise is determined by the limit.

ESSENTIAL

In card rooms and poker clubs, only the dealer is allowed to touch the pot. When you make a bet, don't toss your chips into the pot; instead, place them in front of you. This allows the dealer to make sure you have the right number of chips for your ante or bet.

Most public poker games are played with table stakes, which means you can bet only the money you have on the table, and you must wait to buy more chips until the table is between hands. If you run out of chips in the middle of a hand, the dealer will announce that you are "all in." You're still eligible to win the pot, but if other players continue to bet, their chips will be placed "on the side" in a new pot, and you cannot win that pool of money.

It's a good idea to start out playing at the lowest-limit table you can find. Learning to play in a public game can be nerve-wracking enough without worrying about whether you can afford to lose your bankroll. Use the low-stakes games to hone your skills, and move on to higher-stakes games when you have some experience behind you.

Poker Clubs and Card Rooms

Most casinos offer poker rooms or clubs where players pay a fee to sit at the table. Sometimes this fee is a time-based charge, perhaps $5 or $10 per half-hour, depending on the stakes of the game; some rooms offer twenty-four-hour "club memberships," which allow you to play as long as you like for the duration of your membership for a set price. Standalone card rooms usually use the membership structure for their fees.

Some card rooms make their money by "raking" a percentage of the pot in each hand. The percentage is usually around 5 or 10 percent with a maximum dollar value, say $3 to $5, and only players who win the final pot pay the fee. Another method is the "button charge," in which the player with the dealer button is charged a flat fee, usually a couple of dollars, before each hand begins.

If you're new to the poker room, it's a good idea to let the dealer know as you take your seat. The dealer will then know to explain your options when the action comes to you, and other players will be more forgiving when you slow down the game. The action can move surpris-ingly quickly in a public card room; it's not uncommon for novice players to find the action coming to them before they've even had a chance to look at their cards.

Card Room Etiquette

A public card room can be a frightening place for the novice player. Even if you've spent hours playing simulated games on your computer or playing with friends around your kitchen table, you might find yourself intimidated by the staff, players, and general atmosphere of the card room. Knowing what to expect, and what's expected of you, can help calm those natural jitters.

Given the rapidly increasing popularity of poker, most card rooms are busy places these days. They handle the crowds by having sign-up sheets or boards; you indicate which type of game you want to play and for what stakes. If the tables are full, you might have to wait for a seat to open up. If this happens, be alert; if a member of the staff calls your name and you don't respond, you'll be passed over.

If the action is moving too fast for you, and particularly if another player is impatient to act out of turn, call "time." This gives you an extra moment or two to decide what to do; it also makes it clear to the dealer and the other players that you haven't acted yet. Refrain from any nervous tapping while you're thinking. This is usually interpreted as a signal to check, and it will be binding.

ALERT!

Never put your cards in your lap or intentionally show them to another player; these are grounds for declaring your hand dead, and you're out of the game. Also be sure to place a chip on your cards while they're on the table; cards that aren't so "protected" may be mistaken as a fold.

Dealer Tokes

Poker dealers, like their counterparts elsewhere in the casino, typically make a relatively low hourly wage and depend on tokes, or tips, for much of their income. Most poker players tip fifty cents to $1 every time they win a pot, depending on the individual and the size of the pot. You'll find some players who won't tip if they have to split the pot. Whether to tip is up to you. Remember, though, that the dealer is just delivering the cards; it's not the dealer's fault if your luck or your skills aren't in the game.

Tournaments

Thanks to the game's growing popularity, especially among younger bettors, poker tournaments are pretty easy to find. Many card rooms and casinos offer weekly tournaments with relatively modest buy-ins or entry fees. Some of the bigger rooms and casinos even offer daily tournaments.

In a tournament, players compete for a prize pool, which might be winner-take-all or might be divided up among the top four to seven finishing players. Rules vary from tournament to tournament. Players buy in for a set fee, and each player begins with the same number of chips as every other player. Some allow rebuys, in which busted players can purchase additional chips to stay in the game. Rebuys might be offered to all active players or only to players with short stacks (a smaller-than-average stack of chips), or they might be limited to one rebuy or certain times. Some tournaments also offer "add-ons," which is a one-time opportunity for players to buy a certain number of additional chips. Each of these options, when offered, increases the total prize pool. If rebuys and add-ons are not offered, the tournament is called a "freeze-out," and players are limited to the number of chips they receive at the start of the tournament, plus any chips they win during the course of play.

Betting structures also vary from tournament to tournament, but the betting limits almost always increase during the later rounds of play. This is done in part to hasten the end of the tournament; the bigger the bets, the more quickly players will be forced out in late rounds. Betting limit increases may occur based on time—every thirty minutes, for example—or based on rounds of play.

QUESTION?

What should I look for in a tournament?
If you're new to tournament play, look for one that features a game you're comfortable with at a modest buy-in, and view it as an investment in increasing your experience. Your goal in your first few tournaments should be to learn as much as possible while spending as little as possible.

General Odds

Knowing what the odds are of being dealt a specific hand in poker doesn't do much to improve your game. But knowing the difference between "pot odds" and "card odds" can help you formulate your betting strategy and, in the long run, help make you a winning player.

Pot odds are easy to figure: it's a ratio of the amount of money you have to put in, to the value of the pot. If the pot is worth $500 and you have to put in $5 to continue playing, the pot odds are 100 to 1. If you have to put in $50 to stay in the game, the pot odds become 10 to 1.

Card odds describe the probability that you'll improve your hand with a draw or the next round of dealing. For example, if you hold a pair in your first three cards, your odds of improving your hand range from about 2.5 to 1 to a little over 3 to 1, depending on what the other players are showing. If you hold four cards to a flush, you have about a 1-in-5 chance of getting the card you need. In either case, your betting strategy will be influenced by both the pot odds and the card odds.

Let's say you have a pair of 10s and a 7, with no other 10s or 7s showing. The pot is $100, and you have to kick in $10 to keep playing. The odds of you improving your hand are about 2.5:1, and the pot odds are 10:1. In this case, it's probably worth your while to stay in the game, because the pot odds are good and your card odds aren't bad.

But what if the pot is only $20, and you have to put in $5 to stay in the game? That drops the pot odds down to 4 to 1, and your card odds don't look quite as good in comparison.

Card odds can vary significantly depending on the type of game, the number of players, and other factors. The following chart shows the general odds of drawing one card to complete a hand, using a fifty-two-card deck with no joker.

Hand to Complete	Probability of Drawing Needed Card	Odds Against Drawing Needed Card
Inside straight	8.5 percent	About 11 to 1
Open-ended straight	17 percent	About 5 to 1
Flush	19 percent	About 4 to 1
Inside straight flush	25 percent	About 3 to 1
Open-end straight flush	32 percent	About 2 to 1

Both card odds and pot odds change according to the type of game and the betting structure. Pros spend years learning the nuances of the odds and adjusting their betting patterns accordingly. As a beginning player, your best bet is to watch other players as much as possible, and stick with a fairly conservative approach while you're learning the game. (E)

Chapter 6

Playing Poker Against Other Players

There are several variations of poker that have developed over the years. Many of the most popular games pit the players against each other, not against the house. In these games, your chances of winning depend as much (or even more) on your skill level and the skill level of your opponents as they do on the cards themselves. Here's what you need to know to get started playing poker in a casino.

Draw Poker

Draw poker is considered the standard from which all other variations of poker are derived. Still a common ingredient in many home games, draw has been pushed aside at many casinos, where more exotic and interesting varieties like Omaha and Texas Hold'em have captured larger pools of players. If you find yourself intimidated by those games, however, draw poker is a good place to begin your poker education.

The name of the game comes from the fact that players can draw replacement cards after the deal. Some games allow you to draw up to three cards; others allow you to draw four cards as long as you show that your remaining original card is an ace; a rare few allow you to replace all your cards.

Basic Rules

Before the deal, each player places an ante—a bet for the right to play the hand. After the ante, each player receives five cards, dealt face-down, and the first round of betting begins.

Betting begins with the player on the dealer's left and proceeds to the left around the table. In the first round, the first player to bet has the option of passing (also called checking), which gives the right of the first bet to the next player. If the next player also passes, the right of first bet goes to the third player, and so on. Once someone has opened with a bet, the next player must at least call that bet to stay in the game; he or she also may raise the bet.

ESSENTIAL

If no one opens in the first round of draw poker, the hand is considered over. Ante bets remain in the pot, and each player adds a new ante; then the cards are shuffled and a new hand is dealt.

After the first round of betting is complete, players then decide whether they want to draw replacement cards. Discards are always placed face-down on the table. When all players have received their replacement cards, there is a second round of betting. Again, the first player in the second betting round has the option of checking, and each subsequent player can check as long as no one has bet yet in this round. Once a bet is made, the other players must fold, call, or raise.

If only one player remains active after the second betting round—i.e., has not folded—he or she wins the pot. Under these circumstances, the winner does not have to show his or her cards. In fact, most poker players strongly recommend not showing your cards unless you have to.

If two or more players are still in the game at the end of the second betting round, they enter what is called the "showdown." In this case, each player lays his cards face-up on the table, and the highest hand wins.

Variations in Draw

There are several versions of draw poker that involve modest changes in the rules. One of the most common variations in casino draw games is a version called "jackpots," in which you must have a pair of jacks or better to open the betting. Some casinos offer high/low draw, in which the highest and lowest hands split the pot. There also is a version called "lowball," in which the lowest, rather than the highest, hand wins. In lowball, the ace always counts as a low card.

The size of the pot may dictate whether it's worth taking the chance or not. Multiply your bet by the card odds; if the pot is lower than that total, it makes good sense to fold. For example, if you have to put $10 into the pot in the hopes of beating 1 in 23 odds on the draw, it probably isn't worth the risk unless there's at least $230 in the pot. On the other hand, if your card odds are 1 in 5 and the pot is worth $100, you should stay in.

How to Bet Draw Poker

As with most versions of poker, your betting strategy for draw depends on the cards in your hand, your chances of drawing the cards you need to complete your hand, and the size of the pot. In general, if you have nothing in your first five cards, chances are you'll still have nothing after the draw, and your best option usually is to fold. This is likely to happen about half the time: the odds of being dealt five mismatched cards are about 1 in 2, while the odds of being dealt a pair are around 1 in 2.5.

A Pair or Better

Say you hold a pair of 4s, a 7, a jack, and a king, all of different suits. Should you keep the king as a potential tie-breaker? Or should you dump it and hope for something better in the draw?

Though it's tempting to hang onto that high card, chances are you'll get more help from the deck if you toss it. When you have a pair and draw three cards, you have about a 1 in 3.5 chance of improving your hand. But if you keep the kicker and only draw two cards, your chances of improving drop to about 1 in 4.

Suppose you have three of a kind with a kicker. Should you draw one or two cards? Again, your chances of improving your hand are better when you toss the kicker. If you draw two cards to your three of a kind, you have about a 1 in 9.5 chance of increasing the value of your hand. If you only draw one card, your chances of improving are only about 1 in 11.

As for three-card flushes and straights, your chances of filling either on the draw are pretty dismal—almost 1 in 30 for the flush, 1 in 68 for a closed straight (such as A-2-3, 4-5-8, or Q-K-A), and 1 in 23 for an open straight (3-4-5 or 10-J-Q, for example). In most games, the size of the pot won't be large enough to justify taking those kinds of odds.

Drawing One Card

When you have four good cards to build your hand on, the odds become quite a bit more favorable. You stand about a 1 in 5 chance of completing a flush, and about a 1 in 6 chance of filling a straight that's open at both ends (e.g., a 4-5-6-7, when a 3 or an 8 can complete the sequence). A straight that's open on only one end (such as A-2-3-4) or an inside straight (such as 4-5-7-8) is more difficult to fill, with about 1 in 12 odds. You have about a 1 in 23.5 chance of filling a straight flush that's open at both ends, but the odds against you double to about 1 in 47 for an inside straight flush or one that's open only on one end.

Seven-Card Stud

Seven-card stud is one of the most popular games for beginning players because the rules are easy to learn and the betting sequence tends to build healthy pots—and therefore substantial potential winnings. Players make the best five-card hand out of seven total cards. Each player receives two hole cards, dealt face-down, and one up-card. Betting starts with the player who has the lowest card showing, and proceeds to the left of that player. Players can match or increase the bet or fold at this point.

After the first-round bets are made, each player receives another card face-up. For the second betting round, the player with the highest hand showing begins the betting, again proceeding to the left of that player. This process is repeated until each player has four up-cards. For the final round, also called "the showdown round," each player receives a seventh card face-down. When all bets have been placed, the dealer calls for players who are still in the hand to show their cards, and the highest hand wins.

Under most house rules, a raise must be at least equal to a previous bet or raise. For example, if the player to your right has raised $3, you can call the $3 or raise $3, $4, or $5, but you cannot raise another $2.

How to Bet Seven-Card Stud

According to most experts, the outcome of any seven-card stud game is almost always determined by the first three cards you're dealt. Smart players will make their betting decisions based on their first three cards and will throw away hands that don't carry a reasonable expectation of winning.

Three of a Kind

If you're lucky enough to be dealt three of a kind—the odds are around 400 to 1 against, but it does happen occasionally—chances are you can win the pot if you bet carefully. With this kind of hand, your goal is to let the pot grow so you don't want to scare off the other players. Remember that one of your cards is showing; if you happen to be dealt the fourth in your sequence, you'll have a pair showing, and that may be enough to encourage other players to fold, especially if you're betting aggressively. To keep the pot growing, cover the bets during each round, but avoid raising until the sixth card is dealt.

Pairs and High Cards

A pair of aces, kings, queens, or jacks puts you in a fairly good starting position. If one of your pair is showing (called an "open pair"), it reduces the value of the hand somewhat; other players will assume you have the other half of the pair in the hole. Watch the up-cards during the rounds to see whether other players have been dealt cards that would improve your hand. If you haven't bettered your hand by the fifth card, you're probably better off folding.

If you have a low pair (10s or lower), three high cards (jack, queen, king, or ace), or three cards to a straight, most experts recommend staying in until the fourth card is dealt. If you don't get a card to help this hand by the fourth card, your best option is probably to fold and wait for a better hand.

FACT

A hand that has potential to be really good but which requires another card—for instance, if you have four cards to an ace-high flush—is called a "drawing" hand. Your hand isn't big yet, but if you draw the right card (in this case, another card of the same suit) it will be.

Potential Straight Flush

If you have the first three cards of a straight flush—consecutively numbered cards of the same suit—you're in good shape for at least the next two rounds of betting. There are several ways to improve this kind of hand: you can complete the straight flush, get a straight (with consecutively numbered cards of different suits), or get a flush (five nonconsecutive cards of the same suit). Many players recommend betting or even raising during the first round in this situation. On the other hand, if you haven't drawn anything to help you by the fifth card, most experts recommend folding.

Potential Flush

If you hold three cards to a flush (cards of the same suit), the odds say you'll complete the flush once out of every six hands. Stay in for at least two more cards. If you haven't received another card in your suit after the fifth card is dealt, you're better off folding.

Any Other Combination

If you don't have one of the previous combinations in your hand after the first three cards are dealt, the odds against you winning the hand are astronomical. Don't throw your bankroll away; drop out and wait for the next hand. Take the opportunity to observe the other players and pick up pointers on their betting strategies and skill level.

Texas Hold'em

If you've ever watched the World Series of Poker on the Travel Channel, you've seen Texas Hold'em, widely considered the game of choice among professional poker players. Like seven-card stud, Hold'em is played with seven cards, from which players form the best five-card hand. There are four rounds of betting in Hold'em. Players build their hands from two hole cards (dealt to them face-down) and a series of five community cards dealt face-up in the center of the table.

Basic Rules

The person to the left of the dealer (designated by the dealer button, as explained in Chapter 5) pays the small blind (forced bet), and the person to his or her left pays the big blind. The dealer deals two cards to each player, and then the first round of betting takes place. Betting begins to the left of the person who paid the big blind. Players may call, raise, or fold.

After the first round of betting is concluded, the dealer burns (or discards) the top card on the deck, then deals the first three community cards, called "the flop." Players then make the second round of bets. The fourth face-up card in the middle of the table is called "the turn," and it is followed by another round of betting. The fifth community card is called "the river," and the final round of betting follows this deal. Each player makes his best hand from the two cards he holds and the five cards in the middle of the table.

In limit Hold'em games, the amount of the bets is set. In the first two rounds of betting, players who choose to bet or raise must do so in increments of the lower betting amount. For example, in a $2–$4 game, bets during the first two rounds are in increments of $2. During the third and fourth rounds of betting, bets and raises must be made in increments of the larger bet amount ($4 in this example).

In no-limit Hold'em, typical in tournaments, players may bet as much or as little as they wish when it is time to act.

FACT

Texas Hold'em is by far the most popular tournament poker game. This typically is the game you'll see being played in televised poker tournaments, such as "Celebrity Poker" and the World Series of Poker events. Sometimes, particularly in larger tournaments, the format calls for alternating rounds of Texas Hold'em, Omaha, and other variations of poker.

How to Bet Texas Hold'em

Experts caution that Texas Hold'em is seldom won with any hand lower than a pair of aces. In most cases, if you don't have high-value hole cards and the community cards haven't already given you a good hand, you'll probably be better off dropping out after the fourth community card is dealt.

Betting strategies for Texas Hold'em are similar to those for seven-card stud, but you make your decisions based on your first two cards. If you don't have either a pair or two high-value cards—queens or better—in your hand, experts recommend withdrawing and waiting for the next hand. Again, you can use the time to study the other players.

The best starting hands in Texas Hold'em are a pair of aces, kings, queens, or jacks, but even with a good start, it's important to pay attention to the community cards. If you're lucky enough to start with a high-value pair, you should stay in and cover the bets at least until the fourth up-card is dealt. With aces or kings, most experts recommend playing the entire hand, regardless of what the up-cards show. With a pair of queens or jacks, play until the fourth up-card is dealt, and withdraw if you haven't improved your hand by then.

The same strategy is recommended for lower-value pairs and high-value cards, either of the same or different suits. If you hold any combination of ace, king, or queen, cover all bets until the fourth up-card. If you haven't bettered your hand, fold.

FACT

Because you use the best five of seven cards to build your hand in Texas Hold'em, there are more ways to be dealt winning hands than in a game using only five cards. For example, with five cards, there are only about 10,000 ways to build a straight. But with seven cards, there are more than 6 million ways to do it.

Omaha

In Omaha, sometimes called "Omaha high," players get four down-cards and must use two of them—and only two—along with three community cards, to make their hands. Before the cards are dealt, the two players to the left of the dealer—or the player acting as dealer—post bets called "the big blind" and "the small blind." The small blind, posted by the player to the dealer's immediate left, is half of the lower bet limit (usually rounded to the next highest dollar, so at a $3–$6 table, the small blind would be $2). The player to the left of the small blind player posts the big blind, equal to the table's lower bet limit. After each player has her four down-cards, the first round of betting starts with the player to the left of the big blind. In this round, players can check, fold, call, or raise.

After the first round of betting, three cards are dealt face-up in the center of the table, called "the flop." Then the second round of betting takes place. From this round on, betting action begins with the player to the left of the dealer's button and proceeds clockwise around the table. After the second round of betting is complete, a fourth community card, called "the turn" or "fourth street," is dealt, followed by the third round of betting.

The size of the bet is doubled on the third round in Omaha. For example, at a $3–$6 Omaha table, all bets and raises during the first two rounds would be $3; in the third and fourth rounds, all bets and raises are $6. After the third round of betting is finished, the final community card, known as "fifth street" or "the river," is dealt, and players make their final rounds of bets before showing their hands.

"Omaha 8 or better" is a split-winnings variation of Omaha, in which the high and low hands divide the pot. In this version, the high hand automatically wins, but the low hand must consist of different-valued cards between ace and 8 with no pairs. (If there is no qualifying low hand, the high hand wins the entire pot.) As in regular Omaha, you must use two of your hole cards and three of the five community cards to build your hand. However, you can use one set of cards to make a high hand and another set to make a low hand; when this happens, you "scoop" the entire pot.

On the low side, the win goes to the player with the lowest high card. For example, a player with 2-4-5-6-7 would beat a player with 2-4-5-6-8. The best low hand is A-2-3-4-5, sometimes called "a bicycle" or "the wheel"; straights and flushes are not counted against you for a low hand. If two players have the same high card, the next highest card determines the winner. If all cards have the same numeric value, the two players split the low half of the pot.

How to Bet Omaha

Your cutoff for bad cards in Omaha should come after the flop is dealt and before the third round of betting, when the bet size doubles. As in seven-card stud and Texas Hold'em, you should cover all bets until the third round if you have a pair of aces or better; if you haven't improved your hand with the first three community cards, you're better off folding. Most Omaha hands require a straight or better to win; don't waste your bankroll if you don't have the cards. Ⓔ

Chapter 7

Poker Games Against the House

Several poker games pit the player against the casino, instead of against other players. This makes them fun, social table games, which many players enjoy. Because you're playing against only the dealer, you don't have to worry about bluffing. Several popular variations on poker that are played against the house are covered in this chapter, so you'll be ready to sit down and play in no time.

Pai Gow Poker

Pai Gow, a Chinese phrase meaning "makes nine," is a seven-card game in which the player tries to build two hands that have a higher value than the banker's two hands. The role of the banker moves from player to player, or in some cases, the dealer is the banker. Any player can decline to be banker, but your odds of winning typically are better if you are the banker.

The Pai Gow poker table has space for six players. Usually, the dealer acts as banker for the first hand, then passes the banker's role on to a player. A special marker called a "chung" is placed next to the player who is acting as banker. When a player is acting as banker, the dealer plays the hand in the same way as any other player.

Basic Play

Pai Gow poker uses a standard fifty-two-card deck plus a joker. In a few casinos, the joker may be used as a wild card, but usually its use is limited to filling in straights, flushes, and straight flushes, or as an ace in any hand. Players place their bets, and each player, including the dealer, receives a stack of seven cards. The four leftover cards are discarded.

Players separate their seven cards into two hands, one containing five cards and one containing two cards. The two-card hand is called the "low hand" because its value must be lower than the five-card hand; if the two-card hand has a higher value than the five-card hand, it's considered a "foul" and you lose your bet. The two-card hand is also sometimes called the front hand, and the five-card hand is the high or back hand.

When all the players have set their cards, the dealer turns the banker's cards face-up. The banker (not the dealer) then sets those cards into five- and two-card hands, and his hands are compared, one at a time, to the players' hands. To win, both of the player's hands must beat both of the banker's hands. Equally ranked hands are called "copies," and the banker wins. If one of the player's hands is better than the banker's, but the other is not, it's considered a push and no money is exchanged.

If the player wins, the dealer pays even money from the banker's funds. If the player loses, the dealer gives the player's bet to the banker. The house takes a 5-percent commission on winning bets.

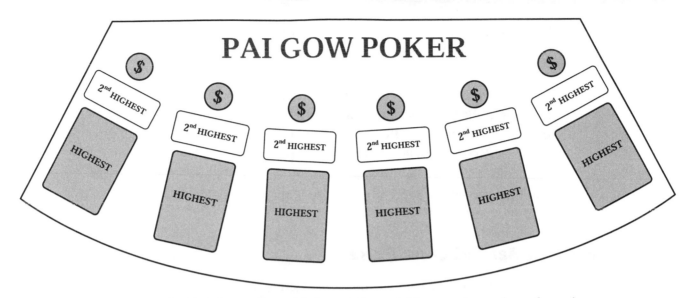

▲ A typical Pai Gow poker table layout. Some tables may have places for only six players, and marking for hands and bets may vary by casino. Some, for example, mark the hands "high" and "low", while others, like this one, use "highest" and "second highest."

Winning Hands in Pai Gow Poker

The hands in Pai Gow poker are valued the same way that standard poker hands are valued. The exception is the five-aces hand, built with four aces and a joker, which is the highest possible hand in Pai Gow poker, beating a royal flush. The two-card hand either contains a pair or a nonpair, and the highest two-card hand is a pair of aces.

The rank of hands in Pai Gow poker, from highest to lowest, are:

- Five aces
- Royal flush (ace, king, queen, jack, 10, all the same suit)
- Straight flush (five consecutively numbered cards, all the same suit)
- Four of a kind
- Full house (three of a kind and a pair)
- Straight (five consecutively numbered cards, not of the same suit)
- Three of a kind
- Two pair

- One pair
- High card

The player has to ensure that her high and low hands are properly set. The five-card hand must rank higher than the two-card hand, so it's critical in this game that you're familiar with the standard poker hand rankings. For example, if you're dealt a pair of 3s and five mismatched cards, the pair must be included in your five-card hand. Likewise, if all you have for either hand is a high card, the highest high card must be in your five-card hand.

How to Bet Pai Gow Poker

The strategy for Pai Gow poker is different from any other version of poker because you have to build a high hand and a low hand. How you build your hands depends on what your seven cards hold. If you have seven mismatched cards that don't include a straight or a flush, you must put your highest card in your five-card hand. Your two-card hand should contain your second- and third-highest cards. If you hold a pair, the pair goes in your five-card hand, and your two highest single cards make up your two-card hand.

With two pair, put the higher pair in the five-card hand and the lower pair in the two-card hand. However, if you have a single ace, use it and another singleton in the two-card hand and keep the two pairs together in the five-card hand. If you hold three pair, your highest pair should go in the two-card hand, and the other two pairs should go in your five-card hand. When you hold two pair and a straight, ignore the straight and play the hand as you would two pair. The same rule applies if you have two pair and a flush.

If you have five cards of a straight, use those five for your high hand and put the two mismatched cards in your low hand. If you have six cards of a straight, use the singleton and the highest card of the straight for your low hand, and play the remaining straight in your high hand.

If you have a flush and no pair, place the flush in your five-card hand and use the highest cards you can (without breaking up the flush) for your two-card hand. For a full house, place the pair in your two-card hand and the three-of-a-kind in your five-card hand.

Playing the Banker

You have a better edge in Pai Gow poker when you play the banker. This may seem counterintuitive, because you pay the winning players out of your own money when you're the banker. But remember that the banker wins all copies, and ties don't cost you or the player anything. You might want to place a bigger bet than usual when it's your turn to be the banker.

House rules on the banker's limits vary, so check with the dealer before you sit down. Some places require you to cover all the players' bets, while others allow you to "play short," with less than the total of all the other players' wagers. And some places limit the other players' bets to what the banker has on the table.

Let It Ride

Let It Ride is a variation of five-card stud. The object of the game is the same—to get the highest hand—but it differs from five-card stud in three important respects. First, players play against the house, rather than against each other. Second, you build your hand using three cards dealt to you, plus the dealer's two hole cards. Third, and perhaps most important, players are allowed to withdraw bets in Let It Ride.

Let It Ride is played at a table similar to a blackjack table, with space for up to seven players. Each place at the table has three circles for bets, labeled 1, 2, and $. Before the cards are dealt, you must place the minimum bet on each of the three circles. At a $5 table, that means you place $15 on the table. Don't let this worry you too much, though; if the cards look terrible, you can remove two of those three bets. If the cards look good, you let your bets ride, hence the name of the game.

ESSENTIAL

If you want to let your first or second bet ride, place your cards face-down under your chips in the 1 or 2 circle. If you want to withdraw either of these bets, scratch your cards on the table toward you. If your first three cards are terrific and you intend to play all three bets, place your cards under your chip on the $ circle; this lets the dealer know you're in for the duration.

Basic Play

You place your bets on the circles in front of you, and the dealer gives you three cards, face-down. The dealer gets two cards, also face-down. The fate of your first bet is decided by your own cards. After you look at your three cards, you can withdraw the bet on the circle labeled 1, or you can let it ride. Either way, the dealer will turn over his first card after you've indicated what you want to do with your first bet.

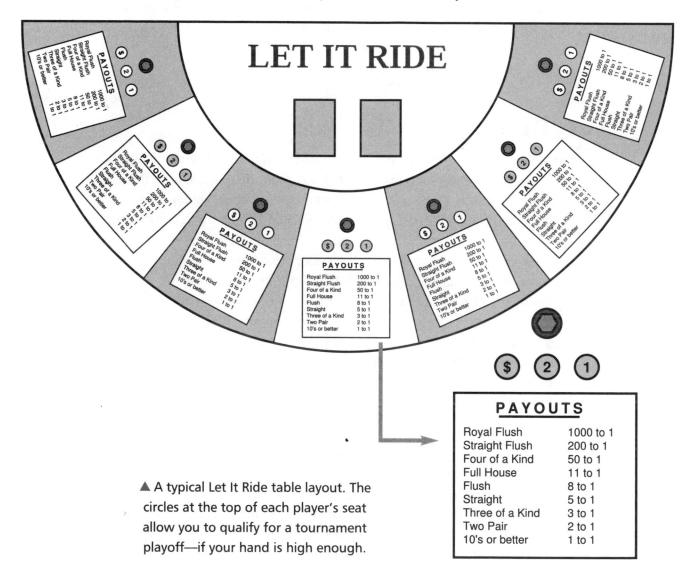

▲ A typical Let It Ride table layout. The circles at the top of each player's seat allow you to qualify for a tournament playoff—if your hand is high enough.

PAYOUTS

Royal Flush	1000 to 1
Straight Flush	200 to 1
Four of a Kind	50 to 1
Full House	11 to 1
Flush	8 to 1
Straight	5 to 1
Three of a Kind	3 to 1
Two Pair	2 to 1
10's or better	1 to 1

This dealer's card counts as the fourth card in your hand. This is when you decide whether to withdraw your second bet, in the circle labeled 2. Again, no matter what you decide, the dealer turns over his second card, which counts as the fifth card in your hand. After both the dealer's cards are face-up, all players lay down their cards face-up, and the value of each player's hand is calculated.

As in any casino game, don't touch your chips once you've made your bet and the hand is in play. If you want to withdraw your 1 or 2 bet, let the dealer push your chips toward you. This will avoid any misunderstandings or disputes.

Winning Hands in Let It Ride

Hands in Let It Ride are ranked the same as in regular poker, but you must have at least a pair of 10s to win. From highest to lowest, the winning hands in Let It Ride are:

- *Royal flush* (ace, king, queen, jack, 10, all the same suit)
- *Straight flush* (five consecutively numbered cards, all the same suit)
- *Four of a kind*
- *Full house* (three of a kind, and a pair)
- *Straight* (five consecutively numbered cards, not of the same suit)
- *Three of a kind*
- *Two pair*
- *One pair* (10s, jacks, queens, kings, or aces)

If you don't have a pair of 10s or better when you combine your three cards with the dealer's two cards, you lose whatever bets are still live on the table. This means you'll always risk losing the $ bet, because you don't have the option of withdrawing that wager. If your 1 and 2 bets are still on the table, you lose those as well. On the other hand, if you have at least a pair of 10s among all five cards, you win on all your live bets.

Payout Schedules

Payouts on these hands can vary from casino to casino. However, a pair (10s or better) typically pays even money, while two pair usually pays

2:1, and three of a kind usually pays 3:1. A straight typically pays 5:1, a flush 8:1, a full house 11:1, four of a kind 50:1, a straight flush 200:1, and a royal flush 1,000:1.

Payout Limits

Now for the bad news: Most casinos limit their Let It Ride payouts. The payout limit can range from a couple thousand dollars to $50,000 or higher, and in most cases it won't affect you. But if you happen to get that elusive royal flush, the payout limits mean you might not collect the full value of your wager.

Here's why: Assume you're playing at a table with a payout limit of $5,000. You place three $5 bets, for a total of $15, and you let all your bets ride. Between your cards and the dealer's, you have a royal flush, which pays 1,000:1 for each live bet. You should collect $15,000—$5,000 for your 1 bet, $5,000 for your 2 bet, and $5,000 for your $ bet. Even if you withdrew your first bet and left only two bets on the table, you should get $10,000. But because of the table limit, you'll only get paid $5,000.

E

ALERT!

Once you decide whether to withdraw your first bet or let it ride, that decision stands; you can't change your mind later. You can, however, decide to withdraw your first bet and let your second bet ride, or vice versa, or withdraw both. The bet in the $ circle cannot be withdrawn.

Because payouts and payout limits can vary, make sure you check these schedules before you sit down. Both figures should be posted on the table. If you have any questions, ask the dealer. Your best plan is to choose a table with a high payout limit, say $25,000 or more, but keep in mind that the minimum bet may (and often does) increase with the payout limit.

How to Bet Let It Ride

Betting strategies for Let It Ride are fairly easy to master. You want to let your bets ride when the cards are favorable, and you want to withdraw your bets when the cards are not favorable. Properly utilizing the option to remove two-thirds of your bet on each hand will minimize your losses and stretch your bankroll.

The First Bet

The decision about whether to withdraw your first bet is based only on the three cards dealt to you. Remember that you must have at least a pair of 10s in order to win; a pair of 6s doesn't do you any good in this round. However, three 6s is a winning hand.

Experts recommend that you let your first bet ride when you hold a high pair (10s or better) or any three cards to a royal flush (the ace, queen, and jack of hearts, for example). If you have three almost-consecutive cards to a straight flush—7-8-10, for example, or 8-9-Q—you should let your first bet ride, especially if you have at least one high card and there's a spread of four or five cards in the sequence.

You should let it ride when you have three consecutive cards to a straight flush, but only when the lowest card in the sequence is a 3 or better. If you're holding A-2-3 or 2-3-4, the odds are pretty stiff against filling that, and you're better off withdrawing your first bet. If your three cards don't contain any of these combinations, withdraw.

The Second Bet

You get another chance to evaluate your hand after the dealer's first card is revealed. Remember that this represents the fourth card in your hand, so you want the dealer's cards to be good. If the dealer's first card doesn't add to the value of your hand, withdraw your second bet.

Remember that you win 1:1 on each of your live bets if you have at least a pair of 10s. If your first three cards are a 3, a 5, and a 10, basic strategy calls for you to withdraw your first bet. If the fourth card is a 10, you've got a paying hand, so let your second bet ride. If it's not a 10, withdraw your second bet, and hope the fifth card is a 10.

Let your second bet ride when you have four cards to a royal flush, straight flush, or flush. You also should let it ride when you have four of a kind, three of a kind, two pair, or a pair of 10s, jacks, queens, kings, or aces. If you have four consecutive cards to a straight, and at least one of them is a high card, let your second bet ride.

Caribbean Stud

Like Let It Ride, Caribbean Stud is based on five-card stud and is played at a blackjack-style table; like blackjack, the player has to beat the dealer. The most unusual feature of Caribbean Stud is that it is the first table game to offer a progressive jackpot.

Basic Play

Players place an ante bet before the cards are dealt; the minimum is $5 at most tables. Each player receives five cards, face-down. The dealer takes four face-down cards and one up-card. The player then decides, based on her own hand and the dealer's up-card, whether to fold or call.

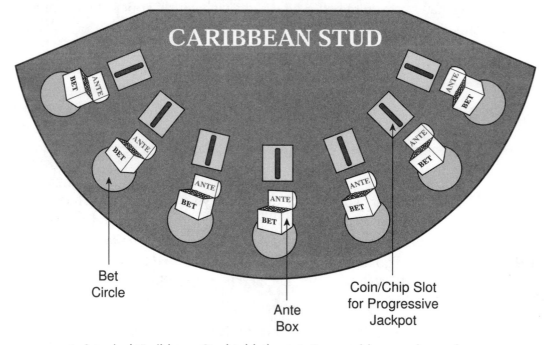

CARIBBEAN STUD

▲ A typical Caribbean Stud table layout. Some tables may have places for only six players, and markings for bets and antes may vary in design.

If you fold, you forfeit your ante bet. If you decide to play, your call bet must be double your ante. If your ante is $5, your call bet must be $10; if your ante is $10, your call bet must be $20. After the call bets are made, the dealer reveals his four down-cards.

The Progressive Jackpot Bet

The bet on the progressive jackpot in Caribbean Stud is a side bet on your hand, not dependent on whether you beat the dealer. At most casinos, this is a $1 bet. You are not required to place the jackpot bet to play the game, but you won't be eligible for any payouts from the progressive pool if you don't.

At most casinos, the jackpot bet pays only if your hand is a flush or higher. A flush typically pays $50, a full house pays $75, and four of a kind pays $100. This varies from casino to casino, so look for the payout schedule at the table or ask the dealer.

If you get a straight flush, you receive 10 percent of the jackpot pool. A royal flush pays 100 percent of the jackpot. The jackpot pool is usually displayed in lights above the Caribbean Stud table, and it can grow quite large, well into the tens of thousands of dollars.

Winning Hands in Caribbean Stud

Winning hands in Caribbean Stud are ranked the same as in regular poker. However, the dealer must "qualify" to play the hand with at least an ace and a king (or a better-ranked poker hand). If she doesn't have an ace and a king, the hand is over. In this event, players get even money on their ante bets, and the call bets are a push—that is, you don't win any money but your bet is returned.

If the dealer qualifies, then her hand is compared to each player's hand, and the highest hand in each case wins. If your hand beats the dealer's hand, you get even money on your ante bet and a bonus on your call bet. The typical call bonus is 1:1 if you have an ace-king high or a pair; 2:1 for two pair; 3:1 for three of a kind; 4:1 for a straight; 5:1 for a flush; 7:1 for a full house; 20:1 for four of a kind; 50:1 for a straight flush; and 100:1 for a royal flush. If the dealer's hand beats yours, you lose your ante and call bets.

The house edge for Caribbean Stud is about 5.2 percent on the ante bet. It's high because the dealer has to "qualify" to play a hand. On the combined ante and call bets, the house edge drops by half, to around 2.6 percent.

How to Bet Caribbean Stud

Basic strategy for Caribbean Stud is perhaps the simplest of all the poker-based games. Remember that you're trying to beat the dealer, and you can't replace any of your cards. You have to make your decision based on your own cards and the dealer's up-card.

If you have a pair or better, you should call. Keep in mind that the dealer has to qualify with at least an ace and king high (or better) hand. If he doesn't qualify, you can win even money on your ante even with a lowly pair of deuces. You also should call if you hold an ace and a king, if one of your cards matches the dealer's up-card. In this case, chances are good that you can beat the dealer with a high card if nothing else.

If you don't have either of these combinations, fold.

Three-Card Poker

Three-card poker is one of the newest variations of the game, designed to move along at a quick clip, almost like a version of blackjack. It is played with a standard deck of cards, and you can bet on your own hand as well as against the dealer. Both the player and the dealer receive three cards, face-down; as in blackjack, each player's hand is played against the dealer's hand and not against the other players.

Winning Hands in Three-Card Poker

The hands in three-card poker are based on standard poker, but the ranking is different because the probability of getting each hand is different when you only use three cards. A flush in three-card poker is three cards of the same suit, while a straight is three consecutively numbered cards of any suit and a straight flush is three consecutively numbered cards of the same suit. Pairs and three-of-a-kind hands also are possible in three-card poker; four of a kind, full house, and two pair are not possible.

Unlike standard poker, you're more likely to be dealt a straight in three-card poker than you are to be dealt three of a kind, and you're more likely to be dealt a flush than a straight. Three-card poker hands, ranked from highest to lowest, are:

- Straight flush
- Three of a kind
- Straight
- Flush
- One pair
- High card

FACT

There are 52 possible three-of-a-kind combinations in three-card poker, and 720 possible straight combinations, which is why three-of-a-kind beats a straight in this game. Likewise, there are more than 1,000 ways to get a flush, which is why a straight beats a flush.

How to Bet Three-Card Poker

Players have three betting options in three-card poker: the ante, the "pair-plus" bet, and the "play" bet. As in standard poker, the ante is your buy-in for the hand. The pair-plus bet is a wager that your hand will contain a pair or better; like the ante, this bet has to be made before the cards are dealt. At most casinos, the pair-plus bet cannot exceed the ante.

Typical payouts on the pair-plus bet are:

- *Pair*—1:1
- *Flush*—4:1
- *Straight*—6:1
- *Three of a kind*—30:1
- *Straight flush*—40:1

After looking at your cards, you decide whether to play your hand against the dealer or to fold. If you fold, you forfeit your ante and pair-plus bets. If you want to play, you make your "play" wager, which usually must be equal to the ante.

In most casinos, a dealer's hand has to "qualify," usually with a queen or better, in order to play against the player. If the dealer's hand doesn't contain a queen, the hand is considered a push. When that happens, you keep your play bet, and you get a 1:1 payout on your ante bet. In addition, some casinos offer bonuses on the ante bet. Typically, you'll receive even money for a straight, 4:1 for three of a kind, and 5:1 for a straight flush.

Chapter 8
Craps

There always seems to be a party going on around a craps table. The shooter, the bettors, even the table staff—all contribute to the convivial atmosphere by shouting encouragement, hollering out bets, and whooping with delight at a successful throw. To the novice, the energy can be just as intimidating as the rules, the crowded table layout, and the lingo surrounding the game, but the game itself is simple. Once you penetrate the mystique, it's easy to join the party.

History of Craps

Humans have been using some variety of dice since ancient times, sometimes as a tool to predict the future or interpret the will of the gods, and sometimes as a form of amusement. Cubical dice, similar to our modern version and dating to about 600 B.C., have been found in Egypt; ancient Indian texts speak of warriors throwing dice and betting on the outcomes. Roman emperors, among them Nero and Caligula, are said to have been devoted dice players, and both Roman warriors and American Indians are believed to have shaped animal knuckle bones into cubes, with which they played various games; this may be the origin of the phrase "roll the bones."

The main theory about the modern game of craps is that it evolved from an Arab game, which made its way to France and England under the name "hazard." It is believed to have made its way to the New World in the early 1700s, when the French colonized Acadia in present-day Nova Scotia. When France lost Acadia to the English, the Acadians took the game with them to present-day Louisiana, where it continued to flourish as a popular pastime. The name *craps* is probably derived from the term "crebs" or "crabes" from "hazard," which described the lowest-value roll in the game. By the mid-1800s, "craps" had officially entered the American English language as the name of the dice game, which moved up the Mississippi River on gambling boats.

FACT

Early dice were made from animal bones, ivory, porcelain, or other hard, opaque materials. Today's casino dice are molded from translucent hard cellulose, which allows you to see into the interior and decreases opportunities to "load" or "fix" the dice.

Early versions of the game allowed only two kinds of bets—"field" or "come" bets—and the use of "loaded" dice to skew the outcome of a roll was common. Then, dice-maker John H. Winn introduced new variations that allowed bettors to wager with or against the dice, which effectively eliminated the usefulness of loaded dice. By 1910, this new improved version of craps was one of the most popular casino games in the world.

The Object of Craps

Appearances aside, the object of craps is really quite simple. As the shooter (the person rolling the dice), you win if the first roll is a 7 or 11. If you roll a 2, 3, or 12, you "crap out," or lose automatically. If you roll any other number—4, 5, 6, 8, 9, or 10—you keep rolling the dice until you roll that number again, which is called the "pass-line point." When this happens, your goal is to avoid rolling a 7 on your next rolls; to win, you have to match the pass-line point before 7 comes up. So, for example, if your first roll is a 5, you keep rolling until you hit a 5 again; if you roll a 7 before a 5 comes up, you lose.

The other players around the table bet either that you will match your pass-line point or that you won't. Usually, perhaps because of the party atmosphere around the craps table, other players will bet with the shooter; it's considered bad form to "disrupt the vibes" by betting against the shooter, particularly if he or she is on a hot streak.

How to Play Craps

Typically, there are four casino staff members at a craps table: the boxman, who is responsible for overseeing the game and resolving disputes; two dealers, one for each side of the table, who take care of the bets; and the stickman, who delivers the dice to the shooter and announces rolls and betting options.

Players take turns acting as the shooter, but you are free to pass the dice if you don't want to shoot. The stickman usually offers the shooter five dice, and the shooter picks out two to play with. The first roll is called the "come-out" roll, and the result of this roll determines what happens next. If the shooter rolls a 7 or 11, she—and those who bet with the shooter—wins even money, and the next roll effectively begins a new round of play. If the come-out roll is a 2, 3, or 12, the shooter—and, again, those who bet with the shooter—loses, and the dice are passed along to the next player.

If the come-out roll is a "point"—that is, a 4, 5, 6, 8, 9, or 10—then players bet on whether the shooter will roll that point again before rolling a 7. The shooter continues to roll until either the point is made or a 7 comes up. If the point is made, the shooter can continue rolling, trying to make the point again, or he can relinquish the dice to a new shooter.

A plastic disk called a "puck," with one black side and one white side, is used to keep track of the game. When the black side is up, that signifies that the current throw is a come-out roll. When a point is established on a roll, the puck is flipped white side up and placed on the numbered box corresponding to the point.

At virtually every casino, you must place a pass-line or don't-pass wager in order to be the shooter. If you don't want to shoot, you can elect to pass and let the next person roll the dice.

Craps Superstitions

There are several myths and superstitions surrounding craps. One is that you should never be the first player when a craps table opens up because the dice will be "cold;" they need to be handled for a while to warm up. Another superstition forbids putting money on the table while a shooter is rolling the dice, especially in the middle of a hot streak; if the dice hit the "new" money, the belief goes, the next roll will be a 7.

Many craps enthusiasts also believe the next roll will be a 7 if one or both dice bounce out of the table during a roll, but this can be avoided (according to the superstition) by making sure you use the same dice on the next throw. That's why you'll sometimes hear the shooter, or even bettors, call, "Same dice!" Along the same lines, hitting someone's hand with the dice is believed to be bad luck, so you'll often hear bettors, shooters, and even casino personnel yelling, "Watch your hands," as the shooter begins to roll.

The Virgin Principle

Finally, there is the so-called "virgin principle," a piece of craps mythology that states a woman who has never acted as a shooter before—a dice virgin—will have a hot streak her first time out. This superstition is so ingrained that when a woman who has never played craps before comes to the table, often you'll find veteran players placing bets for her in an attempt to win her favor, or the favor of her gambling gods. Interestingly, the virgin principle does not apply to men; in fact, it is firmly believed that men who have never thrown the dice before are jinxes at the craps table.

How to Bet Craps

The betting is where craps gets complicated and tends to intimidate the novice player. You have several options, depending on where in the round you are. Payouts and house edges vary according to the type of bet you make, and may vary slightly from casino to casino; the figures discussed here are typical but by no means universal. As always, if you have any questions about the odds or payouts, ask a member of the casino staff for help.

Pass-Line and Don't-Pass Bets

These bets are the most common and are placed before the shooter makes his or her first roll. With a pass-line bet, you're wagering on two possibilities: first, that the shooter will roll a 7 or 11 on the first throw; or second, that the shooter will roll a point (4, 5, 6, 8, 9, or 10) and will repeat that point before rolling a 7. You lose if the first roll is a 2, 3, or 12. Most casinos pay even money on a pass-line bet.

The don't-pass bet is the opposite of the pass-line bet. In this case, you're wagering that the shooter will either crap out on the first roll (that is, throw a 2, 3, or 12) or, if the shooter rolls a point on the first roll, that he or she will roll a 7 before repeating the point. You lose if the first roll is a 7 or 11.

Come and Don't-Come Bets

Come and don't-come bets are the same as pass-line/don't-pass bets, except that they are made after the shooter makes his or her first throw and establishes a point. With a come bet, you're wagering that the shooter will repeat a point before rolling a 7; with a don't-come bet, you're wagering that the shooter will roll a 7 first.

On a come bet, you win even money if the next throw is a 7 or 11. You lose if the throw is a 2, 3, or 12. If the throw is any other number, that number becomes the point for your come bet, and your chips are moved to the numbered box corresponding to your point. If the point is repeated before a 7 is rolled, you win. If a 7 shows up first, you lose.

The don't-come bet is the opposite, and it's much less popular than the come bet. On this bet, you win even money if the next throw is a 2 or 3; a 12 is a push, or tie. You win on this bet if a 7 is rolled before the point is repeated, and you lose if the point is repeated first.

One of the reasons don't-come bets are less popular than come bets is that you're betting against the shooter. Because of the peculiar camaraderie around the craps table, it's considered bad form, if not actually bad luck, to bet against the shooter.

Place, Buy, and Lay Bets

The place bet is the most straightforward bet in craps. You choose one of the possible points—4, 5, 6, 8, 9, or 10—and bet that the next roll will come up on your point. The payoffs on place bets vary according to how likely it is your chosen number will come up. For example, the payoff on a 4 or a 10 is typically 9:5, but it's usually just 7:5 on a 5 or 9, and only 7:6 on a 6 or 8. The higher payoff means it's harder to roll the number. For example, a 5 or 9 each will, on average, show up about 11 percent of the time on random dice rolls, while a 4 or 10 each shows up only about 8 percent of the time. A 6 or 8, on the other hand, will come up about 14 percent of the time—hence the lower payout on those two numbers.

A buy bet is the same as a place bet, except you pay a 5 percent commission up front to the house; in return, you are paid true odds if you win. Under a buy bet, you're paid 2:1 on 4 or 10, 3:2 on 5 or 9, and 6:5 on 6 or 8.

A lay bet is made on a point number—4, 5, 6, 8, 9, or 10—but you're actually betting against the dice. That is, you're betting that a 7 will come up before the point number you selected. A 7 is, statistically, the most likely number to come up on any given roll of two dice; that's why the casino charges a commission on this bet. Typical payoffs are 1:2 if you bet on 4 or 10, 2:3 if you bet on 5 or 9, and 5:6 if you bet on 6 or 8.

Field, Big 6, and Big 8 Bets

Field bets give you a chance to bet that the shooter will roll any one of a field of numbers—2, 3, 4, 9, 10, 11, and 12. The typical payoff on a 2 or 12 is 2:1, while the other numbers usually pay even money. You lose if any other number outside the field comes up.

Big-6 and big-8 bets are even-money wagers; you win if the number you selected is rolled before a 7 comes up.

Proposition Bets

Proposition bets are one-roll wagers on a specific number or group of numbers. You can, for instance, bet that a 7 will come up on the next roll; this bet typically pays 4:1. You also can bet "any craps," and you'll usually win 7:1 if 2, 3, or 12 comes up. Other proposition bets include 2 or 12, with a payout of 30:1; 3 or 11, with a payout of 15:1; craps-11, sometimes called a "C&E" or a "horn bet," with a payout of 3:1 on a 2, 3, or 12 and 7:1 on an 11.

Most casinos also offer hard-way bets on 4, 6, 8, and 10. To win, your number has to come up "the hard way," or as a pair, before it comes up in any other combination and before a 7 comes up. For example, if you bet on a hard-way 6, you only win if a pair of 3s shows up before a 2 and a 4 or a 1 and a 5 (or a 7). Payouts on hard 4s and 10s typically are 7:1. Payouts on hard 6s and 8s usually are 9:1.

Although the payoffs on proposition bets can be appealing, most experts recommend avoiding them. The house edge on proposition bets usually is quite high—between 11 and 16 percent—and the odds are against you cashing in on those big payoffs.

Odds Bets

Most experts agree that in craps the easiest way to trim down the house edge to virtually nothing is to take advantage of the odds bet option. You won't find a place for this on the table layout, but it exists. Odds bets give you true odds (not casino odds). However, the house edge is still the same on the pass-line bets, so the house still has an advantage.

ESSENTIAL

There is no designated space for the odds bet on the craps table layout. Typically you place your odds bet half-on and half-off the bottom of the pass-line or come fields. For don't-pass and don't-come odds bets, place your chips above and to the side. If you aren't sure where to place your chips, ask the dealer.

Odds bets complement bets on pass-line, don't pass, come, and don't come. Depending on the casino, you're allowed to wager up to 100 times your original pass-line bet; in most cases, your odds bet must at least equal your pass-line bet. The odds bet cannot be placed until a point is set, so you can't make this bet on the come-out roll.

For example, assume you made a $10 pass-line bet, and the point is set at 5 on the come-out roll. If the next roll also comes up 5, you win even money on your pass-line bet. Now, assume you placed an additional $10 odds bet. Not only do you win even money on the pass-line bet, but you win 3:2 on your $10 odds bet, or another $15.

Payouts on odds bets depend on the point. Usually 4 and 10 pay 2:1, 5 and 9 usually pay 3:2, and 6 and 8 usually pay 6:5. Additionally, at most casinos, you can remove your odds bet at any time.

Betting Strategies

The best craps strategy for the novice is to take advantage of the pass-line and odds bets. With these wagers, you can enjoy the game without worrying too much about technicalities. As has been shown, some of the other options offer poor odds or a high house edge and should be avoided.

Some experts recommend that you continue making come bets until all the possible points are covered, but that may be too risky for the casual player. A more moderate approach is to make come bets until you have three numbers covered; if you win on one point, then you can place another bet so that you still have three numbers working for you.

You also can try hedge betting, which is a wager that more or less wipes out another wager. For example, you can combine a come bet with an "any craps" proposition bet. You'll win even money on the come bet, but lose your proposition wager, or you'll win 7:1 on the proposition wager and lose your even money wager.

The craps table layout may display payout ratios both as "to" and "for." Remember the difference: If the payout is 10 *to* 1, or 10:1, you'll get your $5 bet back plus $50. If you bet $5 on a 10-*for*-1 payout, you'll get $50 back when you win, but not your original $5 bet.

General Odds

It's fairly easy to calculate the odds of any given number coming up in a craps roll. Each die has six numbered sides, and each craps roll involves two dice, so there are thirty-six (6 × 6) possible outcomes for each roll of the dice. The odds of any given number coming up in any given roll, therefore, are 1 in 36.

However, for every number except 2 and 12, there are several combinations that add up to the same total. The following chart illustrates this and shows statistically how often one of those combinations will come up in a series of 100 rolls.

As shown in the chart on page 98, 7 is the single most likely number to come up, at just under 17 percent. When you combine the chances of a 7 or 11 coming up, you're looking at 22 percent, or almost 1 in 4. By contrast, the combined chance of rolling a craps—2, 3, or 12—is just over 11 percent. That's why the game centers around the numbers 7 and 11.

Of course, most of the time you won't get true odds at a casino craps table. The house edge on the most popular bets—pass-line and come—is less than 1.5 percent, making it one of the best deals on the gaming floor. But other options on the craps table, such as the proposition bets, give the house an edge of 11 to 16 percent, which makes them very poor wagers unless they're combined with more advantageous bets.

Number Rolled	Dice Combinations (Dice A/Dice B)	Percent Chance
2	1/1	2.77
3	1/2, 2/1	5.55
4	1/3, 2/2, 3/1	8.33
5	1/4, 2/3, 3/2, 4/1	11.11
6	1/5, 2/4, 3/3, 4/2, 5/1	13.88
7	1/6, 2/5, 3/4, 4/3, 5/2, 6/1	16.66
8	2/6, 3/5, 4/4, 5/3, 6/2	13.88
9	3/6, 4/5, 5/4, 6/3	11.11
10	4/6, 5/5, 6/4	8.33
11	5/6, 6/5	5.55
12	6/6	2.77

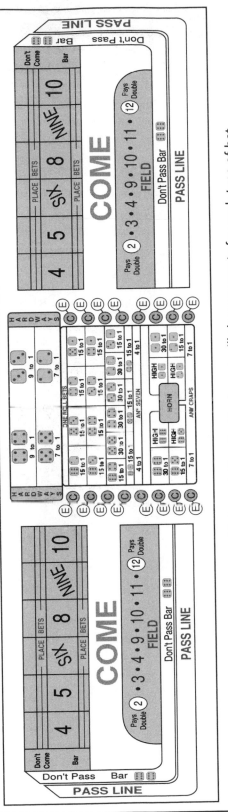

▲ A typical craps table layout. Usually, the layout will show payouts for each type of bet.

Chapter 9
Roulette

Although it isn't as popular in the United States as it is in Europe, roulette is nevertheless the universal symbol for casinos and gambling halls. Its elegant setup and dignified pace evoke images of tuxedo-ed men and gowned women in the exotic surroundings of Monte Carlo or the French Riviera. Roulette is one of the least complex games on any casino floor, with easy-to-understand rules and easy-to-follow action.

History of Roulette

The origins of roulette are uncertain. Some speculate that a game of chance involving a spinning wheel evolved almost immediately after the invention of the wheel itself. One theory states that the game originated in China and was brought to Europe via the spice trade routes. But whatever its ancient history, most historians agree that the modern version of roulette is about 300 years old and was probably introduced in France. Indeed, *roulette* means "small wheel" in French.

The first modern roulette wheels had pockets numbered from 1 to 36, plus one pocket labeled 0 and one labeled 00. Frenchman Louis Blanc is credited with creating the single-zero roulette wheel in the mid-1800s and introducing it in his gaming hall in Germany. With just one pocket labeled 0, the new form of roulette gave gamblers a much better chance of winning, and the game grew in popularity.

When Germany outlawed gambling, Blanc accepted an invitation from Monaco's Prince Charles to open a casino in his tiny country. Blanc used his many political connections to convince the French government to extend the rail line and other essential services to Monte Carlo, and Monaco became the premier gambling destination in Europe, an exclusive playground for the rich. Blanc's casino was the only place in Europe offering roulette until the 1930s.

FACT

Roulette has racked up its share of fantastic stories, both of winners and losers. England's Lord Jersey, it is said, won the maximum bet on seventeen consecutive spins at the roulette table and retired to the country, never to gamble again. On the other hand, in 1974, an Italian player lost more than $1.9 million playing roulette at Monte Carlo.

Meanwhile, the traditional double-zero wheel found its way to the United States and was a staple of gambling halls, especially in frontier towns of the mid- to late-nineteenth century. It's possible to find single-zero roulette in the United States today, but the double-zero version, with its higher house edge, has always been more common here. Perhaps for this reason, or perhaps because the game is played at a much slower pace than other table games, roulette has never achieved the same heights of popularity in the United States that it enjoys in Europe and elsewhere.

The Object of Roulette

The object of roulette is to correctly guess which number a small marble will land on when the roulette wheel slows or stops. The roulette table consists of a wood and metal bowl-shaped wheel, about three feet in diameter, and a table layout for placing bets. The wheel is divided into thirty-eight pockets numbered 1 through 36, plus 0 and 00. The 0 and 00 pockets are green; of the remaining pockets, half are red and half are black. The dealer, or croupier, spins the wheel and releases a small white ball that travels in the opposite direction around the top of the wheel. As the ball loses velocity, it falls into the bowl of the wheel and skips over the buffers that separate each pocket, eventually coming to rest in one pocket. Most roulette tables in U.S. casinos allow up to six people to play at one time.

How to Play Roulette

The roulette table is the only table game where regular casino chips are not used. Because bets are placed on a common layout and not directly in front of each player as in other games, the roulette dealer needs a different system to keep track of every player's bets. When you sit down at the roulette table, you use your regular casino chips (or cash) to purchase roulette chips, which are simply colored disks. You can assign any denomination you choose to these colored chips. For example, if you want $1 chips and you give the dealer $100 in cash, she will give you a stack of 100 colored chips in exchange. If you want $2 chips, the dealer will give you fifty colored chips.

Each player gets a different color so the dealer knows whom to pay, and the dealer will put one of the colored chips on the table rail along with a marker that tells her what that color chip is worth. These colored chips have no value anywhere else in the casino, so you must cash them in for regular casino chips at the roulette table when you are done playing.

Don't be alarmed if you want to make a specific bet and find that someone else has placed a chip on your spot. Because each player's chips are a different color, players can "share" bets at the roulette table; everybody can choose black, for example, or 15, or the same group of numbers.

Minimum bets and table limits are posted at the roulette table. You can make any number of bets, up to the table limit, on any one spin. You simply place your colored chips on the corresponding number, series of numbers, or colors (red or black) on the betting layout.

Usually, the dealer will accept bets in between spins and even after dropping the ball into the wheel—at least until the ball begins to slow down. Then the dealer will wave his hand over the betting layout and will probably announce, "No more bets." When the winning number is determined, the dealer places a clear marker on that number on the betting layout. Losing bets are cleared off the table, and then winning bets are paid. When the dealer is ready for the next spin, he'll announce, "Place your bets."

As with any table game, it's very important that you wait for the dealer's okay before placing a new bet. In some casinos, only the dealer is allowed to touch the chips on the betting layout after a winning number is announced; failure to follow this etiquette might result in the dealer or pit boss asking you to leave.

The placing and paying of bets make roulette take longer between rounds than other table games. You won't find the fast-paced excitement of craps or blackjack here. But if you're a novice at the casino, the roulette table is one of the easiest and least intimidating places to start.

How to Bet Roulette

Roulette offers several betting options for the player. The typical roulette layout consists of forty-nine boxes—one for each of the numbers on the roulette wheel, and colored red, black, or green to match the number's color on the wheel, plus eleven boxes around the perimeter for special bets such as red/black, odd/even, and high/low. Bets on specific numbers are called "inside bets." Other bets are called "outside bets."

Each bet has its own payout. Outside bets typically pay even money for even/odd, red/black, and high/low, and 2 to 1 for column or dozen bets. Inside payouts range from 5 to 1 on a six-number bet to 35 to 1 on a straight bet.

The most important thing to remember is that, no matter what you do, and with very few exceptions, the house has an advantage of at least 5.26 percent on every bet you make on a double-zero wheel. On a single-zero wheel, the house edge is about half that, or roughly 2.7 percent. So, unless you are clairvoyant or incredibly lucky, chances are you'll lose at roulette more than you'll win.

ROULETTE

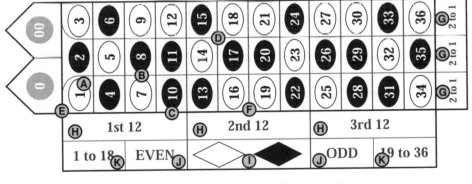

A. Straight Bet (Single Number)
B. Split Bet (Two Numbers)
C. Street Bet (Three Numbers)
D. Corner Bet (Four Numbers)
E. Top Line (Five Numbers)
F. Line Bet (Six Numbers)
G. Column Bet
H. Dozens Bet
I. Red / Black Bet
J. Odd / Even Bet
K. High / Low Bet

▲ A typical roulette table layout. The letters indicate where various types of bets are placed on the table.

The house edge in roulette comes from the difference between true odds and casino odds, or the amount of each bet the casino keeps. On a standard American roulette wheel (one with zero and double-zero pockets), the true odds of hitting any given number are 1 in 38, or 37 to 1. But virtually every casino pays only 35 to 1 on a straight, one-number bet. If you bet $1 on the number 10 and you win, the house will pay you $35—not the $37 you would get if the house paid true odds. The house keeps the $2 difference, which works out to 5.26 percent.

At most roulette tables, you can split up your inside bets to meet the table minimum, but you can't split your outside bets. At a $5 table, you can place several $1, $2, or $3 inside bets, as long as all of these bets total $5 or more. If you opt for outside bets, each bet must be at least $5. If you want to bet red and odd, for example, you have to place $5 on red and another $5 on odd.

Outside Bets

Outside bets are those placed in the eleven boxes around the numbered boxes on the roulette layout. You have five options for outside bets: dozens, columns, even/odd, red/black, or high/low. The payouts on these bets are lower than on inside bets because you cover more pockets; instead of having a 1-in-38 shot at winning, you have up to an 18-in-38 shot.

Dozens and Columns Bets

Columns and dozens bets usually pay 2 to 1. Each of these bets lets you cover twelve numbers on a spin. In a dozen bet, also known as an "any twelve" bet, you choose a set of twelve consecutive numbers—1 through 12, 13 through 24, or 25 through 36.

Place your chip on the box marked "1st 12," "2nd 12," or "3rd 12." If the ball lands on any number within your dozen, you win. If it lands on 0 or 00, you lose.

Column bets also give you twelve potential winning numbers, but they aren't consecutive. You place your bet on the column headed with 1, 2, or 3; your chip goes in the box underneath the column, which usually reads "2 to 1." If the winning number falls in the column you've chosen, you win. Again, 0 and 00 are losing numbers for this bet.

Even-Money Outside Bets

The other outside bets in roulette are red/black, even/odd, and high/low. Each of these is an even money wager, paying 1 to 1 if you win. The boxes for these bets are found farthest to the left of the numbered boxes. Again, 0 and 00 are losing numbers for any of these options.

These even-money bets are just what they sound like. You bet that the ball will land in either a red or black pocket, that the winning number will be odd or even, or that the winning number will be high (19 or higher) or low (18 or lower).

There are eighteen red pockets and eighteen black pockets, eighteen even numbers and eighteen odd numbers, and eighteen low numbers and eighteen high numbers, so it's easy to think that the probability of the ball landing on red or black, odd or even, or high or low is fifty-fifty. Because of the 0 and 00 pockets, which are both green, the probability of winning on any of these even-money bets is closer to 47 percent.

Inside Bets

Inside bets are those that gamble on specific numbers, up to six at once. There are six kinds of inside bets: straight, split, street, corner, five numbers, and six numbers. Correct placement of the chip for these bets is crucial; the dealer will pay based on where the chips are placed, and you don't want to watch your money get swept away because you put your chip on the wrong line. Payouts on inside bets are higher because the probability of the player winning is lower.

Straight Bets

A straight bet, sometimes called a "straight-up bet," means choosing one number to come up the winner. You can bet on 0 and 00 in a straight bet. The straight bet has the lowest probability of winning—37 to 1. But this type of bet also has the best payout; at 35 to 1, which is what most casinos pay on a straight bet, a $5 wager can return $175.

Split Bets

A split bet is one that touches two numbers on the layout. Again, you can bet 0 and 00 if you like. Place your chip on the line separating the two numbers you want to play; you win if either of the numbers you chose comes up. Playing two numbers doubles the probability of winning, so the payout is reduced to 17 to 1 on a split bet.

Street Bets

A street bet covers a row of three consecutive numbers. Place your chip on the outside line of the row you want to play. As in a split bet, you win if any one of your three numbers comes up. Your probability of winning on this bet is three times higher than on a straight bet, and the payout is 11 to 1.

Corner Bets

A corner bet covers four numbers and derives its name from the fact that the chip is placed where the corners of the four numbered boxes meet. Unlike the street bet, the corner bet doesn't cover consecutive numbers. You win if any one of your four numbers comes up. The typical payout on a corner bet is 8 to 1.

Five-Number Bet

The five-number bet, also called the "top-line bet," covers 0, 00, 1, 2, and 3; this is the only place on the layout where one chip can cover five numbers at once. Most experts recommend avoiding this bet because the house edge, almost always a discouraging 5.26 percent, shoots up to more than 7 percent on this bet. The payout on a five-number bet typically is 6 to 1.

Six-Number Bet

The six-number bet covers two rows of three consecutive numbers. Place your chip on the outside line so that it touches the line between the two rows you want to play. If you don't put your chip on the outside line for this bet, you're really playing either a split bet or a corner bet. If any of your six numbers come up, you'll be paid 5 to 1.

General Odds

There is very little you can do to improve your odds in roulette. On a double-zero wheel, the house edge will always be at least 5.26 percent. On a single-zero wheel, it will always be about 2.7 percent.

The House Edge

The reason you can't change the house edge is because roulette is just about as random a game as you can find. Unlike blackjack, for example, where each card dealt changes the makeup of the remainder of the deck and you can improve your odds of getting a winning hand by following a specific strategy, roulette spins are not affected by anything that happened earlier at the table. Roulette spins are independent of each other, like tosses of a coin. When you toss a coin, there's a fifty-fifty chance that it will land heads up; that probability factor is the same every single time, no matter what happened on any previous toss.

FACT

Sometimes roulette tables have a display showing which numbers have come up on recent spins. Some players will bet on numbers that *haven't* hit for a while on the theory that these numbers are "due." Don't fall for the psychological scam here. Remember, every single spin of the roulette wheel is utterly independent of any other spin.

Each time a dealer drops a ball onto the roulette wheel, the chances of it ending up on any given number are exactly the same—36 to 1 on a single-zero wheel and 37 to 1 on a double-zero wheel. You could see a run when the balls lands on, say, 19 five times in a row. But even so, on the sixth spin, the odds of the ball landing on 19 are still 36 to 1 or 37 to 1.

Improving Your Odds

Serious players usually prefer to play outside bets because, although the payouts are smaller, the probability of winning is higher. But the easiest way—and really the only sure-fire one—to improve your odds at roulette is to play European wheels, or single-zero wheels. The single zero drops the house edge to about 2.7 percent on every bet and eliminates the extremely bad (for the player) five-number bet. Payouts are the same on European wheels as they are on double-zero wheels, which makes them even more attractive to the player.

Aside from that, the only other thing that will improve your odds at roulette is playing at casinos that offer the "surrender" rule. It applies only to outside, even-money bets—that is, red/black, high/low, and odd/even. If you have placed one of these bets and the ball lands on 0 or 00, you lose only half your bet. This variation cuts the house edge on these bets in half, to about 2.7 percent. The surrender rule is extremely rare on single-zero wheels, where the house edge is already only 2.7 percent. Before you start playing, ask the dealer whether the house offers the surrender rule.

There are quite a lot of books and Web sites that claim to have workable systems for winning at roulette. The truth is, roulette is a game of chance, not of skill, so no system can guarantee a winning outcome. This sheer randomness is part of what makes roulette stimulating and enjoyable. Sit down at the table with that in mind, and you'll be able to revel in the elegance and relaxation of the game that made Monte Carlo famous. Ⓔ

Chapter 10
Baccarat

Ever since the French nobility latched on to it as their game of choice, baccarat (pronounced "bah-kah-rah") has been the milieu of cultured high rollers everywhere. At most casinos, baccarat rooms are separated from the main gaming floor, tucked away behind velvet ropes and often guarded by impeccably dressed hosts. But beneath all the fancy trimmings, baccarat is an exceedingly simple game of chance.

History of Baccarat

There are conflicting theories about the origins of baccarat. Some believe it's a variation of the French game *vingt-et-un,* or twenty-one, which we know as blackjack today. Others believe it dates from the Middle Ages, when it was played with a deck of Tarot cards. But most historians agree that the modern version of the game originated in Italy and was introduced in France in 1490 by Charles VIII. The name "baccarat" is believed to derive from the Italian word *baccara,* which means "nothing," probably a reference to the fact that 10s and face cards are counted as zero in the game.

Though it gained immense popularity in Europe and particularly in the French Riviera, baccarat has lost its high ranking on that continent to *chemin de fer,* yet another variation of the centuries-old game.

The version of baccarat played in the United States was developed in Great Britain, exported to Central and South America, and finally introduced in Nevada at the famous Dunes Casino in the 1950s. Today it is perhaps most popular in the Portuguese territory of Macao, near Hong Kong. The protocol for the game there is more chaotic than the orderly American version; multiple players often bet on the same spot at the same time, and it falls to the dealers to keep track of each player's wins and losses, and house commissions.

The Object of Baccarat

The object of baccarat is simple: to get a total of 9, or as close to 9 as possible, in two or three cards. Cards 2 through 9 count at their face value; aces count as 1; 10s and face cards count as 0. If the face value of two cards totals more than 9, 10 is subtracted from the total. For example, a 5 and a 9 would equal 4 (14 minus 10). Each hand is limited to three cards, and the player cannot take a third card if the total of his first two cards is 6 or higher.

There are two "natural" hands in baccarat, occurring when the first two cards in either the player's or the banker's hand total 8 or 9. If the player has a natural 8 or 9, the dealer cannot draw a third card. If the dealer has a natural, the player cannot draw a third card. Natural hands beat all other hands in baccarat. The only hand that can beat a natural 8 is a natural 9.

To make the game more accessible to the less affluent gambler, many casinos now offer a version of the game called "mini-baccarat." The rules are the same as in the full-fledged version, but mini-baccarat tables are located on the gaming floor with the rest of the table games, eliminating the exclusive atmosphere and posh accoutrements of regular baccarat. Mini-baccarat also offers much lower minimum bets, making it a more affordable game for most casino patrons. The mini-baccarat table is similar to a blackjack table, usually accommodating six or seven bettors.

FACT

Players don't handle the cards in mini-baccarat. The dealer distributes the cards, calls out the totals, and collects the cards and losing bets at the end of the round. This, combined with fewer players than in regular baccarat, makes for a much faster pace—up to 150 hands per hour instead of the average 50 to 70.

How to Play Baccarat

Baccarat and mini-baccarat are played with multiple card decks, usually six or eight. In regular baccarat, the dealer shuffles the cards and places them in the shoe, and the players take turns dealing the hands from the shoe. There are three dealers at a full table. The one in the middle is the caller, responsible for announcing the total of each hand and determining third-card draws according to the prescribed rules. The dealers on either end of the kidney-shaped table are responsible for keeping track of players' wins and losses and commissions owed on winning banker bets. In mini-baccarat, one dealer handles all these responsibilities in addition to dealing the cards.

Table Layout

A regular baccarat table layout has numbered slots for up to fourteen players to place bets, as well as corresponding slots to keep track of the house commission each player owes. Above the player numbers on the table layout is a row for betting on the player's hand, and above that is a row for betting on the banker's hand. Tie bets are placed in the topmost row on the layout.

FACT

Regular baccarat has seats for fourteen players, but the table layout corresponding to each player's bet is numbered 1 through 12, then 14 and 15. The number 13 is omitted to avoid superstitions of bad luck.

Mini-baccarat table layouts are even simpler, using marked circles to differentiate between player and banker bets; another series of circles or a row for tie bets is located above the player and banker circles. The mini-baccarat table also has designated areas for the player's cards and the banker's cards.

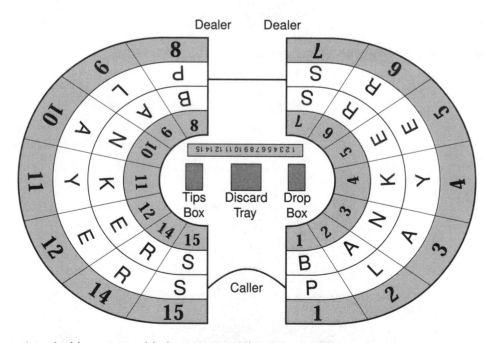

▲ A typical baccarat table layout. Note there is no "13" on the layout.

MINI - BACCARAT

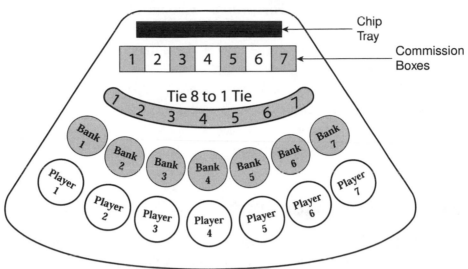

▲ A typical mini-baccarat table layout. The marked areas for player, banker, and the bets may vary in design.

Beginning Play

Whether the dealer is a casino employee or a player, the person who deals the cards plays the role of "banker." Two hands of two cards each are dealt, one for the "player" and one for the "banker." Bets are made on whether the banker or the player will win the hand or whether they will tie.

Other than betting on which hand will win, the player has no choices to make in baccarat. The rules of the game require the player's hand to stand if the first two cards equal 6 or more. If the first two cards equal 0 to 5, the player's hand gets one more card.

The dealer doesn't have any choices to make, either. If the player's first two cards total 6 or higher, the banker's hand draws a third card only if its first two cards total 5 or lower. Otherwise, the banker's hand stands at two cards.

If the player's hand takes a third card, the banker's hand will always draw if its first two cards total 0, 1, or 2. If its first two cards total 7, 8, or 9, the bank hand will always stand. For banker's hands totaling 3, 4,

5, or 6, the decision about drawing a third card depends on what the player's third card is. For example, when the banker's first two cards total 3, the banker takes a card *unless* the player's third card is an 8. If the banker's first two cards total 6, the banker hits only if the player's third card is a 6 or 7.

These rules may sound complicated, but you don't have to worry about studying them in order to play. The dealer makes all decisions regarding the player's and banker's hands and even calls out the totals, so all you have to do is place your bet.

How to Bet Baccarat

Even the betting rules are simple in baccarat. You only have three choices: betting that the banker's hand will win, that the player's hand will win, or that the two hands will tie. You have to place your bet before the cards are dealt, and each bet has its advantages and disadvantages. The house edge on baccarat is very slight for the first two betting choices—less than 1.2 percent on banker bets and about 1.35 percent on player bets.

At American casinos, the house usually takes a commission of 5 percent on winning banker bets. You don't have to pay this commission after each round; instead, the dealer keeps track of what each player owes the house and collects either at the end of the shoe or when the player is ready to leave the table.

Banker's Hand

A winning bet on the banker's hand pays even money, but the house usually charges a 5 percent commission on each winning banker's bet. This means that if you win $100 at the baccarat table, you'll have to give the dealer $5 before you leave. The probability of the banker's hand winning is about 50.7 percent. Even with the 5 percent commission, you're likely to lose less money betting on the banker than betting on the player. If the house commission is 6 percent or higher, you're better off betting on the player's hand.

Player's Hand

The player's hand also is an even-money bet. The difference is that the house rarely, if ever, charges a commission on winning player bets. The player's hand is slightly more likely than the banker's hand to lose. If the commission on winning banker bets is 5 percent or less, your bankroll will last longer betting on the banker's hand.

QUESTION?

Why should I bet on the banker, even with the commission?
In 100 hands of baccarat, the probability of the player's hand winning is about 49.3 percent, versus the banker's 50.7 percent. If you bet $100 over those 100 hands, you probably would lose $1.30 by betting on the player every time, but you would only lose $1.17, even after paying the 5 percent commission, if you bet on the banker every time.

Tie Bet

The tie bet in baccarat is similar to the insurance bet at blackjack—widely considered a sucker bet because the house edge is so high. Statistically speaking, ties will happen less than once in every ten hands. Tie bets usually pay 8 to 1, which is a good payout. But the house advantage on this bet is at least 14 percent, astronomical compared with the tiny edges on banker and player bets. That's why the experts are more or less unanimous in steering you away from it.

The Scorecard

Around the baccarat tables at many casinos, you'll find players busily keeping track of the outcome of each hand, scrutinizing the results for a pattern on which to base their next bet. Casinos actually encourage this, providing pencils and scorecards for the players' convenience. And some diehard players might tell you that they have accurately predicted the outcome of a baccarat hand by filling out the scorecard and discerning a pattern in the number of hands won by the player or the banker.

Analyzing baccarat hands like this can be amusing, but it is absolutely worthless as a predictive activity. Unlike computer-controlled games, where a flaw in the random number generation program can lead to repetitive and predictable patterns in the outcomes of the game, baccarat is a simple game of chance, like roulette or a coin toss. What happens in one hand has no bearing on what will happen in the next.

Card Counting

You may have read the last sentence in the previous section and said to yourself, "Wait a minute. Baccarat is a card game, and when cards are played and taken out of the deck, that changes the odds for the next hand." That's true. But the change in the odds is infinitesimal, for a number of reasons. First, the maximum number of cards played in any one hand is six, and in an eight-deck shoe, six cards is only 1.5 percent of all available cards. Second, already-played cards are usually shuffled back into the shoe long before the last card of the shoe is dealt. So as a practical matter, the cards that are dealt in one hand of baccarat have virtually no impact on the odds for the next hand.

Another reason card-counting techniques don't work well in baccarat is that the betting rules are so rigid. In blackjack, you can alter your betting strategy in certain situations, so keeping track of the cards makes sense. But in baccarat, you have only three betting choices and you have to make your choice before the cards are dealt, so you don't have any opportunity to change your bet midway through the hand.

That said, some sharp mathematical minds have figured out that you might be able to give yourself a very slight advantage by keeping track of the 4s and 6s that are played. As 4s leave the deck, the banker bet becomes slightly more advantageous for the gambler. As 6s leave the deck, the player bet becomes slightly more advantageous. But even the minds that discovered this minute variation in the odds warn that the probability factors in baccarat never change significantly.

Winning and Losing Streaks

Baccarat requires no decision-making or skill from the player, and bets have to be placed before cards are dealt, so there isn't any strategy to maximize your payout per hand. The best you can do in this game is to try to take advantage of the occasional streaks that seem to show up in every game of chance, commonly called "following the shoe." All the term means is that if the player wins one hand, you bet on the player for the next hand. If the banker wins one hand, you bet on the banker for the next hand. By following the shoe, you stay on the right of a winning streak when it appears.

Whether you want to adjust your betting pattern while you follow the shoe depends on the size of your bankroll and how long you want to make your bankroll last. You can use the following betting pattern independent of or in conjunction with following the shoe. This is a conservative betting strategy that involves increasing your wager after a winning bet, but only for the four hands following that win. This gives you the opportunity to maximize your winnings without unduly jeopardizing your bankroll. Here's how it works, based on a $5 wager per hand:

1. You bet $5 on the hand.
2. If you win, you bet $15 on the next hand.
3. If you lose this hand, you bet $5 on the next hand. If you win, you bet $20.
4. If you lose the next hand, you revert to your $5 bet. If you win, your next bet is $25.
5. If you lose the next hand, you revert to your $5 bet. If you win, your next bet is $30.
6. No matter the outcome of the $30 hand, you revert to your $5 bet.

Unlike some more well-known betting systems, this strategy has a built-in fail-safe to ensure you aren't wiped out on a single bet. First, you never increase your bet after losing hands, and second, if you keep winning, you repeat the cycle after five rounds rather than increasing your bet indefinitely. This is an important factor in sound wagering, because, as always, the house edge—slight as it is—will catch up with you eventually.

General Odds

According to mathematicians, the probability of the player's hand winning in baccarat is 44.62 percent. The probability of the player's losing is 45.85

percent, and the probability of a tie between the player's hand and the banker's hand is just 9.53 percent. If you eliminate the possibility of a tie, which is fairly rare in any case, the banker's hand will win just under 51 percent of the time.

Baccarat offers one of the smallest house edges of any casino game—usually a slim 1.4 percent. The casino makes money on baccarat mainly through charging commissions on winning banker bets. Banker hands are slightly more likely to win than player hands, and even with the commission, betting the bank is likely to be slightly more lucrative for you than betting the player. Both banker bets and player bets pay even money, but because of the commission on winning banker bets, the effective payout is .95 to 1.

Tie bets offer attractive payoffs of 8 to 1, but the house edge is more than 14 percent—more than ten times the edge on the even-money bets. The recommendation of most gambling experts is the same for the tie bet in baccarat and the insurance bet in blackjack: pretend it doesn't exist.

As with any form of gambling, you should decide on your bankroll and loss limit before you begin to play baccarat. It's an entertaining game, often played in a sophisticated setting, but unless you can afford to bet—and lose—large sums of money, don't expect an hour or two at the baccarat table to make you rich. If you're lucky, you'll leave with a few extra chips in your hand. Ⓔ

Chapter 11
Slots and VLTs

At one time, slot machines were viewed condescendingly as toys to keep wives and girlfriends occupied while the men played the "real" casino games of craps, blackjack, and roulette. Table games were the prime moneymakers for casinos, and the few slot machines were tucked in little-used corners, away from the traffic and excitement of genuine gambling. Today, slot machines dominate most casino gaming floors, generating by some estimates as much as 70 or 80 percent of a casino's revenue.

History of Slots and VLTs

The first mechanical slot machines were introduced in the 1890s and typically rewarded winners with token prizes like cigars or sweets. Players inserted a penny in the slot and pulled on a lever to start the reels spinning; if the proper symbols lined up in the proper order, the player won. These first machines used springs to release and spin the reels and a notched braking plate to stop them. The first electric slot machines were developed in the 1930s and used a motor to activate the reels. Players pushed a button instead of pulling a lever, but the basic principle remained the same: the player won only if the symbols on the reels lined up in the proper order. It wasn't until the 1960s that electromechanical technology allowed for significant variations in both games and payout rates.

Today's slot machines, though they may resemble their mechanical ancestors right down to the lever, are controlled by computers and microprocessors. Computer technology has promoted a greater variety of games and truly stunning visual and audio components, making slots more enticing and exciting to play. Computers also allow casinos to be far more precise in regulating machine payouts and tracking player activity.

Traditional Slots

Traditional slots are those that accept and dispense coins. These machines have hoppers inside that must be filled (and sometimes emptied) by hand; usually the number of coins they will dispense on any given win is limited, and any wins that require a larger payout must be paid by an attendant. Many casino patrons prefer traditional machines because they like the sound of the coins clattering in the tray when they win.

How Slots Work

Although they are controlled by computers, traditional coin machines operate in much the same way that slot machines have always worked. A coin is dropped into the slot, and the machine records it as a credit. A button or lever is used to activate the reels and make them spin, and a mechanical device is used to brake the reels. Each reel in a machine has a finite number of actual "stops," or places where the reel comes to rest. Thanks to computers, each of the actual stops also has several "virtual stops," or places that tell the computer to brake the reel.

The computer system uses a random number generator, or RNG, which continuously generates random whole numbers, whether or not the machine is being played. When the player pulls the lever or pushes the button, the computer records the numbers generated by the RNG at that precise second. Those numbers are plugged into a mathematical formula to match the virtual stops, which then are matched to actual stops on each reel. If the machine has three reels, the computer will record and compute three numbers from the RNG. If the machine has five reels, the computer will record and compute five numbers from the RNG.

This computerized system allows the casino to be extremely precise in setting its payouts; you may see payout rates of 97.7 percent, for example. It also has the advantage of being truly random because of the huge number of possible combinations of actual and virtual stops.

FACT

Minimum payout rates on slot machines are usually established by law, but actual payouts tend to be much higher than the law requires, usually in the mid to high 90-percent range. Payouts also tend to be higher in more competitive gambling areas because casinos and slot halls don't want to lose business to their competitors.

But this system also means that winning at slots is purely a matter of luck. Whether you pull the lever slowly or quickly or with extra vigor, or whether you push the button instead, your odds of winning on any given spin are exactly the same each time. There is no skill involved in playing traditional slot machines.

Types of Slot Machines

The best-known slot machine is the three-reel, one-pay-line machine, but it is quickly losing favor to bigger machines with more reels and multiple pay lines. Many of these newer machines also have more complicated betting systems that can be confusing to the novice.

Perhaps the most confusing machine is the pay-for-play slot. On this type of game, one coin pays only on certain symbols—black bars and oranges, for instance. To win on, say, gold bars and cherries, you have to play two coins, and to win on 7s, you have to play three coins. If you play only one coin and the reels come up 7s, you won't win anything.

Three-reel, three-pay-line machines also are becoming more common. This machine gives you additional chances to line up the proper symbols, but the payouts for each hit are usually proportionally smaller. For example, a single-pay-line machine might pay out forty-five coins on a hit, but a three-pay-line machine will pay only fifteen coins per hit.

Another variation on the multiple-pay-line machine is the so-called "five-line" machine, where winning symbol combinations can be racked up diagonally as well as on the three horizontal pay lines. Some machines now have four or even five reels. Although these machines sometimes make small payouts on a wide variety of symbol combinations, it's much harder to hit the big jackpot, because more reels mean more possible combinations of actual and virtual stops.

FACT

Your chances of hitting the jackpot dwindle exponentially on machines with more reels. The average odds on a three-reel machine are 8,000 to 1. Those odds jump to about 160,000 to 1 on four-reel machines and to a mind-numbing 3 million to 1 on a five-reel machine.

Coinless Slots

Computer technology also has led to the advent of the coinless slot machine. These machines use either a ticket system or an individual account system in lieu of coins or tokens. Casinos and slot halls like them because these machines have little, if any, "down time." Coin hoppers don't have to be filled or emptied, and there are fewer mechanical failures. Coinless slot machines can save on payroll costs as well. If attendants don't have to worry about filling the machines or paying out on large jackpots, it takes fewer of these attendants to serve the players.

There are advantages for players, too. You don't have to carry around heavy rolls or cups of coins, your hands don't get dirty from handling coins, and you don't have to worry about somebody swiping your coins.

Elimination of the coin itself doesn't affect how the machine works or its payout rates. But it does provide better player tracking and accounting for the casino, and it can be a good money management tool for players.

Ticket Systems

So-called "TITO" systems—short for "ticket in, ticket out"—use paper tickets instead of coins. The player goes to the cage cashier, opens an account, and gives the cashier money to put on the account. The cashier then gives the player a ticket that lists (often in bar code format) the player's account number and balance. The player inserts the ticket into the slot machine, where a scanner reads it, and the computer keeps track of the player's initial balance, credits, and debits. At the end of the session, the player pushes a "cash-out" or "end play" button; the machine dispenses a ticket, which the player redeems at the cage.

Individual Account Systems

These systems work much like an ATM account. The player opens an account at the cage, puts money on the account, and receives a plastic card and a personal identification number (PIN). At the machine, the player inserts the card and enters his or her PIN. As with the ticket system, the computer keeps track of the player's initial balance, wins, and losses. These accounts offer additional security because they cannot be accessed without the PIN if the cards are lost or stolen.

ESSENTIAL

The posted payout rates on slot machines are long-term averages. If you start with $100, a 92 percent payout rate doesn't mean you'll get $92 of your $100 back from the machine. It means that over tens of thousands or hundreds of thousands of pulls, the machine will pay out 92 percent of what it takes in. That's why you can lose your $100, and the next person to play that machine can win $500.

Variety of Games

Many slot machines these days are sophisticated electronic video games, offering a wide variety of playing options. Many of these machines might give you the option of playing six to eight, or more, different games, from keno and lotto-type games to video blackjack. Here are some of the games you might find:

Throw the dough
Jacks or better
Triple 7s
Sun, moon, and stars
High-pair stud
Loaded dice
Where's Henry
Easy riches

Note that some of these games, like triple 7s and sun, moon, and stars, are strictly games of chance; the player has no choices to make. Other games, like jacks or better and high-pair stud, involve more skill than traditional slot games because they allow the player to make choices that can affect the outcome of the game.

Video Lottery Terminals

Video lottery terminals, or VLTs, are electronic games played on a video screen. Often they simulate popular casino games like blackjack, poker, or conventional slot games. Action on these machines is incredibly fast; it's possible to play 400 or more games an hour on a VLT.

VLTs derive their name from the fact that, in most cases, they are linked to a state lottery system. Some states, such as Oregon and South Dakota, allow VLTs in bars, restaurants, and convenience stores. Other states, such as Iowa and Louisiana, permit VLTs only at horse and dog racetracks, which has given rise to the term "racino" in gambling circles.

VLTs are highly popular, in part because of the quick action they offer. This has made them huge moneymakers for the states that have them, too. According to the North American Association of State and Provincial Lotteries, the top three states in per-capita lottery sales are Rhode Island, South Dakota, and Delaware—all with populations of roughly 1 million or fewer. In fact, Rhode Island takes in about $823 a year in lottery sales for every one of its residents. By contrast, Minnesota, which has a state lottery but no VLTs, takes in only about $81 for each of its 5 million or so residents.

Depending on the location, VLTs may use coins, a ticket system, or an individual account system.

How to Play Slots and VLTs

Although the specific games differ from slot machine to slot machine and from VLT to VLT, and methods of payment vary from coins to tickets to account cards, the rules of play are the same. You insert your money, pull the lever or push the button, and wait for the game to tell you whether you've won.

Understand the Machine

Every game should have its winning symbol combinations and its payout schedules clearly posted. Always check to see whether the machine has one pay line or multiple pay lines. Be sure you know whether the machine will pay out the maximum on one coin or whether it requires multiple coins per play for the highest payouts.

If you don't understand how a game works, watch others play a while first, or ask an attendant to help you. There's no need to feel shy or uncomfortable about approaching an attendant; remember, the casino wants you to spend your money, so the attendants are likely to be very friendly and helpful.

Also ask about the payout percentages. Some states require that payout percentages be published regularly, but even those published figures are averages of all the machines at a given location. Payout percentages on individual machines within the same casino can vary widely. If you can, you want to play machines with a 95 percent or higher payout percentage.

Join the Club

Before you sit down to play, ask the cashier or an attendant whether the casino has a players club. Most casinos offer these clubs free of charge to help them track player activity. The advantage for players comes in the form of comps on food, lodging, and merchandise, based on level of play, which casinos offer as incentives for players to come back. You can (and should) join these clubs at every casino or slot hall you frequent; even if you lose money at the slots, you'll get some of your investment back in comps.

ALERT!

Don't fall into the "I'm just playing for the comps" trap. Sometimes people stay too long at the slot machines trying to score a "free" meal. Remember that comps are a nominal reward for your loyalty to a specific casino. You'll recoup some of the money you lose, but you will *never* get it all back in comps.

Video Poker and Blackjack

Many of today's games allow the player to make some choices that can affect the outcome of the play. In video poker, for example, players can choose whether to hold the cards they're dealt or draw new cards, so a basic knowledge of poker is helpful. Likewise, games like blackjack and jacks or better require you to do more than wait for reels to come to a stop.

Most machines with these skill-based games have charts posted on or near the screen that describe winning hands. The rules for each game are the same as they are at the tables. For the novice player, the video versions might be less stressful because you don't have to worry about feeling rushed or intimidated by the dealer or other players.

Some machines with simulated card games let you play three or more hands at once. This can add to the excitement, but it also can be confusing for the newcomer. If you are inexperienced at blackjack, poker, or other card games, stay away from the multiple-hand games until you gain more confidence.

How to Bet Slots and VLTs

We've all heard stories of people who played the quarter slots for twenty minutes and hit an $18,000 jackpot (or higher). That kind of luck gets a lot of publicity, but it doesn't happen to very many people. So, when you sit down at a slot machine, keep in mind that this is a form of entertainment. You might be lucky enough to hit the big one, but just in case you don't, remember to be responsible in your betting.

Minimum Versus Maximum Bets

Most machines these days accept multiple coins (or credits, if you're using a coinless system) on a single spin. Sometimes the payouts are different if you play one, two, or three or more coins. Make sure you understand the payout table, and if you have any questions, ask an attendant.

Many experts recommend that you always play the maximum bet. This strategy is suggested to ensure that you'll get the maximum payout if you do hit the big one. It works best on the pay-for-play machines, which don't pay anything for the jackpot symbols if you haven't placed the maximum bet.

ALERT!

Many experts advise you to play the maximum number of coins on every spin to increase your chances of receiving a large payout. Remember, on a $5 machine, you'll risk $25 on a five-coin spin. That same five-coin spin will cost you $5 on a $1 dollar machine and $1.25 on a twenty-five-cent machine. If you go with the maximum bet strategy, pick a denomination that fits within your budget.

However, many machines have a payout ratio that remains constant no matter how many coins or credits you bet. For example, a machine might pay twenty coins on a one-coin bet, forty coins on a two-coin bet, and sixty coins on a three-coin bet. If you win on a three-coin bet, you'll get more coins back, but the payout ratio is still 20:1. And if you lose, you've lost three times as much as you would have on a one-coin bet.

In short, making the maximum bet on each pull means bigger returns for you if you win, while making the minimum bet means your bankroll will last longer.

Straight Versus Progressive Jackpots

Payoffs on slot machines are either straight or progressive. A straight machine pays a fixed ratio on winning pulls or a maximum jackpot, which is posted on the machine. If two players pulled two consecutive jackpot spins on the same $2,500 machine, each player would receive $2,500.

Progressive machines are linked, and a portion of each bet on every machine is added to the jackpot. Linked machines can be within the same bank of machines at the casino, or in different banks, or in different casinos altogether. These jackpots usually have a minimum of several hundred dollars, but they can grow to thousands, hundreds of thousands, or even millions of dollars. When someone wins a progressive jackpot, the jackpot is reset to the minimum and begins growing again until the next winner comes along.

Some experts believe it's more difficult to win a progressive jackpot than a straight jackpot, while others argue that the RNG gives players equal chances of winning on either kind of machine. In the end, it's up to you to decide how to try your luck.

Tight and Loose Machines

There's a popular misconception that casinos can instantly turn a given slot machine "hot" or "cold" with the flip of a switch. This isn't so. That said, casinos do typically have machines that are "tight"—those that don't pay out very often—and machines that are "loose"—the ones that do pay out fairly regularly. The placement of these machines is largely a matter of psychology, and it makes perfect sense when you look at it from the casino's point of view. Nothing sells like success. The lights and sounds of a winning slot machine are designed to attract attention because the casino knows that people are more motivated to play when they see other people winning. Watching other people win makes us want to get in on the action. That's why loose machines often are located in a casino's high-traffic areas; it's good business.

Tight machines are usually interspersed with the loose machines, and sometimes you'll find entire banks of tight machines in lesser-used areas of the gaming floor. This, too, is sound psychology. As a player, you have no way of knowing whether the machine next to the one that just paid out is tight or loose, but you're more likely to try a machine as close as possible to the "hot" one. Conversely, players often assume their chances are better in the obscure corners because of the lack of use of those machines, reasoning that these slots are due to get "hot." That may be true, but it could take hundreds or even thousands of pulls before such a machine heats up enough to hit a big payout.

Don't walk away from your winnings. Traditional slot machines are limited on how many coins they dispense at one time; large payouts have to be paid by an attendant. If a machine is spitting out coins sporadically, that could mean the hopper is empty; again, you'll need an attendant to get your full payout. Always, always, always hit the "cash out" or "end play" button before you leave a machine.

General Odds

In general, you have about 1 chance in 8,000 to win a jackpot on a straight three-reel machine. The odds on video lottery games and the like are even more astronomical. The bad news is that those odds won't change significantly no matter what you do. The good news is that you can take some steps to make playing more enjoyable.

First, look for the highest payout percentages you can find—95 percent or higher. Second, observe other players and the machines they play. If you watch for a while, you can get a pretty good idea of where the looser machines are. It also doesn't hurt to ask the attendant which machines the locals prefer; regular players won't waste their time at persistently tight machines. Third, decide before you begin how much you're willing to invest in a machine before it starts paying out. If a given machine isn't paying out something on every fourth or fifth pull, you might be better off looking for another machine.

Finally, look at playing the slots as a form of entertainment rather than a get-rich-quick scheme. If fortune favors you, that's terrific. But if it doesn't, at least you've had some fun.

Chapter 12

Special Table Games

Casinos offer a variety of easy games and specials to bring more players through the doors. Some of them are time-limited and others are unique to certain casinos, but they all have the same goal of inducing more people to part with more of their cash. Often, these are games of chance, rather than skill, designed to be less intimidating to the novice player than more traditional games; but they often carry high house edges as well.

Wheel of Fortune

Sometimes called "the money wheel" or "the big 6 wheel," the wheel of fortune is a game of chance with no skill involved. In the United States, the wheel typically has fifty-four slots, most of them marked with various denominations. Bets are placed on boxes on the table layout that correspond to the slots on the wheel. Usually, the wheel has twenty-four $1 slots, fifteen $2 slots, seven $5 slots, four $10 slots, and two $20 slots. The remaining two slots may have either the casino's logo or a joker.

Some wheels have a slot marked "respin." When this slot comes up, all bets remain on the table and the next spin determines whether you win or lose your wager.

After all the bets are placed, the dealer spins the wheel and waits for it to stop. A large clapper indicates the winning number or type of bet. The dealer pays all winning bets and collects all losing bets, then calls for new wagers for the next spin.

FACT

Australian wheels of fortune have only fifty-two slots, with a slightly different payout structure. Because there are two fewer slots to bet on, and because of the way the other slots are divided among the betting options, the house edge is reduced to under 8 percent.

Payouts may vary slightly from casino to casino. In general, payouts correspond to the amount of money wagered. Bets of $1 pay even money, while $2 bets pay 2:1. Bets of $5 usually pay 5:1, $10 bets pay 10:1, and $20 bets pay 20:1. The logo or joker slot typically pays 40:1 and even 45:1 at some casinos.

The house edge on wheel of fortune games is quite high, with the lowest being 11 percent on the even-money bets. The 2:1 bets carry a house advantage of almost 17 percent, and the edge on the 5:1 bets is more than 22 percent. The house advantage on the joker or logo bet is more than 24 percent.

Sic Bo

Sic bo traces its roots to ancient Asian dice games; the name means "two dice" or "pair of dice." Today's version uses three dice and offers several betting options, though most of them carry very high house edges. The dice are juggled in a shaker or, often, a small cage, and winning numbers are those facing up. At most sic bo tables, the winning numbers are typed into a computer, which then lights up the winning bets on the table. Any squares not lit are losing bets.

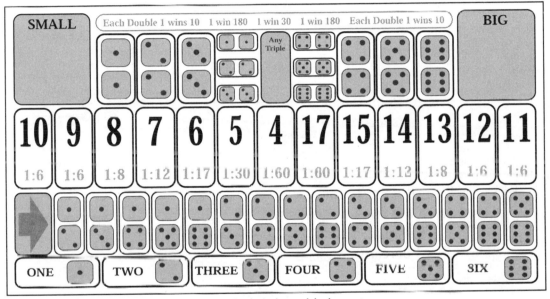

▲ A typical sic bo table layout

There are seven kinds of bets you can make in sic bo. You can bet on a single number from 1 to 6, and if that number shows up on one of the three dice, you win even money. If your number shows up on two of the dice, you get paid at 2:1, and if all three dice show your number, you get paid at 3:1. The house edge on this type of bet runs around 8 percent.

You also can bet on a combination of two numbers; this is called a "two-face" bet and usually pays 5:1, with a house edge of about 17 percent. Another betting option is for any pair, and the payout is usually 8:1. But this bet has one of the worst house edges at around 33 percent.

You can bet on a specific triple—that all three dice will come up 2s, for example—or on "any triple." The payout on a specific triple is a giddy 150:1, while the payout on any triple is a more modest 24:1. In both cases, however, the house edge is about 30 percent.

You also can wager on the total of the three dice, excluding triples. That means you have to select a specific total between 4 and 17; totals of 3 and 18 are losing numbers for a total bet. Because there are different possible combinations for the various totals, the payouts and the house edge vary. Here's a typical payout and edge chart for the possible winning numbers.

Total	Payout	House Edge
4	60:1	29 percent
5	18:1	47 percent
6	14:1	30 percent
7	12:1	10 percent
8	8:1	12 percent
9	6:1	19 percent
10	6:1	12 percent
11	6:1	12 percent
12	6:1	19 percent
13	8:1	12 percent
14	12:1	10 percent
15	14:1	30 percent
16	18:1	47 percent
17	60:1	29 percent

Finally, you can place a "small" or "big" bet, predicting that the total of the three dice will be between 4 and 10 (small), or between 11 and 17. As in the total bets, 3 and 18 are losing numbers here. The small and big bets pay even money, but they carry the smallest house edge of any sic bo bet, at about 3 percent.

FACT

"Chuck a luck," a game similar in its essentials to sic bo, seems to have died out in bricks-and-mortar casinos, but you can still find it at some online casinos. You can bet on single numbers, "under 10" or "over 11," or "the field," which is any number from 3 to 7 or 13 to 18. The house edge ranges from about 8 percent on the single-number bets to about 25 percent on the over/under bets.

Acey Deucy

Acey Deucy, also known as Red Dog or In Between, is another game of chance, but it uses cards instead of dice or a spinning wheel. Players place their initial bets, and the dealer draws two cards and places them on the table face-up. Assuming the two cards are not consecutively numbered or of the same rank—two 3s, for instance—the players have an opportunity to increase their initial wager if they believe the value of the next card will be in between the values of the two up-cards. At most casinos, your additional bet cannot exceed your original bet.

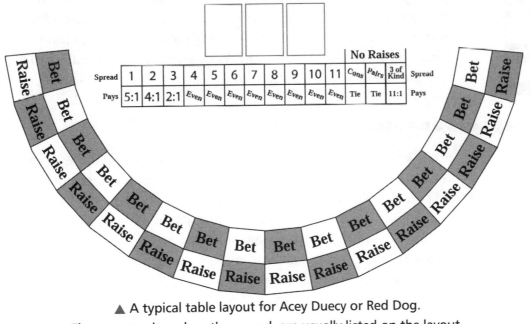

▲ A typical table layout for Acey Deucy or Red Dog.
The payouts, based on the spread, are usually listed on the layout.

As an example, say the dealer draws the 2 of hearts and the 8 of clubs. The spread—the number of cards between two and eight—is five; a 3, 4, 5, 6, or 7 will win the bet. If your initial wager was $5, you can decide to double it to $10. If the third card falls between the 2 and the 8, you win. If the third card falls outside the range of the first two cards— that is, an ace or a 9, 10, jack, queen, or king—you lose. You also lose if the third card matches either of the first two cards.

Card Ranking

In Acey Deucy, cards are ranked the same way they are in poker, and suits are irrelevant. If the first two cards are consecutively numbered, such as a 3 and a 4, the hand is considered a push and your bet is returned to you. If the first two cards are the same rank—two queens, for example—the dealer draws a third card. If the third card matches the first two, you win, with a typical payout of 11:1. If the third card doesn't match the other two, the hand is a push and you get your original bet back.

The highest possible spread is eleven cards, occurring when the first two cards are a 2 and an ace. You'll win in this situation 85 percent of the time, compared with only 8 percent of the time when the spread is just one card. With a seven-card spread, you'll win your bet about 54 percent of the time.

Payouts and Odds

Acey Deucy typically pays 1:1 when the spread is four cards or more. A three-card spread pays 2:1, a two-card spread pays 4:1, and a one-card spread pays 5:1. The overall house advantage on Acey Deucy is just under 3 percent, which is more or less normal for games that don't involve any skill. Most experts recommend against increasing your wager unless the spread is seven cards or more, because the odds go against you quickly as the spread gets tighter.

Casino War

Casinos have turned the popular children's card game of war into a betting game for adults. The object is to have a higher card than your opponent—in this case, the dealer. Casino war is usually played with six decks of cards, which are ranked the same as in poker, except that the ace is always high. As in Acey Deucy, suits don't matter.

To play casino war, you make an initial bet, and you and the dealer each get one card, face-up. If your card is higher than the dealer's, you win even money. If it's lower, you lose your bet. If you and the dealer have the same card, you have two choices: you can surrender, in which case you forfeit half your bet, or you can go to war. If you decide to go to war, you have to place an additional bet equal to your original bet. (At some casinos, the dealer may do the same, but only for show; it doesn't change the payout.) After you place the war wager, the dealer will burn, or discard, three cards and give you and himself another card.

If you beat the dealer on the second card, your raise bet gets even money, and your original bet is a push, which the dealer returns to you. If the dealer's second card is higher than your second card, you lose both your original bet and your raise. Some casinos offer a bonus on the raise bet if the second cards tie. Typically, you get a 2:1 bonus on your raise, and your original bet is a push. Some casinos give you a 3:1 payout on the raise but you forfeit your original bet. Either way, you end up with the same amount.

The house edge on casino war varies with the number of decks used and the bonus structure. A straight six-deck game with no bonus offering carries a house edge of about 2.8 percent. If the casino offers bonuses on second-card ties, the house edge drops to about 2.3 percent.

Three-Way Action

Three-way action goes by a variety of names, but it generally combines three card games: blackjack, a version of war, and a version of poker. You can bet on any one of the games or any combination. Three-way is usually played with a single deck, which is shuffled after each hand.

In the blackjack portion, you play under the regular house rules. If you take seven cards without busting (going over 21), it's an automatic win. The house edge varies according to the blackjack rules, but it averages around 5 percent.

The war portion, sometimes called "combat," pits your first card against the dealer's up-card. The highest card wins, and aces are always high. If your card is higher, you win even money. If your card and the dealer's card tie, you forfeit half your bet. The house edge is just under 3 percent.

The poker portion is sometimes called "seven-card showdown." If necessary, both you and the dealer get additional cards until each of you has seven. The best poker hand wins the bet. The house edge is about 3.25 percent.

In the poker portion of three-way action, the dealer has to have at least an ace high to qualify. If the dealer doesn't qualify, you win half your bet, plus the return of your original wager. If the dealer qualifies and you win the hand, you get paid even money.

Derby

If you're looking for a way to stretch your bankroll while still seeing some action, you might be interested in the electronic horseracing game known as "derby." Derby can usually be found in larger casinos that offer sportsbooks, and often it's located near the sportsbook area of the casino. The minimum bet for this game is usually twenty-five cents, and usually you can bet between one and twenty coins on each race.

The only bet available in derby is the quinella, or choosing the first and second finishers in either order. Odds for each of the possible quinellas are posted on a board before each race. Odds for derby are "for one" instead of "to one," which means you don't get your original wager back. Payouts typically range from 2 for 1 to more than 150 for 1, though these will vary from casino to casino. House edges on derby range from about 10 percent to 20 percent.

"Double Your Paycheck" and Other Specials

Casinos offer dozens of special promotions to attract new players and keep their regulars coming back. One of the most common—and most widely criticized—promotions is an offer to double, triple, or even quadruple your paycheck. This is a device to encourage people to cash their paychecks at the casino. A typical promotion involves a pull-tab, usually given to you free when you cash your check, with prizes ranging from $1 or $2 to $2,000 or more. The idea behind this promotion is simple: casinos want you on their gaming floors when you're flush with cash, and that means bringing you in on payday.

It is best to avoid payday bonanza promotions. Although the pull-tab itself usually doesn't cost you anything, the very act of walking through a casino with your paycheck converted to cash violates two of the most important rules of responsible gambling: you've got a pocketful of "scared money"—funds earmarked for bills, which you can't afford to lose—and you don't have a predetermined budget or gambling plan. Ignore the bait and go to the casino on your own terms.

Drawings

Most casinos offer drawings for cash and prizes on a regular basis. The odds of winning depend on how many people enter, but usually you can count on a lot of competition, especially for those that allow multiple entries. Make sure you understand the rules of the drawing before you enter. Many, if not most, are free, but some are limited to rated players, and many require you to be present at the drawing in order to win. In some cases, if the drawn winner is not present, the casino keeps drawing names until a winner turns up. However, sometimes the casino simply never awards the prize or money if the winner isn't there to claim it.

Double Points

Occasionally, and especially during traditionally slow periods, casinos will offer double, triple, and even up to ten-times comp points for their players' club members. These are usually great deals if you can take advantage of them. Again, be sure to check the rules, because sometimes special points will expire or there will be limits on what you can use them for. Ask the casino host if you have any questions.

Catch a Wave

The Foxwoods Resort in Connecticut introduced this table game, which involves guessing whether your next card will be higher or lower than your last. It is played with eight decks, and cards are ranked the same way they are in poker, except that aces are always high. You have to place your first bet before any cards are drawn; then you and the dealer each receive one card, face-up, and you have to decide whether to hit or stand. If you hit, you have to announce whether you think the next card will be higher or lower than your up-card.

If your call is incorrect, or if the second card is the same value as your first card, you lose. However, if your call is correct, you again decide whether to hit or stand, and again you must announce whether you expect the next card to be higher or lower. This process continues until one of three things happens: your call is incorrect, you decide to stand, or you make six consecutive correct calls. This last is called "catching a wave," and it pays 6:1 on your original bet.

After all the players have taken their turns, the dealer plays his own hand, but with a special set of house rules. If the dealer's first card is a 7 or lower, he must call a higher card; if it's an 8 or higher, he must call a lower card. If the dealer's call is wrong or if his second card matches his first, all the players who are still active get paid even money.

After that first hit, the rules for the dealer change. He is required to stand on 5s through 10s. He must call a higher card on a 4 or lower and a lower card on a jack or higher. The dealer continues to draw cards until he either makes an incorrect call or is required to stand. If the dealer makes an incorrect call, the players who remain active get paid even money on their wagers. If the player and the dealer both stand, the winner is determined by the total number of hits. If the dealer has more, the player loses; if the dealer and the player have the same number of hits, the bet is a push. If the player has more hits than the dealer, the player is paid according to the difference between the number of hits. For instance, if the dealer has three hits and you have five, you would be paid 2:1.

In Catch a Wave, you should always stand on an 8 except in the following situations: if the 8 is your first card and the dealer is showing a 2, 3, king, or queen; or if you have successfully taken five hits and the dealer is showing a 7, 8, or 9.

General Odds

For the most part, special games like those described here are not intended to keep you planted at the table for a long time. Rather, they are "impulse" betting opportunities, designed to catch the eye—and part of the bankroll—of the casual or novice gambler as he or she explores the gaming floor. You can confirm this the next time you're at a casino by watching the wheel of fortune for a few minutes. Chances are you'll notice one or two people stopping to place one or two bets, and then moving on.

With few exceptions, these kinds of games carry a horrendous house edge—in the 30 percent and 40 percent range in some instances. That's why you don't see veteran gamblers crowded around the Acey Deucy table or scrambling to find a spot at sic bo. Unless you want to drop your entire bankroll as quickly as possible, your approach to these games should be to use them sparingly, as an enjoyable break from other games or as a brief detour on your way to the buffet. (E)

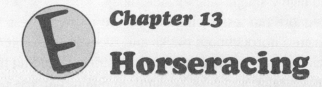

Chapter 13

Horseracing

Horseracing is one of the oldest sports known to man, and today the track remains one of the most interesting places to spend a few carefree hours. Even if you know nothing about horses or betting on horses, it's still exciting to watch these magnificent and graceful animals demonstrate their speed, strength, and endurance. And if you have a little flutter on a horse you like the looks of, that adds some extra zest to the experience.

Harness Racing

Harness racing has been around in some form since the beginning of recorded history, and probably before then. The ancient Greek Olympics featured both mounted horseracing and chariot races, and ancient Rome's Circus Maximus ran two dozen races a day, complete with bookmakers, changing odds, and highly sought-after "inside" tips.

Today, there are more harness racing tracks, and more harness races, per year than there are Thoroughbred tracks and races in the United States. Harness racing also is popular in other countries, including most of Europe, Canada, Australia, and New Zealand. In Spain, harness races are held on beaches, while in Switzerland horses race along snow-covered tracks in the winter. In many countries, harness races are held on grass courses. Most U.S tracks have dirt or clay surfaces.

Harness races don't begin from a dead stop as mounted races do. In a harness race, the horses are lined up on the track before a mobile "gate" attached to a car or truck. The car or truck drives around the track, or a portion of it, allowing the horses to get up to speed. When the gate passes the starting line, the car or truck accelerates and moves out of the way so the race can begin.

FACT

Harness racing has two so-called Triple Crown series. For three-year-old trotters, the Triple Crown comprises the Hambletonian, the Kentucky Futurity, and the Yonkers Trot. The pacing Triple Crown, also for three-year-olds, consists of the Cane Pace, the Little Brown Jug, and the Messenger Stake.

As harness racing grew in popularity, breeders established the standardbred horse, with specific attributes suited for harness racing—endurance, temperament, and anatomy. The name "standardbred" stems from the practice of basing harness racing speed records on a standard distance of one mile. Today's standardbreds all trace their lineage back to Imported Messenger, an English Thoroughbred brought to the United States in the 1780s and bred to both Thoroughbred and mixed-breed mares. One of Messenger's great-grandsons, Hambletonian, greatly influenced the standardbred bloodline. Hambletonian sired four prominent racers that, in their turn, produced lines that included Lou Dillon, the first trotter to run a mile in two minutes.

Standardbred horses are classified as either trotters or pacers. A trotter moves his or her legs diagonally, balancing the weight on the front right and hind left, or the front left and hind right, while running. Pacers, on the other hand, move laterally, with the front and hind legs on the right hitting the ground together, followed by the left front and hind legs.

Young Standardbreds go through a series of training steps while learning to race. In the first stage, the trainer walks behind the horse and teaches it to respond to movements of the reins and harness. In the second stage, the horse learns to pull a training cart, which is usually heavier than the sulky that the horse will pull during a race. All racing horses also go through regular training exercises to develop their speed and skills and to maintain their condition as their careers progress.

Thoroughbred Racing

Mounted horseracing has been around ever since humans learned to ride the animals. During the Crusades, many English knights brought back from their travels fast Arabian horses, which they bred with English horses to produce a line of strong and swift runners. The nobility often paired these horses in head-to-head races to determine which was the fastest—with, of course, a friendly wager as to the outcome—and the "sport of kings" was born.

For the last two centuries, Thoroughbreds have been bred for their speed, agility, and stamina. The breed's long legs allow it to cover more ground with every stride, while its wide girth gives it greater lung capacity. Sloping shoulders and powerful hindquarters also contribute to the Thoroughbred's outstanding running speed.

These common characteristics notwithstanding, Thoroughbreds develop individual running styles through the course of their training and racing careers. Some, called "frontrunners," "pacesetters," or "speedsters," like to lead the field from a race's beginning to the finish line. Others, called "stalkers," would rather hang back from the early leaders and slowly advance during the race. Some, called "closers," "late runners," or "stretch runners," prefer to conserve their energy until the final stages of the races, when they typically come on with furious speed from the back of the field.

To be classified as a Thoroughbred, a horse's lineage must be traceable to sires listed in the General Stud Book. In fact, the breeding has been so selective that every one of today's registered Thoroughbreds can trace its pedigree back to one of three foundation sires: Byerley Turk (1679), Darley Arabian (1700), or Godolphin Arabian (1724).

OTBs and Simulcasting

In the days before satellite technology and the Internet, you had to go to the track if you wanted to see a race other than the Kentucky Derby or the Preakness. These days, with off-track betting parlors (OTBs), live nationwide simulcasting of daily races, and virtual tote boards, you need never see the inside of a racetrack if you don't want to. Several states have OTB parlors, and the advent of simulcasting—where races from tracks around the country are televised on closed-circuit or satellite television—has brought the thrill of horseracing to thousands of new fans. Indeed, even as track attendance has dropped over the years, the handle—the total amount of money wagered on a given day—has increased.

Many OTBs and some tracks even offer online betting, with virtual tote boards displaying odds and results in close to real time. Some OTBs and tracks also accept bets over the phone. To take advantage of these services, you have to open an account and may need a daily password to access online betting options.

OTBs in most states are "public benefit" corporations, which means the profits they generate are funneled into state coffers. Like traditional tracks, they use a pari-mutuel betting system, with a portion of each wager removed from the prize pool to cover operating expenses and state and local taxes. The races they cover depend on the way the OTB is structured; some may cover only the tracks in their state, while others may have multistate arrangements.

FACT

Pari-mutuel is a French phrase meaning "gambling amongst ourselves." The track or betting parlor acts as an agent for placing bets; all bets are pooled, and the track deducts a certain percentage, usually between 14 and 30 percent, to cover expenses, state and local taxes, and the track's or parlor's profit.

Reading the Race Sheets

Horseracing sheets offer a huge amount of information about a specific horse—everything from its past performances in various races to its lifetime earnings, and even the records of the trainer and jockey. The sheer wealth of data can be intimidating in itself, and the abbreviations can make you feel like you're looking at a page of obscure computer code. A typical race sheet might look like this:

TIME TO FLY	Smith, P.G. (175-30-52-26-15)	Life: 20 4 4 1 $160,000
ch c 2 Sir Deeds-AnneMarie-Cash Flow		Tr-Darlene Jones (81-17-9-15)
Or-Randall Jackson, Goshen, N.Y.		Br-Randall Jackson

12Jul03 FL ft78 INV HCP $15,000 1 26 55^3 123^1 154^4 4 $4^{11/2}$ $2^{1/2}$ 1^1 1^1 $1^{1/2}$ 26^4 154^4 Smith, P.G. *1.40 Time To Fly, Sunnyside, Flower Girl

It looks confusing, doesn't it? But we're going to break it down so you know what you're reading the next time you visit the track.

Race Sheet Abbreviations

To fit all the relevant information on a race sheet, and still make it readable, race sheets use a lot of abbreviations. Here are some of the most common ones.

Horse's Color

b	bay	ch	chestnut
blk	black	gr	gray
br	brown	ro	roan

Horse's Sex

c	colt (four years old or younger)	h	horse (a male, five years old or older)
f	filly (four years old or younger)	m	mare (a female, five years old or older, or a younger female that has been bred)
g	gelding (a castrated male)	r	ridgeling (a male whose testicles aren't fully descended)

Track Sizes

1/2	one-half mile	7/8	seven-eighths of a mile
5/8	five-eighths of a mile	1	one mile
3/4	three-quarters of a mile		

Track Condition

ft	fast (the best condition)	my	muddy (wet, with a soft base)
gd	good (still wet in spots but mostly dry or drying)	hy	heavy (not as difficult to run as muddy, but not as fast as a good track)
sy	sloppy (there may be puddles, but the base is firm)		

Race Types (often called "race conditions")

CD	Conditioned race	FFA	Free-for-all
5000CL	Claiming race (the number indicates the value on this horse)	INV	Invitational
OP	Optional	OPN	Open
EC	Early closer	HC	Handicap
LC	Late closer	MDN	Maiden
STK	Stakes race	QUA	Qualifying race
FUT	Futurity	MAT	Matinee race

Once you understand what the abbreviations mean, the race sheet begins to make more sense. The next step is to know where the information is on the sheet.

Who's the Horse?

The top of the race sheet gives information about the horse, its age and pedigree, its owner, driver or jockey, trainer, and the horse's career highlights. A typical sheet (using a fictional horse, for this example) might look like this:

3 TIME TO FLY	Smith, P.G. (175-30-52-26-15)	Life: 20 4 4 1$160,000
ch c 2 Sir Deeds-AnneMarie-Cash Flow		Tr-Darlene Jones (81-17-9-15)
Or-Randall Jackson, Goshen, N.Y.		Br-Randall Jackson

In this example, the horse is named Time to Fly, and it is horse number 3 today. The jockey is P.G. Smith, and the numbers behind his name indicate how many times he has ridden this year (175), followed by the number of first-, second-, and third-place finishes he has had in those races. He has won thirty of the 175 races, come in second in fifty-two, and finished third in twenty-six.

A jockey or trainer who has a win rate of 15 percent or higher is probably both skilled and talented, and therefore worth considering for a wager. To figure out the win rate, divide the number of wins—in this case, thirty—by the total number of races, like this: 30/175 = .17 = 17 percent.

The "life" numbers provide an overview of the horse's racing career. In this example, Time to Fly has raced twenty times and won four of those races. He has come in second in another four races, and finished third in one race. His lifetime money earnings total $160,000.

The second line contains more information about the horse. The "ch" indicates the horse's color; in our example, he's a chestnut. How do we know Time to Fly is a "he"? The letter immediately following the color indicator tells you the sex of the animal; the "c" tells us he's a colt. The number next to the sex indicator tells you how old the animal is. In our example, Time to Fly is a two-year-old.

The names that come next show the animal's lineage, giving the names of its sire, its dam, and the dam's sire. Next comes the trainer's name, as well as his or her record, which is displayed in a similar format to the driver's or jockey's record. Finally, the top of the sheet indicates the owner and the breeder; this may be the same individual or stable or two different people or stables.

Past Performance

The past performance lines, which are directly underneath the general horse information, give you details about this horse's performance in specific races. The Daily Racing Form, widely considered the bible for racing bettors, also tells you the horse's Beyer Speed Figure, a formula for calculating a horse's running speed that takes into account such variables as time of day, track surface and condition, and so on. Most other racing forms do not include this number, so our example will omit it.

The left half of a typical past-performance line looks like this:

| 12Jul03 | FL | ft78 | INV HCP | $15,000 | 1 26 55^3 123^1 154^4 |

This part of the past-performance line gives the date of the race (July 12, 2003), the track at which the race was held (FL is the abbreviation for the Finger Lakes track in upstate New York), the track conditions and the temperature at the time of the race. In this example, it was a fast track, and it was 78 degrees. The next column indicates the type of race, in this case an invitational handicap race, followed by the purse for the race. The next series of numbers shows the length of the race (one mile in this case), then the time of the horse who *led* the race (not necessarily this horse) at the quarter-mile, half-mile, and three-quarter poles. The final number in this section indicates the time, in seconds, of the horse that won the race. The smaller superscript numbers are increments of one-fifth of a second.

The right half of a past-performance line looks like this:

4 4$^{1\frac{1}{2}}$ 2 $^{\frac{1}{2}}$ 1^1 1^1 1$^{\frac{1}{2}}$ 26^4 154^4 Smith, P.G.   *1.40   Time To Fly, Sunny-
                                                                                      side, Flower Girl

This section of the chart gives information on *this* horse's performance in the race. The first number shows the horse's starting, or post,
position. The next three numbers show the horse's position at the quarter-
mile, half-mile, and three-quarter-mile poles. The superscript numbers show
how many lengths behind the leader, or, if the horse is in the lead, how
many lengths ahead of the second horse. In this example, Time to Fly
was 1½ lengths behind the leader at the quarter-mile, ½ length behind at
the half-mile, and 1 length ahead at the three-quarter-mile post.

The next two numbers show where the horse was positioned entering
the homestretch, and where he finished the race. Again, the superscript
numbers indicate how far ahead or behind the horse was at these two
points in the race. Following these numbers are two times. The first is
the time, in seconds, it took this horse to finish the last quarter-mile of
the race; the second is the total time, in seconds, it took this horse to
run the entire race. The superscript numbers here indicate increments of
one-fifth of a second.

The next piece of information is the name of the jockey or driver for
this race, followed by the payout for this horse in the win pool. In this
example, Time to Fly paid $1.40; the asterisk next to the payout figure
shows that this horse was the betting favorite. Finally, the past-performance line shows the first-, second-, and third-place horses for this race.

FACT

An asterisk next to a jockey's name on a race sheet indicates that
the rider is an apprentice, sometimes called a "bug." This can be a
factor in choosing a winner, especially over long distances;
apprentice riders often don't have the experience needed to
"pace" a long race, and that can hurt their chances of winning.

How to Bet Horseracing

Most tracks these days offer two ways to place your wagers—either at the traditional teller window or through self-service automated kiosks. If you're new to the track, you might prefer to go to the teller window, because the teller can help you with any questions you might have. For live, at-the-track racing, you'll usually have thirty minutes or so between races, but you should get to the teller window at least fifteen minutes before the start of the race you want to bet on. This will give you plenty of time to place your bet without worrying about "shutting out" the people in line behind you.

To place your bet, you need to give the teller the track, the number of the race, the amount you want to bet, the horse's number, and the kind of wager you want to place. For example, if you were to bet on the race described previously in the race sheet section, you would tell the person at the window, "Finger Lakes, race two, two dollars on number three to win."

Be sure to specify the track when placing your bet. With simulcasting, you can bet on races at virtually any track anywhere in the country. If you don't specify the track, the teller may assume you want to bet on the race at the home track.

Types of Races

Different classes of horses compete in different classes of races. Stakes and handicap races generally attract the best horses, trainers, jockeys, and drivers, and they usually carry the highest purses. Owners have to pay a fee to nominate, enter, and run their horses in these types of races, and those fees are added to the prize money or purse for the race. Usually, horses must be nominated at least two weeks before the running of a stakes race. In handicap races, faster horses may be required to carry additional weights to ensure a more equal competition.

One variation of the stakes race is an overnight stakes, in which horses can be nominated as late as a week before the race. Usually, owners don't have to pay the nominating, entry, and starting fees required for a stakes race. Nevertheless, overnight stakes races usually attract high-quality racehorses and offer good-sized purses.

In claiming races, the horses entered can be purchased for the amount indicated by the owner. The value of a horse that easily beats a field of $5,000 claimers will usually be increased to avoid having that horse claimed, or purchased, for the lower claiming price. Maiden races are for horses that have never won a race.

Types of Bets

You have several options for wagering on a given race. The most basic is a straight "win" bet, in which you bet that your chosen horse will win the race. A "place" bet means you bet that your horse will finish either first or second, and a "show" bet means you bet that your horse will finish first, second, or third. The "show" bet is sometimes called an "across-the-board bet," because it covers first-, second-, or third-place finishes. If you prefer, you can choose two, three, or even four horses in a given race. For two horses, you can place a quinella bet or an exacta bet. In a quinella, you win if your two horses finish first and second in either order. In an exacta, you have to pick which horse will finish first and which will finish second, and you win only if your two horses cross the finish line in the exact order you predicted. If you want to predict the exact order of the top three finishers, you can place a trifecta bet; as in the exacta, you win only if your horses finish the race in the exact order you predicted. A superfecta bet allows you to choose the top four finishers of a race.

Most tracks and betting parlors have a $2 minimum on bets for win, place, or show. If you place an across-the-board wager, you have to bet $6—$2 for the win bet, $2 for the place bet, and $2 for the show bet.

You can bet on multiple races, as well as multiple horses. In a daily double bet, for example, you choose the winners of two consecutive races (usually the first two races of the day at a track, although some tracks offer later doubles). Both of your horses have to win in order for you to win your wager. Some tracks also offer daily triples, or pick three, bets, in which you choose the winners of three consecutive races.

Many tracks feature six-race bets, called "pick six," "classix," or "super six," in which you choose the winners of six consecutive races. Usually, these are the last six races of the day. The money pool, like a lottery jackpot, is divided among all bettors who correctly chose the six winners. If no one correctly picks all six winners, part of the money is divided among those who picked five correct winners, and the rest of it goes into the next day's six-race pool.

Odds and Payouts

Racing odds and payouts are based on how many people bet on a given horse. You aren't betting against the track or betting parlor; you're pitting your judgment against that of all the other bettors. A popular favorite, therefore, may be offered at very short odds, say 1:5, but may not necessarily be the best horse in the race. Unlike sportsbook (see Chapter 14), your odds are not locked in at the time you place your bet. Instead, you get whatever the closing odds are on your particular horse.

At the track, the tote board (shorthand for totalizator board, the original name for the board) continually updates the odds for the next race to reflect wagering activity. When a race is completed, the tote board shows the horses that finished "in the money," the odds, and the payout for each. The payout figure includes the return of the original wager. The payout on a 3:1 horse, for example, will be displayed as $8—$6 in winnings, plus the return of the $2 wagered.

In most states, the return on a $2 bet is rounded to the nearest ten cents after the winners' pool is divided. For example, if the actual share comes out to $5.22, the official payout will be $5.20. The track keeps the difference, called the "breakage," and this forms a significant portion of a track's profits.

Payouts may vary according to how much the track keeps to cover operating expenses and state and local taxes. This take can be between 14 percent and 25 percent, depending on the state and, sometimes, on the type of wager. With these differences in mind, following is a typical payout table for a $2 bet (remember that the payout includes the return of your original wager).

Odds	Payout	Odds	Payout
1:5	$2.40	5:2	$7.00
2:5	$2.80	3:1	$8.00
1:2	$3.00	7:2	$9.00
3:5	$3.20	4:1	$10.00
4:5	$3.60	9:2	$11.00
1:1	$4.00	5:1	$12.00
6:5	$4.40	6:1	$14.00
7:5	$4.80	7:1	$16.00
3:2	$5.00	8:1	$18.00
8:5	$5.20	9:1	$20.00
9:5	$5.60	10:1	$22.00
2:1	$6.00		

Judging horses is a fine art that professionals spend years perfecting. If you're new to racing and are unsure what to look for in a horse, here are a few suggestions to help you get started. First, look at the early odds posted by the experts. These are usually a good indication of which horses will finish in the money, and you conceivably could cover first, second, and third place with across-the-board bets on six horses.

Second, look for winning horses and winning drivers or jockeys. Horses, like human athletes, experience streaks and peaks in their performances. A horse that has won before is more likely to win again. A driver or jockey who has a high win rate clearly is doing something right as well.

Finally, as in any other form of gambling, establish a bankroll before you get to the track or betting parlor, and stick with it once you're there. Set a stop-loss limit; for example, you might start with $100 and decide to quit when you're down to $50. Also set a limit for your winnings. If your goal is to win $50, stop when you reach that goal. Horseracing is entertainment, and the wagering is just another way to keep it interesting. If you aren't enjoying yourself, it's time to leave.

Chapter 14

Sportsbook

Betting on sports is one of the most popular forms of gambling in the United States, whether it's through an office pool, a casino sportsbook, or increasingly, an online sportsbook. Aside from the entertainment value, sports betting offers the knowledgeable gambler one of the best options for profit over the long term. First, though, you have to solve the mystery behind sports odds, point spreads, and money lines.

How Betting Lines Are Set

Sports betting lines are created by oddsmakers, who analyze a team's or player's past performance as well as such variables as the weather, player injuries, the home field advantage, and anything else that might affect the outcome of the game. Statistics, and any patterns or trends the oddsmakers discern in the statistics, form the basis for a betting line. For example, if Team A is strong on defense and Team B has a strong offense, an oddsmaker will look at how effective Team A has been in containing other teams with strong offenses and how Team A has performed in previous contests against Team B. Virtually every aspect of a game, from location to time to mental distractions, is used to predict how a given team or player will perform.

Some Las Vegas sportsbooks have in-house oddsmakers, but most use the services of a group called Las Vegas Sports Consultants to establish their odds and betting lines. LVSC also provides this service to the Oregon State Lottery—the only other state in the United States that permits and regulates sports betting—and to licensed European bookmakers. According to some estimates, LVCS sets the initial betting lines and odds for up to 90 percent of the licensed sportsbooks in Nevada.

FACT

Nevada and Oregon are the only states where betting on sports is legal. Nevada sportsbooks will set up telephone accounts for gamblers, but they are not allowed to accept out-of-state wagers. Though there are dozens, if not hundreds, of online sportsbooks, the legality of gambling through them is unclear.

Betting lines on sports are usually adjusted many times between the posting of the initial line and the time the game or event begins. There are two main reasons for this. First, injuries, weather, and other factors can change the statistical outlook of a game, so oddsmakers will adjust their lines to reflect those changes. Second, virtually no sportsbook wants to risk its own money on any given sporting event. Sportsbooks make their money from the commission—often called the "juice" or the "vigorish"—they charge on bets placed, so their ideal situation is to have approximately the same number of bettors on either side of a line. That way, the money from the losing bettors goes to pay the winning bettors, and the sportsbook still gets its juice.

In general, your betting line is locked in at the time you place your wager. Sometimes you'll get better odds by placing your bet early; other times, it might be to your advantage to wait. This is where your knowledge of both the sport involved and the way sportsbooks work comes in. If too many people bet on the favorite, the sportsbook likely will adjust the betting line to encourage more people to bet on the underdog. When this happens, the underdog often gets better odds than it deserves from a strictly statistical point of view, so it might be worthwhile to place your bet closer to game time. On the other hand, if you want to bet on the favorite, you might be better off to get your bet in early to give yourself the best odds.

Reading the Lines

Sports betting lines can be confusing to the novice because of the way the odds are expressed. To begin with, although it seems counterintuitive, the favorite in virtually any betting line is indicated by a negative number— -110 in a money line, for example, or -6 in a point spread, two of the most common sports betting lines. Conversely, the underdog is indicated by a positive number. A typical betting line for a professional football game, for example, would look like this:

Team	Line	Total	Money Line
Giants	-6	32	-110
Bills			+91

The Money Line

The number on the money line shows how much you have to bet to win $100. In our example, you have to bet $110 on the Giants to win $100 (plus the return of your original wager). If you wager on the Bills, however, you only have to bet $91 to win $100 (plus the return of your original wager). You don't have to place $100 bets on a money line; the payoff is proportional to the amount of your wager.

The key thing to remember in reading money lines is that they are not even-money bets. A negative money line means you win less than you wager; a positive money line means you win more than you wager.

The Point Spread

The point spread is a way of handicapping opposing teams. In our example, the Giants are favored to win (as shown by the negative number next to the Giants in the "Line" column), and the point spread is 6. This means that the oddsmakers expect the Giants to beat the Bills by 6 points. Depending on how you wager, you're hoping that the final scores of each team are more or less than 6 points apart.

Let's say you bet on the Giants. To win your bet, the Giants have to beat the Bills by 7 or more points. This is called "covering the spread." If the Giants don't cover the spread—that is, if they win by 5 points or less—you lose the bet. If they win by exactly 6 points, the bet is considered a push and your wager is returned.

QUESTION?

Is there a sportsbook system I can use to improve my odds of winning?
Any "system" based on anything other than knowledge of the game is most likely a scam. Professional sports bettors, on average, win fewer than 60 percent of their wagers. If someone is hawking a system that promises outrageous win rates, ask yourself why this person is selling the system instead of using it.

If you bet on the Bills, on the other hand, you could win in a number of ways. Of course, you win if the Bills pull off an upset and win the game by any margin. You also would win your bet if the Bills lose by fewer than 6 points or if the game ends in a tie.

Point spreads are prone to change many times between the initial posting of a betting line and the start of the game. For example, if too many people are betting on the Giants, the sportsbook might increase the point spread to 9 to encourage more people to bet on the Bills. In this case, the Giants now have to win by more than 9 points to cover the spread, but the Bills don't have to win; they only have to finish the game within 8 points of the Giants.

Types of Bets

Sportsbooks offer a variety of ways to wager on your favorite athletic events. The most common wagers are so-called straight bets, either on a money line or a point spread. But you can add to the fun by selecting parlays or proposition bets, or minimize your risk by opting for teasers.

Money Line Bets

Sometimes sportsbooks will offer only money line bets on a game, with no point spread. This is a straight bet, where you choose the team you think will win. On a straight money line bet, it doesn't matter what the margin of victory is; if your team wins the game, you win your bet.

A straight money line looks like this:

Team	Money Line
Giants	-150
Bills	+130

As shown here, the negative number on the Giants' line indicates they are favored to win the game. On a negative money line, you wager more than you win. In this example, you would have to bet $15 on the Giants to win $10, plus the return of your original $15 wager. To win $100, you would have to bet $150.

If you choose to bet on the Bills, however, you would win more than you wager. For this example, you would win $13 for every $10 you bet. If you bet $100 on the Bills, your payoff would be $130.

Spread Bets

The point spread is perhaps the most common sports bet. The odds-makers determine a favorite and predict the difference in the two teams' scores. When you place your bet, you're pitting your knowledge of the game against the oddsmaker and deciding whether the favorite can cover the spread. A point spread looks like this:

Giants	-3
Bills	+3

In this example, the Giants are favored to win by 3 points. If you bet on the Giants, their final score has to be at least 4 points higher than the Bills' final score in order for you to win your bet. If the Giants win by exactly 3 points, you don't win any money, but your wager is returned. If you wager on the Bills in this example, they have to win the game, tie, or lose by 1 or 2 points in order for you to win your bet. If the Bills lose by 3 points and you bet on the Bills, you lose your wager.

Point spread bets typically carry 11:10 odds, which means you have to wager $11 to win $10.

ESSENTIAL

In almost all sportsbooks, the team listed on the bottom is the home team. This is true for all team sports and for all types of sports bets. Sometimes the home team is listed in all capital letters as an additional indication.

Over/Under Bets

Over/under bets also are 11:10 wagers, but instead of betting on the difference between the teams' scores, you bet on whether the total points scored will be higher or lower than the oddsmakers' predictions. Point totals often are expressed in half-points—for example, 291/2 in football, or 1921/2 in basketball. Here's what an over/under posting would look like:

Giants	-3	-150	4 P.M.
Bills	+3	+130	44 ½

This posting gives you the point spread, the money line odds, the time the game is scheduled to begin, and the predicted total score. If you wager that the total points will be higher—also known as "betting the ball"—you win if the Giants' and Bills' scores, added together, total 45 or more. If you place an "under" wager—also called "betting the clock"—you win if all points scored total 44 or less.

Parlays

Parlays allow you to bet on two or more games for a better payoff. The catch: you have to win all the events in your parlay to win the bet, and the payoff odds are more heavily skewed from the true odds. In fact, the more games you parlay, the bigger the advantage for the sportsbook.

The true odds on a two-team parlay are 3:1, but the typical sportsbook payout is 13:5. A three-team parlay usually pays around 6:1, instead of the true odds of 7:1. Six games might net you 40:1 or even 45:1 odds, compared with the true odds of about 63:1, while seven games will pay between 80:1 and 90:1, compared with the true odds of 127:1. Remember, you must win each contest in a parlay in order to win the bet. With even one loss, you lose your wager.

FACT

Some sportsbooks offer parlay cards that allow you to wager as little as $2. You fill out the cards by filling in a circle next to the teams you choose and the amount you want to bet. The rules for these kinds of parlays vary; always read the back of the card before you place your bet.

If any game in a parlay is postponed for any reason, that game is simply removed from the parlay bet as though it had never been included. A four-game parlay, for example, becomes a three-game parlay. A two-game parlay becomes a straight single-game bet.

Proposition Bets

Proposition bets—often called simply "props"—can be made on virtually any aspect of a particular game. In football, a sportsbook might offer proposition bets on how many field goals will be made, how many interceptions or completed passes will be thrown, how many fumbles will result in turnovers, and so on. In basketball, a sportsbook might offer a proposition bet on how many 3-point shots will be made, or how many free throws will be made. In baseball, the proposition might be how many home runs or how many strikeouts are made. In hockey, the proposition might involve hat tricks or penalties.

Props can be very broad or highly specific, ranging from totals in a given game to which wide receiver will catch the most passes. Most of these types of bets are over/under propositions. If the sportsbook predicts that there will be three field goals scored in the Giants-Bills game, for instance, you would bet that the total number of field goals will be higher or lower than 3. The typical prop bet offers 11:10 odds, but check with the sportsbook to make sure. Some props, especially the more exotic ones, offer better—or worse—odds.

Teasers

In a teaser bet, you essentially change the point spread to give yourself a better chance of winning, but in doing so you reduce the payoff amounts. At most sportsbooks, a teaser must involve at least two games, and, like the parlay, you have to win both games to win your bet. The payoff amounts vary according to how much you change the point spread. For example, a straight two-team parlay typically offers 11:10 payoff odds. If you tease half a point—that is, you add half a point to the point spread—the payoff on a two-team parlay drops to 5:6. Teasing a full point drops the payoff to 5:7.

Here's a look at how teasing changes the payoff amounts:

Number of Teams	5-Point Spread	5½-Point Spread	6-Point Spread
Two teams	11:10	5:6	5:7
Three teams	8:5	3:2	6:5
Four teams	5:2	2:1	9:5
Five teams	4:1	7:2	3:1
Six teams	6:1	5:1	4:1

When placing a teaser bet, you change the point spread by a set amount. You can change the spread on all the games in your parlay by the same amount.

Buying Half Points

This is a rarer form of sports bet, which allows you to move the point spread half a point in your favor by accepting 6:5 payoff odds instead of the standard 11:10. Most experts recommend ignoring this option except on 3-point spreads in football. For those games, buying the half a point—sometimes called "buying the hook"—gives you a better chance of winning the bet, but at a reduced payout.

Futures

Futures bets allow you to wager on the outcome of an entire season—who will win the Super Bowl, the World Series, the NBA Championship, the Stanley Cup, and so on—even before a single game has been played. Odds for each team winning are posted at the beginning of the season and adjusted from week to week or day to day during the season. Your odds on a futures bet are locked in at the time you place the wager. For example, assume that in April you bet on the Chicago Cubs to win the National League Championship at 100:1 odds. By September, if the Cubs are still in the pennant race, the odds might be only 12:1. But, if the Cubs win the pennant, you get paid at the original odds of 100:1.

Many sportsbooks offer futures bets on major events in horseracing, such as the Kentucky Derby or the Breeder's Cup. Usually, if the horse you pick for such an event doesn't start the race, you lose your wager.

However, the odds on a horserace are locked in at the time you place your bet, regardless of what the odds are on the day of the race.

FACT

Nevada sportsbooks are not allowed to accept bets on anything other than athletic contests. You might find odds posted on Most Valuable Player, the Heisman winner, Rookie of the Year, or even on the outcome of presidential elections or the Grammy Awards, but these are for amusement only—you can't legally bet on them.

Some futures bets are over/under bets; you bet that the St. Louis Cardinals will win more or fewer than eighty-five games in the baseball season, for example. Typically, these kinds of bets are offered on professional football and major league baseball teams, and occasionally on professional basketball teams. Other futures bets are more specific, such as betting that baseball player Barry Bonds will hit the most home runs during the regular season, or that quarterback Drew Bledsoe will have the most passing yards.

Oregon Sports Action

The Oregon Lottery allows people to bet on professional football during the National Football League season. The minimum bet is $2, and you must pick the winners in at least three games. Oregon also offers a number of "special play games," where you can bet on such things as total points scored, sacks, field goals, completed passes, lost fumbles, rushing yards, and interceptions. A winning three-game ticket pays $5 for every $1 wagered; five- to fourteen-game tickets are paid out on a pari-mutuel basis.

Football

Professional and college football games are the most common sports events for bettors to gamble on. Most sportsbooks offer straight bets—picking what team will win, with no point spread—as well as point spreads and over/under bets, at the typical 11:10 odds. Odds for parlays vary according to how many games you play and to the sportsbook you place your bet with. Remember that in a parlay, you must win each game in order to win the bet.

Teasers also are available on football wagers, but you must play at least a two-game parlay. When you elect a teaser, you improve your odds of winning the bet in exchange for a lower payoff rate. As with a regular parlay, you have to win all the games in your teaser in order to win the bet.

Baseball

Odds for major league baseball teams are usually determined in large part by the starting pitcher, and changes in the pitching order can dramatically change the odds. At most sportsbooks, you can specify that either one or both of the listed pitchers must start the game. If one or both of the starting pitchers change before the game, your bet is considered a push and is returned to you.

A typical baseball betting line looks like this:

Team	Pitcher	Odds	Total	Money Line for Total
Cubs	Wood	-120	8.5	Over -110
Braves	Ramirez	+110		Under -110

The bottom team listed is usually the home team. The negative number on the Cubs' line indicates they are favored to win. The money line for the total refers to total runs scored in the game; you can bet that the two teams will score 9 or more runs or 8 or fewer runs.

ALERT!

In baseball, over/under bets have two specific rules. First, the game must go at least 8½ innings if the home team wins, or 9 innings if the visiting team wins. Second, both listed pitchers must start the game. If either of these rules is not satisfied—if the game is rained out after 6 innings, for example—the bet is a push and your wager is returned.

Basketball

Basketball betting lines always include a point spread, and you must cover the spread in order to win the bet. If the Lakers are favored over the Bulls and the point spread is 3, you would win your bet on the Lakers only if they won by at least 4 points. If you bet on the Bulls, they have to win the game or lose by 2 points or 1 point in order for you to collect on your wager. If the Lakers win by exactly 3 points, your bet is considered a push (no matter which team you bet on) and your wager is returned to you.

You can bet parlays in basketball. As in other sports parlays, all of your teams must cover the spread in order for you to win the parlay. Payoff odds vary depending on how many teams you bet on and the sportsbook where you place your bet. Teasers also are available in basketball betting; as usual, you must play at least two teams to use the teaser option.

Boxing

Boxing bets use a money line to show the odds. As in other sports, a negative money line indicates that boxer is favored to win, and a positive money line indicates the underdog. Remember, money lines show either how much you have to wager to win $100 (a negative line), or how much you win if you bet $100 (a positive line).

A typical boxing betting line looks like this:

Boxer	Odds
Lennox Lewis	-280
Roy Jones	+240

Lennox Lewis is favored to win. A $280 bet on Lewis would win $100, plus your original wager. On the other hand, a $100 bet on Roy Jones would pay $240, plus the original wager. If the match is a draw, your bet is returned to you.

Sportsbooks usually offer a number of proposition bets on boxing matches, with varying odds. Propositions might include how many rounds the fight will go, how many knockdowns there will be, or whether the fight will conclude with a knockout.

As always, the odds can change dramatically from the initial posting to the day of the fight. If too many people are betting on Lewis to win, the sportsbooks will shade the odds in Jones's favor to encourage more people to bet on Jones. This doesn't mean Jones's chances of winning the fight are any better; it just means that the sportsbooks are trying to even out the action.

Hockey

Hockey betting lines combine the money line and the point spread. The team you choose must cover the spread in order for you to win the bet. A typical hockey betting line looks like this:

Team	Line	Money Line	Total
Rangers	+1.5	+120	
Islanders	-1.5	-130	4

In this example, the Islanders are favored to beat the Rangers by 1½ goals. If you bet on the Islanders, they must win by 2 goals to cover the spread, and a $13 wager will win you $10, plus the return of your original bet. If you bet on the Rangers, they must win the game, tie, or lose by only 1 goal in order for you to win the bet. A $10 bet on the Rangers would win $12, plus the return of your $10 wager.

You also can play an over/under bet on the total number of goals scored. In our example, the oddsmakers have predicted that a total of 4 goals will be scored in the game; you decide whether you think the combined score of the two teams will be higher or lower. As in other sports, an over/under bet in hockey typically offers 11:10 odds.

Hockey bets also can be parlayed, with the payout on the first game being applied to the second game, and so on throughout the parlay. You must win each game in order to win a parlay bet. If a game is postponed, it is removed from the parlay, so a three-game parlay would become a two-game parlay, and a two-game parlay would become a straight bet.

Auto Racing

As NASCAR's appeal continues to grow around the country, betting on NASCAR races has become increasingly popular. The most common betting option is to pick the winner of a given race. In most auto racing books, the sportsbook will list ten to twenty individual drivers at various odds, plus one set of odds for the rest of the field. Many sportsbooks offer betting lines on NASCAR events as well as lesser-known racing circuits.

A typical (though abbreviated) auto racing line looks like this:

Driver	Odds
Jimmie Johnson	6:1
Jeff Gordon	8:1
Sterling Marlin	12:1
Terry Labonte	15:1
Field	100:1

If you bet $100 on Jimmie Johnson and he wins the race, you would win $600, plus the return of your original $100 wager. If you bet $10 on the field, and none of the listed drivers win the race, you would win $1,000, plus the return of your $10 wager.

Many sportsbooks offer match-up proposition bets on auto racing, pitting two drivers against each other. In these wagers, the driver doesn't have to win the race; he just has to finish the race ahead of the other driver. Say you bet on Dale Earnhardt Jr. in a match-up with Jeff Gordon. If Earnhardt finishes third and Gordon finishes fifth, you win the bet. If Earnhardt finishes third and Gordon finishes second, you lose.

Match-up propositions are usually posted with money lines, like this:

Driver	Money Line
Earnhardt	-135
Gordon	+120

In this example, Earnhardt is favored, and a $135 bet on him would win $100 if he beats Gordon. If you bet on Gordon and he finishes the race in a higher position than Earnhardt, your $100 bet would win $120. For match-up propositions, both drivers must start the race; if either driver doesn't start, the bet is a push and your wager is returned.

Sometimes you'll find more unusual proposition bets in auto racing, such as an over/under bet on the number of cautions or a straight bet on which auto manufacturer (rather than which driver) will win a given race. Unless otherwise posted, these bets usually offer 11:10 odds.

Golf

Along with auto racing, professional golf is one of the fastest-growing sports for betting action. The most common way to bet on golf is to pick the winner of a given tournament. As in auto racing books, golf tournament books typically list twenty to thirty—and sometimes more—individual players at specific odds, with the rest lumped into a field with one set of odds.

Competition for sports bets is fierce, and it's worth your time to shop around for the best odds. Some sportsbooks now offer parlays in which the bettor wins in case of a tie. This gives you an advantage, so if you want to place parlay bets, look for this feature.

Golf betting also offers match-up propositions similar to those offered in auto racing. These are money line bets, with the negative number indicating the favorite. The main difference in golf matchups is that if one player fails to make the cut in the tournament, the bet is still considered action and the golfer who does make the cut wins the matchup.

Increasingly, as a handful of individuals seem to dominate the professional golf tournaments, you can find a variation of a matchup in which one player is pitted against two or more other players. For example, a sportsbook might offer a matchup among Tiger Woods, Phil Mickelson, and Tom Lehman. To win your wager on Woods in this kind of matchup, his score has to be better than both Mickelson's and Lehman's.

Some sportsbooks offer other proposition bets in golf, such as over/under bets on the winning score, the lowest score, or where a given player will finish in the tournament. Ⓔ

Chapter 15
Player Incentives

There's a saying among casino gamblers that there's no such thing as a free lunch, except at the buffet. Casinos spend hundreds of millions of dollars every year giving away "comps"—complimentary drinks, meals, hotel rooms, tickets to shows, and even free plays on slots and table games—to their loyal customers. In fact, those incentives often are the key to keeping customers loyal. It isn't hard to get your share of comps, but you do have to know how to go about it.

Player's Clubs

Every casino in the world has a player's club. But not every player takes advantage of these clubs, and that is a sure-fire way to miss out on a full menu of comps. Player's clubs help the casinos keep track of who their customers are, including how often they play and how much they wager. Interestingly, for some, this is the main argument *against* joining these clubs; critics contend that they don't want casinos to know how much they spend or how often they play, and they worry that government agencies also can use that information.

The fact is, if you win anything substantial, the federal and state governments are going to know about it and you will pay taxes on those winnings, whether you join the player's club or not. As for the casino, you want the house to keep track of how much you spend and how often; this is how the casino determines what comps you're eligible for. If you pass up joining the player's club, you're essentially giving up the freebies the casino would offer just for gambling the way you normally do.

FACT

There's a popular misconception that comps are reserved for the high rollers, those betting hundreds or even thousands of dollars per hand. But there are a lot more "low" and "moderate" rollers out there, and the casinos willingly give out comps to keep these players happy and coming back. No matter what your level of play, chances are you'll qualify for some sort of comp.

Joining the player's club is free and easy. Usually, you fill out a brief form with your name and address. Sometimes the form will ask for your e-mail address, phone number, and even your date of birth; this latter helps the casino ensure that its patrons are of legal gambling age, but it also is used for special promotions, such as birthday slots tournaments or match-play coupons. You present the form and a photo I.D., usually a driver's license, at the player's club booth, and you are issued a plastic card, similar to a credit card, with an account number and a personal identification number (PIN).

QUESTION?

If I join a player's club, won't I get put on a mailing list?
Yes, and that's a good thing. You will probably receive a mailing only once or twice a month. Casinos use their mailing lists to let you know about special promotions and discounts, such as "double points" days and match-play coupons. You can't take advantage of these offers if you don't know about them.

Using Your Player's Card

When you play slot machines, video poker, or other machine games, you insert your card into the machine, enter your PIN, and begin playing. The card keeps track of each bet you make and how many bets you make per hour. The casino's computer system translates your level of play into a point system, which determines what kind of comps, and how many, you're entitled to.

Most player's clubs have brochures explaining the comp system. At most casinos, you have to rack up a predetermined set of points to earn a free meal, hotel room, or other comp. When you register, be sure to ask how the comp system works so you know what your bankroll is working toward. Also be sure to ask if the casino offers any specials for new club members or out-of-state members; some casinos have additional one-time incentives for these players.

You also can ask a casino host for help. After you've been playing for a while, say thirty minutes or so, ask an attendant to page a casino host for you. When the host arrives, give him or her your card and ask him or her whether you've earned any comps; if you haven't, ask how much more you'll have to play.

Multiple Cards

Most experts recommend asking for at least two player's club cards when you join. There are a couple of good reasons to do this. First, if you go to the casino with a spouse or friend, both of you can use the cards to earn comp points, and those comp points will add up more quickly on one account than they would if each of you opened separate accounts.

Second, if you play alone, sometimes you can insert your second card into an adjacent slot machine and earn comp points from someone else's play. If you notice another player who isn't using a player's club card, ask for permission to insert your card. The worst that can happen is that the player will say no; if he or she agrees, you have a chance to significantly boost your own comp rating.

If you should lose your player's club card, or if you forget to bring it with you on a visit, you can always get a duplicate at the player's club booth.

Don't start playing a slot machine until you've inserted your player's club card and made sure the machine has accepted it. If, for some reason, your card isn't accepted or stops tracking play in the middle of a session, ask a casino host for help; usually, they'll give you at least partial credit for the play that wasn't recorded on your card.

Tracking Your Play

The point system used by most player's clubs focuses your attention on the rewards you've earned rather than the money you've spent. Your account will show that you've racked up 1,000 points, for example, but it won't tell you that you dropped a total of $3,500 into the quarter slots to get those 1,000 points. So, while the club card is a great way for the casino to keep track of your wagers, it's not a very useful tool for the player when it comes to figuring out your gambling budget.

However, because you do earn comps, it is important to keep track of your play. Pay attention at the slot machines and make sure your card is recording your play. If there's a problem, ask a slot attendant or casino host to adjust your account. At the table games, keep track of how long you play and your average bet per hand so you can ask the floor person or pit boss to rate you correctly. Finally, pay attention to the rules for using your comps.

Getting Rated

Getting rated as a table game player sounds more impressive, and more difficult, than it actually is. All getting rated means is that the casino is keeping track of how much time you spend at the table games and how much you wager while you're playing. For rating purposes, it doesn't matter whether you win or lose—or how much you win or lose—during any particular session or visit.

The Rating Formula

Here's why wins and losses don't matter. Every game at the casino has a built-in house edge, which varies from around 1 percent to 30 percent or more. That house edge is the amount of each wager the casino expects to keep as profit over the long run. Comps, whether they're for meals, drinks, hotel rooms, or airfare (for the really high rollers), are a fraction of the house edge, usually around 20 percent but sometimes as high as 40 percent. Since all of these figures are calculated over the long term, it doesn't matter, from a comps standpoint, whether you lose $500 or win $1,500 in a given session. All that matters is how long you play, how much you wager, and how much the house edge is.

Suppose you're playing craps, betting $5 at a time, with a house edge of 1.4 percent. This is what a typical casino's comp formula might look like:

Average Bet	Total Throws	House Edge	Expectation	Comp Rate	Comp Value
$5 ×	75/hour ×	1.4% =	$5.25 ×	20% =	$1.05

The expectation is how much, on average, the house expects to win from you at your level of play. In this example, you're wagering an average of $375 an hour ($5 per throw times 75 throws an hour), but the house only expects to keep $5.25 of that total. They'll give you back about a dollar of that in comps, which still leaves them a comfortable profit but makes you feel better about spending your money there.

E
ALERT!

Never play any casino game just for the comps. Comps are rewards you earn for wagering your money, but their value is only a tiny percentage of what you gamble. It makes no sense to drop an extra $50 at the blackjack table or into a slot machine just to get a "free" $9.95 buffet.

Improving Your Rating

The difference between table game ratings and player's club cards is that, with the card, a computer is keeping precise track of each spin and wager you make. At the table games, casino personnel are estimating how much time and money you spend at the table. At many casinos, you might meet some resistance to getting rated unless you're betting $25 or more per hand, but don't let that discourage you from asking. Some places will rate you—and give you comps—for betting as little as $1 per hand.

There are some things you can do to improve your table game rating without going over your budget. Perhaps most important is being friendly with the dealer and tipping appropriately. Remember that the dealer reports to the floor person, and a friendly dealer can be an advocate for you when it comes time to figure out your comps.

You also can get credit for playing even when you're sitting out a hand or absent from the table. When a waitress asks you for a drink order or brings your drink to you, for example, you can miss a couple of hands without losing your seat at the table. If you take a restroom break, you can ask the dealer to "mark" your seat, or save it until you get back. In both cases, you'll get credit for playing even when you didn't place a wager.

Merchandise Comps

Casinos often give away so-called "logo items"—things like key chains, decks of cards, sport bottles, hats, and so on, marked with the casino's name and logo. These trinkets may be part of a welcome pack for new player's club members or hotel guests, or they may be part of a special promotion. For example, some casinos celebrate their anniversaries by offering free merchandise to, say, the first 200 people at the buffet that day.

Most casinos also have a player's club store or catalog where you can exchange your comp points for merchandise like jewelry, electronics, clothing, and luggage. Instead of price tags, the merchandise has tags that show how many points you need to "purchase" the item. Some players save up their comp points for this purpose, rather than using them for meals or something else. The casino host can tell you how the comp points system works at that particular casino.

When it comes to handing out comps, not all casino personnel are created equal. Typically, a dealer can't give out comps, but he or she reports to the floor person, who fills out the rating slip and can give out meal comps. The pit boss has authority to give out room and meal comps, and the shift supervisor or VIP host has the authority to give out any kind of comp.

Free Play

Free play is just what it sounds like, and it's the equivalent of cash for your bankroll. It can take several forms, and the rules governing how you use it vary from place to place. For example, some Las Vegas casinos offer a free roll of nickels; you aren't required to play the nickel slots with it, but you are expected to drop at least some of them into the machines.

Match Play

Match play coupons are issued for table games and usually are valid only on even-money bets like blackjack, red/black or odd/even bets at roulette, or pass or come bets at craps. They come in different denominations, too; you might get a $5 or $10 match-play coupon, or one that pays $7 to $5, for instance. It's called "match-play" because you have to match the coupon's value with your own bet.

Match play coupons essentially double your money without risking more of your bankroll. Here's how it works: You place your bet, along with the match-play coupon, on the table. If you win, you get paid for your bet, plus whatever the value of the match play coupon is. For example, suppose you have a $5 match-play coupon and place a $5 bet on red at the roulette table. If red comes up, you'll get your original $5 bet back, plus your $5 winnings on that bet, plus $5 for the match-play coupon. If you lose, you've bet $10, but you've only lost $5.

Many people, particularly those who prefer the slots, ignore match play. But this is an easy way to see some action at the table games, and you can do it one wager at a time. It's also an easy way to stretch your gambling dollar.

Coupons

Funbooks, vouchers, and coupons are particularly prevalent in Las Vegas, where competition for the casino visitor is fierce. The offers vary from discounts at shops to free slot tokens, double points, half-price show tickets, or match-play coupons. If you're a member of a player's club, you also can expect to find coupons and other promotional offers in the mail or, more rarely, in your e-mail. Often such promotions will be cyclical, designed to boost attendance and revenues during a casino's slack times. Keep an eye out for offers that make the most sense for you.

Online Bonuses

Online casinos can't offer you free drinks, free food, or free hotel rooms, so the only way they can build loyalty among their players is by offering cash-equivalent bonuses. Most offers are either a fixed dollar amount, advertised as "$100 free," or a percentage of your initial deposit, advertised as "100 percent deposit bonus." As with match play at a bricks-and-mortar casino, these bonuses extend your bankroll without putting more of your own money at risk.

Usually, you have to make wagers totaling three to five times the amount of the bonus before you can cash out at online casinos. For example, if you get a $100 cash credit for signing up, you have to bet $300 to $500 before you can close your account. As with land-based casino comps, it doesn't matter whether you win or lose for most online bonuses (although the longer you play, the more likely you are to lose); the important thing is the amount you wager, not the amount you end up with in your account.

Of course, comps at online casinos have the same goal as those at land-based establishments: to keep you playing as long as possible. With most online bonuses, you have to "play through" a predetermined number of times before you can cash out. This is to prevent you from signing up, getting your $100 bonus, betting $5, and then cashing out. Always read the terms and conditions to find out the rules for bonuses. If possible, call the online casino and ask them to explain their bonus program to you, then ask if there are any other offers you might be eligible for, especially any "frequent player" programs.

Room, Food, and Beverage Comps

RFBs—room, food, and beverage—comps are considered the mother lode for most gamblers. Nearly everyone, no matter what the level of play, can get at least one of these. Food and beverage comps are the most common and the most freely given comps for even relatively low rollers; if your level of play is a bit higher, you can qualify for at least discounted, if not totally free, hotel rooms.

Room Comps

Most casinos keep a block of hotel rooms open at all times for their rated players. Typically, you need to play the tables at least four hours a day at a set wager-per-hand—usually at least $25 and at some places up to $100 per hand—to qualify for free hotel nights. If you're a slots player, you have to pump a set amount of money through the machines every day during your stay in order to get the free room. But there are discounts you can earn at a lower rate of play.

The most common discount is the "casino rate," which may be 25 percent off the regular room and could be as much as 50 percent off. Some casinos automatically offer this discount to members of their player's club, while others require a minimum amount of play in order to get the discount. Sometimes you can even get the discount when you make your reservation, just by asking if the hotel has a casino rate.

Though the casino rate is quite common, some casinos are doing away with the practice; they charge everyone the full rate, unless you play enough to qualify for a free room. Because policies vary so widely, it's important to ask up front, either when making your reservation or when you get to the casino.

No matter what your level of play is, always check with a casino host before you check out of your hotel to see whether you've earned any discounts. You might not get a free night's stay, but you may be able to shave a considerable sum off your bill—a savings you won't get unless you ask.

Meal Comps

Most casinos are quite liberal with meal comps, especially to the buffet and coffee shops. High-end restaurant comps are more difficult to come by, and they usually require a higher level of play. Meal comps are usually for two people, and they generally come in two forms: either a fixed dollar amount or a list of menu options. You might get $15 off dinner for two at the coffee shop, or a pass through the buffet line for two people. Sometimes the voucher will list exactly what you're entitled to, especially at the full-service restaurants: appetizer, entrée, two sides, dessert, and nonalcoholic beverage, for instance.

If you have more than two people in your party, you can ask for additional meal comps. Casino hosts and floor supervisors generally have quite a bit of discretion in granting comps. Often they will give you rewards like extra meal comps even if you haven't technically earned them.

Meal comps typically cannot be saved for use on another visit; most of them are valid only for twenty-four hours. Remember that the purpose of comps is to keep you in the casino as long as possible, because the longer you stay, the more you play, and the more you play, the bigger the casino's profit.

FACT

Even when you have meal comps, you are still responsible for gratuities. Your tip should be based on the total of the bill *before* subtracting your comp; if your meal is free, find out what the normal charge is and base your tip on that. Remember that only the food is free. You are expected to pay for the service.

Beverage Comps

Free drinks are far and away the most common comp offered at any casino. Sometimes you don't even have to be playing; a beverage server might come up to you and ask if you'd like a drink even if you're just watching the action. As with meal comps, the drinks themselves are free, but you are expected to tip the server. In fact, if you want the server to come back, you almost *have* to tip.

Although not having to pay for your drinks is nice, there is a danger, especially if you're drinking alcohol. When you don't have to pay, it's easier to lose track of how many drinks you've had and overindulge, which in turn will affect your judgment at the tables or the slots. Consider alternating alcoholic drinks with water or nonalcoholic beverages to lessen the chances of overimbibing.

Entertainment Comps

Some casinos will offer discounted, upgraded, or free tickets to their live shows as comps. Free tickets, especially for headliners in Las Vegas, generally are reserved for the high rollers, that is, those betting $100 or more per hand. But moderate bettors often can get either discounts or better seats by talking to a pit boss or casino host. Just as the casino reserves hotel rooms for its rated players, most showrooms reserve some of their best seats for players. Your best option is to check with the casino host to find out what special entertainment offers you might qualify for.

Chapter 16

Travel Packages

Gambling and traveling seem to go hand in hand, with more options than ever these days for the low, moderate, or high roller. Gambling establishments pride themselves on providing a wide range of "price points," which is the industry lingo for "budget." Whether you're planning an afternoon outing to a casino or a seven-day gambling cruise, a little research should yield the perfect package for you.

Day Trips

If you're fortunate enough to live within 100 miles or so of a major casino, it's easy to plan a day trip. You can drive yourself, or you can check out a bus package. Many bus companies offer day trips that often include transportation, meals, and gambling coupons for one set price. Sometimes bus tours will even include a show. The advantage of these kinds of packages is that you don't have to worry about traffic, and they're easy to plan from a budget standpoint because everything except your own bankroll is included. The disadvantage is that your schedule is not your own, and your meal choice will probably be limited to one restaurant in the casino.

Although some short gambling trips may be taken on the spur of the moment, you should plan ahead as much as possible. Whether you're driving yourself or joining a bus group, you'll have expenses—besides gambling—to pay for. If you're driving, for example, you'll need gas, money for any tolls both there and back, and cash for valet parking at the casino if necessary. You'll also need money for food, drinks, and tips, and for shopping, if that's part of your itinerary. You should keep money for all these things separate from your bankroll; that way, you won't end up short when it's time to eat or get back on the turnpike to go home.

If possible, and especially if your bankroll for your day trip is relatively small, get cash from your own bank or your own bank's automated teller machine before you hit the casino. This will save you fees and service charges, which can add up quickly. Casinos are liberally dotted with ATMs to make it easy for you to get cash, but if your bank isn't on the casino ATM's network, you could take an unnecessary punch in the pocketbook.

FACT

Many ATMs charge service fees of $1, $2, even $3 if your particular card isn't part of their network, and if the ATM charges a fee, chances are your bank will charge you another $1 or $2 for the transaction. You could end up paying $5 or more for every cash withdrawal you make when the fees are added.

The other advantage to taking your bankroll with you in cash is that it helps you stick to your gambling limit (more about this in Chapter 18). If you don't have a preset bankroll, it's awfully easy to keep returning to the ATM every time you're down to your last chip. That can lead to serious financial difficulties, especially if you end up playing blackjack with the rent money.

Weekend Trips

Weekend packages are great ways to create a mini-vacation and are commonly offered in major gambling destinations like Las Vegas, Atlantic City, and Tunica, Mississippi. A typical package includes airfare, two hotel nights, show tickets, and sometimes match play or "lucky bucks" coupons for gambling. Other discounts, such as two-for-one meals, also might be included.

Casinos usually offer the best weekend deals during the off-season, or "shoulder" season—the weeks leading up to peak season—for gambling destinations. In Las Vegas, July, August, and December are usually the slowest months for casinos, so they'll offer deep discounts on packages to entice visitors. You may have to book these specials several months in advance to get the best deal, and it never hurts to shop around for bargains.

Finding a Good Package

Many casinos advertise their packages on their Web sites, so surfing the Internet is a good place to start your search. Travel agents also have a wide range of special offers at their disposal. Planning your trip as far in advance as possible generally will net you better deals; for the most part, the lower the price, the faster the special will sell out.

Be sure to ask about restrictions and conditions before booking your package. Some require that reservations be canceled forty-eight or even seventy-two hours in advance in order to be eligible for a full refund; others might charge a cancellation fee. Packages that include airfare might be completely nonrefundable. If you're traveling alone, you might have to pay a premium over the stated rate, because most hotel deals are based on double-occupancy.

With packages, you can't get comped for your hotel room because it is already included—usually at greatly reduced cost—in your package. However, you still can qualify for other comps through your gambling. The advantage is that you don't have to limit your playing to one casino in order to get a great room rate.

The Midweek "Weekend"

You can save even more money if you can take your weekend trip in the middle of the week. Throughout the hotel industry, room rates typically are cheaper Sunday through Thursday, and this is true for the casino hotels as well. During the off-season, or shoulder season, it isn't uncommon to find hotel rooms in Las Vegas for as little as $25 to $40 a night during the week, and even higher-priced rooms usually carry midweek discounts.

Although it used to be common for airlines to require a Saturday-night stay for their cheapest fares, that restriction seems to be fading. In general, it's still cheaper to fly on Thursdays and Sundays, although you might have to shop around to get the best deal. If you like to look for deals on the Internet, keep in mind that two of the big low-fare airlines, Southwest and JetBlue, do not advertise their fares on the major discount airfare Web sites like Travelocity.com and Orbitz.com. To check the fares for these airlines, you'll have to go through a travel agent or to their Web sites.

Cruises

Gambling cruises are becoming increasingly popular, especially for the traveler who likes to combine sightseeing with gambling. At some major ports like New York City, gambling boats take short daily excursions; for legal reasons, gambling on these ships doesn't start until the vessel crosses into international waters, a few miles off the coast. Larger cruise lines also offer standard three-, four-, and seven-day cruises to the Caribbean, Mexico, and Alaska that include gambling among the shipboard amenities. Some cruises specialize in specific games, such as poker, slots, or bingo, and offer special tournaments for their guests.

You can find gambling cruises by surfing the Internet or checking with your travel agent. Cruise prices are usually based on double occupancy and, depending on the time of year, may require reservations well in advance. For cruises to the Caribbean and Mexico, the peak season typically runs from about November through March; you might get a better deal by planning your cruise for the summer months. On the other hand, summer usually is peak season for Alaska cruises, and rates are usually lower for November or February cruises.

Generally, if a cruise begins and ends at a U.S. port, you won't have to worry about customs on your return. However, because of increased security concerns and scrutiny of various segments of the travel industry, be sure to check the customs and other requirements with your travel agent or cruise line.

Gambling Overseas

Many countries offer a variety of gaming options, from racinos and card rooms to full-fledged casinos. If you're lucky enough to win significant amounts of money abroad, you might have to deal with different reporting requirements, customs declarations, and tax authorities. For example, U.S. winners at Canadian casinos have to pay Canada tax on their winnings, but they can file for a refund of that tax under certain circumstances. U.S. customs rules require you to report large amounts of currency that you bring into the United States from abroad, and other countries may require you to declare how much currency you're bringing in or taking out of the country.

Regulations vary depending on the country you're visiting and, usually, the length of your visit. Keep in mind that with the heightened emphasis on security and antiterrorism efforts, you may find yourself answering more questions and filling out more forms than you did in the past. If you have questions about the requirements, ask the casino personnel; they should be able to give you the information you need. You also can check with your travel agent, especially if he or she handles a lot of gambling-related bookings.

Personal Safety and Security

Because casinos are a cash-intensive business, it's no surprise that they attract their share of thieves and other criminals. By exercising common sense and knowing a little about some common thievery tricks, you can protect yourself and your bankroll without sacrificing your enjoyment.

Inside the casino, you've got a lot of help in the form of the casino's security system. Security guards are always on the gaming floor, keeping an eye on things, and surveillance cameras record everything that happens in virtually every nook and cranny, usually even in parking lots and garages. The main exception is restrooms; usually cameras are trained on the entrances and exits of public restrooms, but they are not in the restrooms themselves. Should you be the victim of a pickpocket or other thief on the casino's property, always report it to casino security. Chances are the cameras caught the act on tape, and the security department can track down the miscreant.

The first rule in protecting yourself and your valuables, of course, is not to make yourself a soft target. Thieves and pickpockets look for easy marks:

- People who wave a lot of cash around or boast publicly about how much they've won
- People who are careless with their cash, leaving coin cups, chips, purses, or wallets lying about
- People who don't seem to be alert to their surroundings or are distracted

Protecting Yourself on the Gaming Floor

The gaming floor is fertile ground for thieves. Players get caught up in the game, whether it's craps, blackjack, or slots, and they forget to pay attention to their valuables and their surroundings. If you carry a purse, keep it on your lap while you're playing. Don't put it on the floor or on the shelf next to the game; it's too easy to lose track of it if you get engrossed in the game. Never hang your purse on the back of your chair, either on the gaming floor or at a restaurant.

At the table games, keep your chips in front of you, and be alert for distractions like an argument, a spilled drink, or even a fall. Thieves have been known to use such measures to take players' attention away from their stacks, and they use the opportunity to pocket some or all of the chips lying unattended on the table. At crowded tables, like craps, keep one hand on your chip rack at all times.

At the slot machines, keep your coin cup in front of you whenever possible; the best place is in the coin tray. Sit close enough to the machine that you would notice if someone reached for your coin cup. Don't put your cup on the shelf next to the machine; someone can reach in from either side to take a handful of coins, or even the entire cup, without you noticing.

Remember that chips and slots tokens are the same as cash at the casino, so protect them the same way. For slots that use ticket systems instead of coins or tokens, the tickets are the same as cash and deserve the same care. Cashless slot machines that use a PIN-controlled account card are more secure; the card can be used only with the PIN code, and if your card is lost or stolen, the casino cage can close your account or issue you a new card.

If you win a jackpot, ask the casino to give you your winnings in check form. At many casinos, if you elect to take your jackpot in cash and later decide you want a check instead, you'll have to either find a bank that will sell you a cashier's check or traveler's checks for the cash, or you'll have to buy a money order from the post office or other outlet.

Protecting Yourself in Your Room

Hotel rooms at casinos also can be targets for thieves. When you're in your room, always use the chain lock and the deadbolt if available. This will prevent someone with a master key from entering the room while you're inside. It's a sensible precaution at any hotel, whether you're taking a shower, changing into evening dress, or simply relaxing in between activities.

Don't leave your wallet or purse out in the open. Put it in the drawer of the nightstand or in the closet, anywhere out of sight. If you have a lot of cash or other valuables with you, make use of the hotel's safe or ask for a safe-deposit box at the casino cage. Remember, the cage counter is under the eye of the ever-present surveillance cameras, and most casinos require their cage personnel to count out money, whether it's coming in or going out, in a specific pattern so the cameras (and the people who monitor them) can easily see what's going on. Make sure the box is securely locked; most require two keys to open and lock them.

If You Are a Victim

Even if you take all the precautions you can think of, you still might find yourself a victim of theft or other crime. If this happens, make sure you file a report with casino security and, if necessary, with the police department. Most casinos work closely with local or state police and will be happy to cooperate with you. For insurance purposes, you'll need a written report to prove your claim.

If credit cards or identification, like a driver's license or social security card, are among the things stolen, take prompt steps to protect your credit rating. You can do this by calling the three major consumer credit-reporting bureaus—Equifax, TransUnion, and Experian—and asking to talk to their fraud departments. You can ask the credit bureaus to mark your file with a "fraud alert" flag, and you can attach a written victim's statement to your credit report. This alerts potential new creditors to the fact that your identification has been stolen, and they generally will take extra steps to ensure that new accounts are genuine before granting credit. You can ask that the fraud alert and victim's statement remain on your credit report for up to seven years, but you must make that request in writing.

Finally, if your wallet or purse is stolen, close all accounts that might be affected. This includes credit cards, bank accounts, and any other accounts a thief might have access to. For example, you might want to contact your phone company, cellular phone carrier, Internet service provider, electric company, and so on; even if the account numbers for these services weren't among the stolen items, the thief might be able to track them down with your address or your social security number, or both.

ALERT!

Always keep copies of police reports, any written report from the casino security department, and your correspondence with the credit bureaus. If a dispute arises, even years after the actual theft or fraud, having the records on hand protects you and helps bolster your case.

What to Look For

Planning a gambling vacation is just like planning any other travel. In most cases, it pays to begin your planning early, at least three months in advance; if you're planning a trip to a popular destination during peak season, you might want to plan as long as a year in advance to get the best deals, particularly on airfare. Think about what kind of trip best suits your style: do you plan to spend most of your time at one casino, or do you want to try several different casinos? Are you flexible on the days and dates of your trip, or do you have a tight schedule for arriving and leaving?

Booking the Hotel

If you aren't taking the package route, be sure to ask for the casino rate when making your hotel reservations. You can save up to 50 percent off the regular posted rate, although at most casinos you have to join the player's club and may have to gamble a certain amount in that casino in order to qualify for the casino rate. If you go with a package, don't worry about room comps or discounts; you've already got a deep room discount built into the package.

Be sure to ask about the different types of rooms available during your stay. Most casino hotels have, in addition to their standard rooms, deluxe rooms or suites with special amenities, such as whirlpool tubs. The rates for these rooms are higher, naturally, but you may qualify for an upgrade on your room based on your level of play. In some cases, you might be able to upgrade your room, even with a package deal, for a fee.

Flying to Your Destination

Some gambling travel packages include charter flights, which operate under different rules than commercial flights. While commercial airlines will often compensate you for significant delays (other than those caused by weather), charter companies are not required to provide any compensation, or even alternative travel arrangements, for delays of up to forty-eight hours that are caused by mechanical problems. Check the contract before you purchase the package to find out what expenses the charter operator will cover—such as meals, lodging, or car rentals—for delays that aren't related to mechanical problems.

If you're flying with a commercial airline and you get bumped involuntarily because the flight is overbooked, you're entitled to compensation that varies according to the severity of the delay, as long as you show up for your flight on time. Under U.S. Department of Transportation rules, the airline doesn't have to compensate you if it can get you to your destination within an hour of your originally scheduled arrival time. However, if the airline can't get you to your destination until one to two hours after your original arrival time, they owe you up to $200 in cash. If you are delayed more than two hours, you're entitled to up to $400 in cash.

These compensation rules apply only if you're bumped involuntarily. Typically, on overbooked flights, airlines will first ask for volunteers to be bumped, and they'll offer travel vouchers that can be used on future flights as compensation. Depending on how many overbooked seats there are and how many people volunteer to get bumped, the airline might kick in additional incentives.

Finally, if you're booking a flight on a commercial carrier, you'll probably be more comfortable in planes that offer more leg room, at least thirty-four inches between seats, especially on longer flights. In general, the smaller the aircraft, the less space between the seats and, usually, the smaller the seats themselves. More and more airlines are using so-called "regional jets," which usually carry between fifty and 100 passengers, for two-hour flights, and some use them for flights up to three hours long. You can tell whether your flight is using one of these smaller jets by looking for the codes "RJ" or "CRJ" in the aircraft description.

Do You Need a Car?

If you're flying for a weekend trip at a casino resort, decide ahead of time whether you'll need to rent a car. Many casinos offer free or low-cost shuttle-bus service to and from the airport, and the major gambling cities are well-equipped with taxi and shuttle services for getting around town. In fact, there's a limousine service in Las Vegas that will take you from the airport to virtually any hotel or casino for a modest fee—$4 or $5 per person—and it's more stylish, and may even be less expensive, than taking a taxi.

If you're planning a stay in downtown Las Vegas or on the Strip, you'll probably prefer to walk most places because that's the best way to see the sights. If you need a taxi, the doorman at your hotel will flag one down for you; in Vegas, most taxis will stop only for doormen. It's customary to tip doormen about $2 for this service; you should tip taxi drivers $2 to $5, depending on the length of the trip, number of passengers, and number of bags.

The sights in other gambling cities are more spread out, so you might want to consider renting a car. If you choose to do this, keep in mind these tips for car rentals:

1. Check to see whether your car insurance or your credit card covers rentals. If so, waive the rental company's insurance.
2. Choose the mileage option that best suits your plans. If you're only planning to use the car to get back and forth to an evening show, you probably don't need the unlimited mileage option. If you plan to drive to the Hoover Dam, however, the unlimited mileage option might make more sense.
3. Compare the daily rates with the longer-rental rates to see which option is cheaper. You might need the car for only two days, but a three-day rental may be less expensive than the daily rate. Ⓔ

Chapter 17

Virtual Gambling

With the Internet and cheap computer software, it's easier than ever to learn how to play casino games. Any store that sells software most likely has a selection of inexpensive CD-ROMs featuring a variety of casino-type games like blackjack, video poker, craps, and slots. Many of the online casinos also allow you to download their gaming software and play, for free, at home.

Computer Games

The advantage of using software on your home computer to learn various casino games is that you can set your own pace for learning. Virtually every casino CD includes an overview of the game, the "house" rules, a description of your options, and a help menu if you get stuck. Many even have "virtual advisers," a small window that appears in the corner of your monitor and suggests your next move.

Learning games on your computer at home is an especially good strategy if you've never played a particular game before and are unsure of the rules or betting options. Craps, for example, can be very confusing to the novice gambler, mainly because there are so many betting options. By practicing with a computer game at home, you can get a feel for the game without worrying about keeping up with the real-life action.

Of course, many casino computer games allow you to immerse yourself in the traditional casino atmosphere—or a reasonable facsimile of it—with high-quality graphics and sounds. At the virtual blackjack table, you can listen to the dealer shuffle the cards while the "crowd" ebbs and flows around you; you can hear your hand tap the table as you ask for another card; you can even hear the bells and whistles of off-screen slot machines. And if you get tired of the noise, you can always hit the mute button.

You can find computer casino games that are as specific or as varied as you like. Some focus on a particular game and its variations, like poker; the menu for a casino poker CD might include everything from draw, stud, and Texas Hold'em to Boston 5, three-card poker, and jacks or better. Others offer a range of different games, covering roulette, baccarat, blackjack, craps, slots, and even keno and bingo.

Online Casinos

If you don't want to go shopping for a CD to use at home, you can simply download software from an online casino. Most reputable sites have a "play-for-free" option that allows you to download their software and play by yourself without opening an account or depositing any money. In fact, it's a good idea to spend some time using the free-play option before signing up with an online casino; this gives you a chance to get familiar with the games a site offers and the rules they play under, without having to risk a penny.

Is It Legal?

The legality of Internet-based casinos is hotly contested in the United States. In 2003, the U.S. House of Representatives passed a bill that would require banks and credit card companies to block all transactions for online gambling, including debit card payments and other electronic transfers of funds. The U.S. Senate proposed its own legislation that included criminal penalties for gambling online and extended the prohibition against online gambling to other high-tech communications venues like satellites and microwave transmitters.

Some online gambling sites give you the option of downloading their software or playing through your Internet browser. Generally, downloading the software gives you the benefit of all the special effects—fancy graphics and sophisticated sounds—while some of these features may be limited if you use the browser-only option.

As of this writing, neither of these bills has become law, but the pressure to regulate, if not prohibit, Internet-based gambling is enormous. A handful of states have enacted laws that bar online gambling. North Dakota authorities have successfully prosecuted at least one online gambler who placed sports bets through Internet gambling sites.

Restrictions

Banks and credit card companies also are facing new restrictions under the U.S. PATRIOT Act, which was enacted in the wake of the September 11, 2001, terrorist attacks to combat, among other things, money laundering for illegal activities. Under the PATRIOT Act, credit card companies cannot transfer or transmit money when they know the funds will be used for illegal activity. In addition, U.S. courts generally have ruled that federal laws prohibiting the use of telephone and telegraph lines for interstate betting also apply to the Internet.

In response to these pressures, most of the online casinos you'll find today are based outside the United States. Since 1995 or so, about 1,800 off-shore gambling sites have shown up on the Internet. Some countries, like Australia and the United Kingdom, regulate Internet gambling sites, even going so far as to license online casinos similar to the way bricks-and-mortar casinos are licensed. Still, although online gambling is legal in about fifty countries, most Internet gambling sites—up to 90 percent of them, according to some estimates—operate from islands in the Caribbean, European countries, or countries in the Pacific Rim.

Protecting Yourself

Given the uncertainty over its legality and the continually changing political pressures surrounding online casinos, you would be wise to exercise a little extra caution before diving into Internet gambling. First, find out whether your state has outlawed online gambling. Second, keep track of legislation in your state and at the federal level regarding online gambling. Third, if you are uncomfortable with the legal issues, forget playing online for real money and confine your Internet casino games to those you can play for free.

According to a survey commissioned by Peak Entertainment, NV, the average online casino player is of middle age, well educated, and has a middle-class household income. Men typically prefer to play blackjack online, while women prefer to play slots, a division similar to the profile of brick-and-mortar gamblers.

If you decide to gamble online for real money, there are some guidelines you should follow to protect yourself from unscrupulous or fraudulent sites. Doing a little research before you begin can save you money and frustration in the future and make your online experience more enjoyable.

Play-for-Free Options

The best online gambling sites allow you to play their games without setting up an account. Many sites even offer strictly recreational games, where players can participate in their favorite games and chat with other players while vying for points instead of cash. The casinos offer the play-for-free option because it's a good way to attract new customers; these days, most Internet-savvy consumers want to try something before they plunk down hard cash for it.

The play-for-free option is good for you because it gives you a chance to explore the software and get comfortable with it before you put any money on the line. You can find out which games are offered, study the rules for each game, and try a few practice hands to get a feel for the action. At some sites, you also can watch as other players gamble before jumping in yourself.

You probably should stay away from any site that does not allow you to take its gaming software for a test run before signing up. Some sites might ask you to fill out a short form before using the play-for-free option. As long as this form doesn't ask for banking or credit information, you're probably safe. If you have to give credit or banking information before you can try the software, leave the site immediately and don't go back.

Bonuses and Play-Throughs

Very few of us take the time to read the "terms and conditions" when we register for Internet sites or sign up for offers we received in our e-mail. But in the case of online casinos, it pays to be diligent about wading through the fine print. This is where you'll find out how the casino's bonuses are delivered, what you have to do to claim your bonuses, which games do and do not qualify in the bonus structure, and how and when winnings are paid.

Bonuses

Most online casinos offer bonuses for signing up, and many have frequent player bonuses or refer-a-friend bonuses. Usually, the bonus will be a certain percentage of your initial deposit, up to a dollar limit; for example, an online casino might offer a 25-percent bonus up to $100, which means you'll get $25 if you deposit $100, and $100 if you deposit $400, but you'll never get more than $100 in bonus money.

Always check out the terms for qualifying for a bonus. Many casinos make the bonus automatic as soon as you sign up, but some require you to claim your bonus within a certain period. If you don't claim your bonus within the prescribed time, you lose it. The terms and conditions will tell you what you have to do to claim your bonus.

Play-Throughs

Virtually all bonuses require a play-through, which varies from site to site. This is the casino's way of making sure that players don't sign up, claim the bonus, and leave without wagering. The play-through is usually expressed as a multiple of your deposit and bonus, like this: 10 × (deposit + bonus). If you deposit $100 and receive a $25 bonus, you can't withdraw any winnings until you've played 10 × ($100 + $25), or $1,250. That sounds like a lot, but it's the equivalent of 250 hands of blackjack at $5 a hand, and it doesn't take long for most players to meet the play-through requirements.

Remember that not all casino games are created equal when it comes to bonuses. Most online casinos exempt certain games from the bonus structure; the most common exemptions are roulette, craps, and baccarat. Some online casinos give only partial credit for certain games. One site, for example, gives you only one-third bonus credit for video poker, black-jack, and craps, which means you have to play $15 at one of these games to get a $5 credit on your play-through requirement. A few online casinos have no restrictions on games that count toward your play-through, but those are rare.

Some companies that operate several online casinos limit your eligi-bility to one bonus for that company's entire group of gambling sites. This should be explained in the terms and conditions section. Also, some sites that exempt games from the bonus structure may not even let you play those exempted games until you've met the play-through requirements. Again, the terms and conditions section on the site should spell out these restrictions.

ALERT!

If you can't readily find the terms and conditions on a gambling site, call the telephone number listed for the site and ask them to e-mail you a copy. If you can't find a phone number on the site, do not sign up for any real-money play. Sites that make it difficult for you to learn the rules of play or to contact them may be scams.

Customer Service and Support

Reputable and legitimate online casinos make it easy for their players to get help and information. Before you sign on with an Internet casino, check out its customer service and support facilities. You should be able to contact the casino via e-mail and via telephone, and there should be a toll-free number for technical support, especially when you download the casino's gambling software.

You can test an online casino's customer service by calling the telephone number and asking a real person to explain the bonus structure, rules, and restrictions. Also ask about withdrawal policies. Some casinos require you to maintain a minimum balance in your account or close it out entirely. The support personnel should be able to explain every item in the terms and conditions; if they hedge or give only vague answers, look for another gambling site.

Check to see if the site offers real-time support in chat mode. This is important if you run into problems or questions with the software; you don't want to be held up with technical issues when you're ready to play, and often chat-based support can resolve problems more quickly than telephone-based systems. You also can test the responsiveness of the site's e-mail support system by asking a question and seeing how long it takes the site to reply. If you don't get a response within twenty-four hours, be cautious about playing at that site.

Find out the hours when support is available. Some online casinos offer twenty-four-hour e-mail and telephone support. Others have twenty-four-hour e-mail support but their phone support hours are limited. The best companies offer several convenient ways for you to contact them, no matter what time of day it is.

Licensing and Regulation

Most countries that permit online casinos also have licensing and regulatory structures for those sites. Companies that operate online casinos may pay fees of $50,000 to $100,000 or more a year for the right to conduct gambling activities on the Internet, and they are usually subject to independent audit requirements to ensure compliance with standards of fairness and even the randomness of their gaming software. Many jurisdictions also require online casinos to post a bond or carry insurance that will cover gamblers' winnings if the company itself is unable to meet its obligations.

If an online casino is licensed in its home country, you should be able to find that information in the "about us" section of the Web site. The personnel manning the telephone support system also should be able to tell you where the company is licensed, whether it is subjected to independent audits, and which company conducts those audits. Typically, online casinos will use the services of large, multinational firms, such as PricewaterhouseCoopers, to conduct independent audits, and the audit findings should be available to the general public.

Some online casino operators are publicly held companies; these companies will be listed on the NASDAQ stock exchange or other exchanges. Public companies, such as Boss Media, have additional reporting requirements under the U.S. Securities and Exchange Commission. You can find a wealth of financial and other information about these companies from the SEC's Web site (see Appendix B).

In addition to meeting the regulations established by governments, many online casinos are members of trade groups or associations that monitor and promote so-called "best practices" for their members. The

Internet Gaming Commission is one of these associations, an independent body that keeps track of licensed and unlicensed online casinos and provides information about the games offered at online gambling sites. Another group that serves as both a watchdog and a consumer-information organization is the e-Commerce and Online Gaming Regulation Assurance, or eCOGRA, group. Web sites for these groups are included in Appendix B.

The Buzz from Other Players

It's always a good idea to find out what others are saying about a specific site. There are dozens, if not hundreds or even thousands, of sites that purport to "rate" the best online casinos, but some of these are affiliated in some way with the gambling sites they promote. When you're reading through a rating site, look for the criteria the site uses in determining a gambling site's ranking. Independent sites typically will base their ratings on the casino's payout percentage, customer support services, ease of use, and other factors. Many of these sites also have message boards where you can find out what players think about a given site.

Ideally, you want an online casino that is free of player complaints. You will likely find complaints from people who are unhappy that they lost money gambling and want to blame the casino site for their bad luck, poor gambling skills, or faulty strategies. Read such complaints carefully, and look for patterns in the types of complaints. Are players having a hard time cashing in their winnings? Are there unreasonable delays in receiving winnings or promised bonuses? You can make allowances for the occasional disgruntled losing player, but if a particular gripe shows up again and again, and from more than one player, that should make you wary about joining that gambling site.

Payouts and Payoff Options

Reputable online gambling sites will post their payout percentages on their Web pages, as well as their procedures for paying out winnings. Look for payout percentages in the very high 90s—97 percent or higher. Like their brick-and-mortar counterparts, legitimate online casinos make their money by building a reasonable house edge into all their games and by taking advantage of players' mistakes in strategy. If you avoid online gambling sites with payouts of 95 percent or lower and exercise the same care in playing that you would use in a real-life casino, you should experience more or less the same win rate no matter where you play.

It also is important to understand how you will receive your winnings. In most cases, an online casino will return your original deposit the same way you made it. That is, if you use a Visa to deposit $100 in your online gambling account, you'll get that $100 back as a credit on your Visa account. Winnings, though, are usually handled differently. Instead of crediting your winnings to your credit card, most online casinos will cut a check and mail it to you; it may take about two weeks to receive it, depending on where the casino is based and which bank it uses. Some online casinos also offer a wire transfer option for receiving winnings. You get your winnings faster, but usually you have to pay a fee for this service.

ALERT!

Many credit card companies, and even some third-party pay services like PayPal, are refusing to authorize charges to online gambling sites because of the questions about the legality of such sites. You may have to do some searching before you find a service that will accept your deposit to open an online gambling account.

Internet Scams

Unfortunately, the same technology that allows you to play your favorite casino games on your computer also allows unscrupulous operators to set up all-too-convincing Web sites and e-mail messages that allow them to steal your money and even your personal information, such as your social security number or driver's license number. Usually, these fake Web sites look enough like the real thing that it's easy to be scammed if you aren't paying close attention. But you can protect yourself by following some basic, commonsense rules for online transactions.

First, make sure any online casino you decide to join uses a secure server to transmit your personal information. In most Windows-based programs, you'll see a dialog box advising you that you are about to enter or leave a secure Web site; when you're on a secure site, a small padlock icon will appear in the lower right corner of the screen. Secure servers use encryption codes to prevent unauthorized people from capturing your data while it's being transmitted; the information is decoded only after it is received by the secure server.

Second, proceed with caution whenever you receive an e-mail from an Internet company that asks you for credit, banking, or other personal information, even if it's from a company you've done business with in the past. This is a popular ploy for Internet scam artists, and it's relatively easy for them to make such messages appear legitimate with copied graphics. If you receive a message asking you to confirm any personal information, *do not* reply via e-mail. Instead, call the customer service number for the company and verify that the e-mail message is legitimate. If it isn't, ask the customer service representative to file a report of the scam with his or her supervisor. You also might want to consider notifying the consumer protection division of your state attorney general's office.

One way to limit your exposure for fraud is to open a separate credit card with a small limit, say $500 or less. Use this card only for your online gambling. This will make it easier to identify fraudulent or unauthorized charges in the event your card number is stolen, and your other credit accounts will be secure.

Third, and perhaps most important, read all information on a gambling site with a healthy dose of skepticism. If something sounds too good to be true, it probably is; don't fall for promises or claims that are vastly different from those you've seen on other sites. If most online casinos are offering a 25 percent sign-up bonus, for example, be sure to read the fine print when you come across one with a 75 percent bonus. There may be a catch—or several catches—to claiming the bonus. Assume there is, and search until you find it.

Chapter 18

Managing Your Money

Gambling experts are virtually unanimous in recommending that players plan their gambling budgets in advance of a trip to a casino, racetrack, or any other gambling venue. Unfortunately, many people fail to do this, and they often end up dropping money they can't afford to lose. You can save yourself much needless stress and anxiety by religiously planning your budget before you set foot inside a casino, taking into account not only your bankroll but also essentials like food, gas, parking or valet fees, and so on.

Setting Your Limits

Before you start gambling, you have to know when to quit. That means knowing exactly how much your bankroll is, how much time you can or should play, and what kinds of bets you should stick with. These limits will vary depending on what kind of trip you're planning. For example, if you live near a casino and want to spend a Saturday evening there, your bankroll and time for playing will be smaller than if you're planning a weeklong vacation in Las Vegas. And if you're eager to try a new betting system at craps, you might deviate from your normal betting strategies.

Players who don't take the time to plan their gambling outings often find themselves playing with so-called scared money—funds that should be reserved for the mortgage, car payment, or electric bill—and chasing their losses, thinking that one big win will return to them what they've lost. In fact, the casino atmosphere is much more conducive to chasing losses than it is to getting up from the table and moving on when you've reached your limit. If you don't set your limits in advance, you might not realize you've exceeded them until it's too late.

Money Limits

Your bankroll is the money you have set aside to gamble with. You should always keep your bankroll separate from other funds. Some players like to keep their gambling money in a special bank account; this can help counter the temptation to withdraw "a little extra" from the household budget for gambling. At the casino, you should keep your bankroll separate from money for food, parking, gas, tips, and other essentials. You can do this by keeping your gambling funds and other money in separate pockets or in separate compartments in your wallet or purse.

Some players recommend keeping your bankroll in one pocket and any winnings in a separate pocket. With this system, you bet only with money from your bankroll pocket; the money in your winnings' pocket goes home with you. This takes some discipline, but it's a good way to make sure you have some money left at the end of your gambling session.

Make sure your bankroll contains only the amount of money you are willing and can afford to lose. Naturally, you hope to win, but inevitably you will encounter times when, no matter what you do, you'll lose every bet. If all you can afford to lose is $100, then take only $100 with you to the casino. If you'd like a bigger bankroll but can't really afford more than $100 right now, postpone your casino visit until you can afford to boost your bankroll to a more comfortable level.

ESSENTIAL

If you keep your bankroll in a separate bank account, you can leave the ATM card for your regular account at home and only take the bankroll account card with you to the casino. This way, you won't be tempted to dip into "scared money" while you're playing.

Getting money to gamble with while you're at the casino is easier than ever before—sometimes too easy. ATMs allow you to take cash advances on your credit cards as well as withdraw money from your checking or savings account. At some casinos, you can even transfer funds from your checking account to your slot club account without ever leaving the machine. If these easy options will tempt you to exceed your set bankroll, leave your credit cards, debit cards, and checkbook at home.

Types of Wagers

Planning for the types of wagers you'll place is another important part of protecting your bankroll and making sure you get the most enjoyment out of your gambling session. Before you go, know the house edge for the various bets on the games you want to play, and stick with the wagers where the house edge is 2 percent or lower. It's easy to get caught up in the moment and make those enticing "sucker bets," such as the insurance bet in blackjack. But if you do your homework in advance, you'll find it easier to resist the temptation of these losing bets.

If you hear or read of a new betting strategy that you just can't wait to try, remember to build the extra risk into your bankroll planning. You might be lucky enough to win on a bet that has a house edge of 11 percent, for example, but the odds are against it. So, when you budget your bankroll, budget for a loss when you try a new system. The extra risk may mean adjusting the length of your sessions, the size of your bets, and even the kinds of games you plan to play.

Stop-Loss Limits

In the stock market, investors regularly issue "stop-loss orders." These are standing orders to the broker to sell a stock when its price dips below a predetermined limit. If you buy a stock for $50 a share, for example, you might tell your broker to sell if the price goes below $25. You don't protect all of your investment with a stop-loss order, but you don't put all of your investment at risk, either.

A solid gambling plan includes stop-loss limits. Most players hit the casino thinking, "I've got $500 to blow," and they won't leave until every penny is gone. But the smart gambler thinks, "I've got $500 in my bankroll for the weekend. I want to have at least $250 to gamble with tomorrow." That gambler has set a stop-loss limit for herself, and she'll stop playing for that day when her bankroll gets down to her predetermined limit.

You can set your stop-loss limits any number of ways. Some players give themselves hourly limits; this forces them to take a break if they're in the middle of a losing streak. Others prefer to set a loss limit for a session or a day. The key to successful stop-loss limits is obeying whatever rule you've established for yourself. If your plan is to lose no more than $100 in an hour, you have to abide by that decision even if you've only been playing for twenty minutes when you reach your limit.

Winning Limits

Successful gamblers—those who end up with a net profit, however small, over the long term—set goals for what they want to win at each gambling session. If you have $100, you might set a goal of increasing your bankroll by, say, 40 percent, or $40. When you reach that goal, you quit playing.

Setting limits on your winnings is just as important as setting limits on your losses, and for the same reason. Many a player has found himself up a huge amount at the table or slot machine, only to go home empty-handed because he continued to play well past the point where he should have quit. Remember, the longer you play any game at the casino, the more the odds swing in the casino's favor.

If you're lucky enough to increase your bankroll with winnings, set a limit on how much of your winnings you're willing to lose. If your loss-after-winning limit is 50 percent and you've won $100, you can wager up to $50 of your winnings. The other $50 stays in your pocket and goes home with you.

Pay attention to your chips, especially during a winning streak. Many casinos train their dealers to "color up" winning players by giving them higher-value chips, and in the rush of the game it's easy to lose track of what your chips are really worth. If you're playing $5 chips, make sure you get $5 chips back when you win.

Time Limits

Planning your time at the casino works hand in hand with planning your gambling budget. The simplest way to make sure your bankroll doesn't run out before you're ready to leave is to divide your bankroll by bets per hand and hands per hour. If you're planning a four-hour casino visit and your bankroll is $500, that gives you $125 per hour to play with. At a $5 blackjack table, that allows you twenty-five hands per hour—a rather slow pace that will require you to sit out a few hands or take frequent breaks, unless you're lucky enough to hit a winning streak. On the other hand, if your game of choice is $1 keno or a twenty-five-cent slot machine, $125 per hour should be ample.

Set a stop-loss limit for each gambling session. In a four-hour visit, for example, you might plan two gambling sessions of ninety minutes each, with a meal break in between. With a $500 bankroll, you've got $250 per session; don't dip into your bankroll for the second session until after the break you already planned.

Breaks are an important part of the gambling experience. They give you an opportunity to walk away from a losing streak, if necessary. Just as important, though, breaks give you time to clear your head, watch and learn from other players, and return to your playing with a fresh mindset.

Meal breaks are perhaps the easiest to plan, but you can plan other breaks as well, even it's just to get up and stretch your legs. Giving yourself a break of even five or ten minutes every hour will help you stay focused during your sessions.

Betting Systems

Virtually any betting system you come across will take one of two forms: increasing the amount of your bet when you lose, or increasing your bet when you win. Beware of any betting system that touts itself as a "sure winner" or "can't-lose system." There is no such thing. If people could predict the outcome of a given draw of the cards, spin of the roulette wheel, or throw of the dice, it wouldn't be called gambling.

Systems that call for you to increase your bet when you lose—such as the Martingale, D'Alembert, or Fibonacci systems—have two inherent problems. First, they assume you have a large bankroll. Second, you're likely to run up against table limits before you can follow these systems to their promised conclusions.

The Martingale system is the most commonly known "up-as-you-lose" system, calling for you to double your bet every time you lose. Consider how expensive this system can be even if you're playing just $5 a hand at blackjack, assuming no bet limits for this example. If you lose the first hand, Martingale calls for you to bet $10 on the next. If you lose that hand, you then bet $20 on the third hand. Lose that hand, and you're at $40 for the fourth hand, and when you lose that one, you're up to $80 for your bet on the fifth hand. After five losing hands, you've dropped $155 ($5 + $10 + $20 + $40 + $80 = $155). If you continue with this system for another five hands and lose those five, you'll have dropped more than $5,000 in ten hands of $5 blackjack.

Why won't the Martingale system work with table limits?
Casinos establish maximum bets, or table limits, specifically to prevent systems like the Martingale from wiping them out. At most $5 tables, the maximum bet is $200. If you play six losing hands using Martingale, you've lost $315; even if you win the seventh hand at the maximum bet, you'll get only $200 back.

"Up-as-you-win" systems, such as the reverse Martingale, call for you to increase your bet when you win and return to your base wager when you lose. So, if you're playing $5 blackjack, you would bet $5 on the first hand and, if you win, you would bet $10 on the next hand. If you win that hand, your next wager would be $20, and if you win again, you would increase your bet to $40. Systems like these are great as long as you're winning. But, like the up-as-you-lose systems, they can get expensive, and they have the added disadvantage of putting your winnings, as well as your base bet, at risk. With these systems, it only takes one losing hand to wipe out everything you've won before.

A more conservative betting strategy—and one that will neither break your bankroll nor run up against table limits—would be upping your bets by one unit as you win for a cycle of, say, five bets, then starting that cycle over. Using our blackjack example again, you would bet $5 on the first hand; if you win, your next bet would be $10. If you win that hand, your bet on the third hand would be $15, then $20, then $25. Whether you win or lose on the fifth hand, return to your $5 bet on the sixth hand, and if you keep winning, you keep repeating the cycle. If you lose, you bet no more than $5 until you win again.

Conservative strategies like this won't make you rich overnight, but they will help keep your expectations at a reasonable level. Remember that any win, large or small, still is a win, and small wins, carefully husbanded, add up quickly. In addition, more conservative betting means longer life for your bankroll, and the longer your bankroll lasts, the more fun you can have playing.

Tips and Tokes

Dealers, keno runners, food and beverage servers, slot attendants, and casino porters are all members of the service industry. Base pay for these workers usually is minimum wage or slightly higher, and they rely on tips for much of their income. In many cases, especially for dealers and wait staff, half or more of their income may come from gratuities.

Tips for Service

Tipping rates vary depending on the kind and quality of service you receive. At the casino's coffee shop or restaurant, you should tip the way you would at any other restaurant. A good rule of thumb is 15 percent of the bill if the service is decent, 20 percent if the service is exceptional. If your meal or a portion of it is comped, calculate the tip based on the total before the comp is applied.

You might give the valet parking attendant a buck or two for bringing your car around. If you hit a decent win at the slots, you might slip a few coins to the attendant who verifies your win. Keno runners also appreciate recognition for the service they provide you. At most casinos, you'll receive free drinks on the gaming floor, but it's a good idea to give the beverage server a dollar every time you get a drink; servers return more promptly to people who tip.

Tokes for Dealers

"Tokes" is casino jargon for tips, especially for dealers. A few casinos allow their dealers to keep their tips, but at most casinos, tokes are pooled and shared among all the dealers on a shift. The sharing system makes good business sense from the casino's point of view. It encourages all dealers to be friendly and helpful. If a dealer has a bad attitude, that will be reflected in the tokes from his or her table, and the other dealers will pressure their colleague to clean up his or her act. Sharing tokes also prevents low-limit tables from becoming "slum tables" that no dealer wants to work. After all, a dealer at a $5 blackjack table deals just as many hands—and often more—as a dealer at a $50 table.

Dealers offer a service the same way waiters and waitresses do. They deliver the game to the player in a cheerful, efficient, and friendly fashion. And, even though the dealer represents the house, and therefore your opponent, at most table games, dealers really want their players to win. The reason is simple: winning players are more likely to toke. But as the player, you should toke even if you're not winning. It isn't the dealer's fault if you lose, and if the dealer is cheerful and friendly and helping you enjoy yourself, win or lose, toking is appropriate.

FACT

Depending on the region, casino dealers can make anywhere from $25,000 to more than $60,000 a year. But at most casinos, starting base pay for dealers is around $5.50 an hour—only $11,440 a year. The rest of a dealer's income comes from tokes.

There are several ways to toke. Some players flip chips to dealers after a winning hand or round. Others prefer to make bets for the dealers once an hour or so. You can do this by placing a chip next to your own bet on the layout. Your bet for the dealer can be any amount; it doesn't have to equal your own bet. Be aware, however, that if the bet wins, the dealer will keep both the bet you placed and the winnings from that bet. That makes this form of toking an expensive proposition, especially if your wins are modest (or even nonexistent).

Another, less expensive method of placing a bet for the dealer is to put a $1 chip on top of your own bet and tell the dealer it's "riding on my coattails." If you win, the dealer also wins, but the $1 bet stays put for the next hand or round. If you keep winning, the dealer keeps collecting a toke. But you're tipping the dealer with the casino's money, not yours. You can place coattails bets at virtually any table game; just let the dealer know that's what you're doing.

Cashing Out

If you've set your gambling budget and goals, you know when it's time to quit playing and cash out. It's a simple process: you take your chips, tokens, or slot card to the cage cashier, who will give you currency or a casino check in exchange. If you'll be tempted to gamble beyond your preset limits, ask for a check instead of cash. It's also a good idea to ask for a check if your winnings are substantial; payment on checks can be stopped if they're lost or stolen, but cash is a more tempting target for thieves and pickpockets.

You'll need to have a photo ID with you when you cash out. Most casinos accept a valid driver's license, government-issued photo ID, or a passport. Depending on the size of your winnings, you also may need to supply a valid social security number (see Chapter 19).

Chapter 19
Record Keeping

The average bettor views gambling as a form of entertainment, but in reality it is a tightly controlled, highly regulated business. Even charitable gambling, such as bingo nights at a church or firehouse, is subject to stringent rules regarding record keeping for both the establishment and the player. You can save yourself a lot of headaches later by being familiar with the rules that affect you both at the casino and at tax time.

Regulatory Requirements for Casinos

Casinos are cash-intensive businesses, but they also handle a broad range of other financial transactions. They can conduct wire transfers, accept deposits, extend credit, issue checks and other noncash financial instruments, and exchange foreign currency. To ensure the integrity of all these transactions, casinos have to comply with layers upon layers of regulatory requirements from several agencies, including state gaming authorities, federal banking regulators, the U.S. Department of the Treasury, and the Internal Revenue Service, not to mention each casino's internal auditing and regulating bodies.

The Bank Secrecy Act

The federal Bank Secrecy Act (BSA) came into being in 1970 and initially was aimed at discouraging illegal transactions at banks, credit unions, and savings and loans. In 1985, the law was expanded to include casinos with gross annual gaming revenues of more than $1 million. Among other things, BSA requires casinos to file Currency Transaction Reports on cash transactions involving more than $10,000, whether the player is paying it in or the casino is paying it out.

Transactions include the purchase of chips or tokens, front money or safekeeping deposits made by a player, the purchase of a casino check, payments on various forms of credit, exchanges of foreign currency, and, of course, wagers. Casinos also are required to file these reports when they pay out more than $10,000 on such things as cashing out chips, advances of credit, wire transfers, check cashing, and reimbursements for a player's travel, lodging, or entertainment expenses. Casinos have to file these reports within fifteen days, and they must keep copies of these records on file for five years.

Casinos also must report multiple transactions for one player in a single gaming day that meet the $10,000 threshold. For example, if you bought $5,000 worth of chips, lost $4,000 at the blackjack table, exchanged your remaining $1,000 in chips for slots tokens, and won a $7,000 jackpot, the casino would have to file a Currency Transaction Report on your activity for the day.

FACT

At Nevada casinos, the threshold for reporting is still $10,000, but multiple transactions are added together only if they are all deposits or purchases by the player or money paid to the player. In the example in the Bank Secrecy Act section, the multiple transactions would not have to be reported because the player neither paid in more than $10,000 nor cashed out more than $10,000.

Suspicious Activity Reports

The requirement for casinos to report suspicious financial activities is nothing new. But since the September 11, 2001, terrorist attacks, personnel at all financial institutions, including casinos, have been on higher alert for such activities. Suspicious Activity Reports (SARs) go to the U.S. Treasury Department's Financial Crimes Enforcement Network, and they are not public record; that is, casino personnel can file an SAR on anyone without that person's knowledge. Because of the heightened awareness of potential terrorist activity, you could inadvertently (and quite innocently) raise questions about your own activities at the casino if you don't know what their staff members are trained to watch for.

Most important, make sure you have a valid form of identification. You'll need it to open a player's club account. If you are dealing with large amounts of money or win a jackpot, you'll also need it for the various forms you'll have to fill out at the cage cashier's desk. A valid driver's license is the most commonly accepted form of identification, but most casinos also accept state-issued ID cards, military ID cards, and valid passports. These days, even an expired driver's license can trigger questions about your real purpose at the casino.

Casino personnel also will be on the lookout for people who try to structure their transactions to avoid the $10,000 reporting threshold. For example, asking what constitutes a "gaming day" at the casino, then making sure you don't go over the reporting threshold by the end of the gaming day is sure to raise suspicions. Similarly, if you and your best friend each buy $3,000 worth of chips separately, play a few hands of blackjack, decide you're not in the mood to gamble, and pool your chips when it comes time to cash out, that might raise a flag for the cage cashier. If you're betting large amounts of money but playing both sides of the bet—i.e., betting odd and even at roulette, or come and don't come at craps—expect casino personnel to keep a sharp eye on you.

ALERT!

Never, never, never ask a casino employee not to file a currency transaction report or to break down your transactions to avoid the reporting threshold. Such requests are unethical and could lead to problems with casino security and even the U.S. Treasury Department.

Withholding on Winnings

If you're lucky enough to land a substantial win on certain games, the casino will issue you a W-2G form that shows your gross winnings, the type of wager you made, the date, the cashier who paid your winnings, and the amount of income tax withheld. The Internal Revenue Service has two withholding rates for gambling winnings: 27 percent for regular withholding on cash winnings, and 30 percent for backup withholding. Only one of these rates will be applied to your winnings. In general, the regular withholding rate will apply as long as you can supply a valid social security number; if you can't, the casino will withhold at the higher backup rate.

Different winnings limits apply to different games. In general, taxes may be withheld on winnings of $600 or more when the winnings are at least 300 times the amount of the bet. So, for example, if you won a $600 purse on a $2 race bet, the casino or race course would give you a W-2G, a copy would go to the IRS, and you would have to report those winnings as income on your tax return.

Games Subject to Backup Withholding

Regular withholding rates apply to almost all gambling winnings. The key exceptions are keno, bingo, and slot machines, which have different reporting limits and different tax rules. Noncash prizes, such as cars and vacations, also have their own set of rules.

For keno, the threshold for IRS reporting is $1,500. You have the option of subtracting the amount of your wager from your winnings before the withholding tax is figured. For example, if you spent $200 at the keno lounge and won $2,100, you could choose to subtract your $200 wager from your winnings and pay withholding taxes on $1,900 rather than on the full $2,100. The IRS requires casinos to use the backup-withholding rate for keno winnings.

The backup-withholding rate also applies to bingo and slot machine winnings of $1,200 or more. As with keno winnings, you have the option to subtract your wager from your winnings. The regular withholding rate is usually applied to winnings of $5,000 or more from lotteries, sweepstakes, wagering pools, and other forms of gambling where the winnings constitute at least 300 times the amount you wagered.

ESSENTIAL

Backup-withholding taxes apply to the entire sum of winnings, not just the amount that exceeds the reporting requirement. In our keno example on this page, the reporting limit is $1,500, but the total winnings (minus the wager) are $1,900. The backup-withholding rate will be applied to the entire $1,900, not just to the $400 over the reporting limit.

Table Game Winnings

The IRS does not require casinos to file W-2G forms on your winnings at table games, such as blackjack, craps, roulette, and baccarat. However, the casino may issue a 1099 form at the end of the year if your winnings exceed $600. In this case, no taxes will be withheld at the time you collect your winnings, and you will be liable for all taxes on your table game winnings when you file your return.

You can ask the casino to issue a W-G2 form any time you win, no matter what the amount. You also can elect to have more than the standard withholding rate taken out of your winnings. If the jackpot is high enough, you could choose to have 50 percent or more withheld for taxes, and that might significantly reduce your overall income tax bill at the end of the year.

Noncash Prizes

Noncash prizes also are subject to taxes, under a different set of rules. Generally, prizes like merchandise, vehicles, and vacations must be given a "fair market value" for tax purposes. If you decide to pay the tax when you win the prize, the tax rate will be the regular withholding rate, based on the fair market value minus the amount of your wager. If you choose to have the casino pay the withholding tax, you'll be taxed at a higher special withholding rate.

IRS Requirements for You

As far as the IRS is concerned, all gambling winnings are taxable and must be reported as income. This applies to charitable gambling and online gambling as well as the commercial variety; it even applies to illegal gambling. Whether your gambling is legitimate or not, the federal government expects you to report it.

Because tax laws and regulations change often, your wisest move is to consult your tax adviser about your specific situation. However, keep in mind that the burden of proof is on the taxpayer. If you get audited and don't have the documentation to support your claims of gambling wins and losses, you could end up paying penalties.

FACT

The IRS considers *all* gambling winnings taxable, even if your winnings don't meet the reporting requirements for a W-2G. If you wager and win only small amounts, these easily can cancel each other out on your income tax return. However, you can claim gambling losses as a deduction only if you itemize.

If your winnings meet the reporting limits discussed previously, you'll receive copies of the W-2G form from the casino, usually by the end of January for the previous tax year. On your tax form, you enter the amounts from your W-2Gs as "other income." If you itemize, you can deduct your gambling losses, but only up to the amount of your winnings.

For example, if you won $10,000 but lost $18,000, you can only claim $10,000 in losses.

Proof of Wins and Losses

The IRS requires you to keep an accurate record of your wins and losses, plus supporting documents that will prove those wins and losses during an audit. In addition to your W-2G forms, the IRS recommends keeping validated keno or bingo tickets, canceled checks, payment slips, and other records you routinely get from the casino. You should keep these records for as long as you keep other income tax records—usually a minimum of seven years.

On your tax return, you can claim gambling losses as a deduction only if you itemize. If you take the standard tax deduction and don't itemize, you have to report your gambling income but cannot claim your losses. Married couples must combine their wins and losses when they file a joint tax return. You cannot "lump" your wins and losses; that is, you can't just report zero dollars in gambling winnings if you ended up losing more than you won. Finally, the IRS requires taxpayers to report wins and losses only in the year in which they occur. You can't carry losses forward or apply them to previous years to offset your winnings.

State Income Tax Requirements

Tax laws vary from state to state. Some levy income tax on your gambling winnings; some allow you to deduct the federal income tax you paid on those winnings; and some don't bother with gambling winnings at all. You also might have to file a tax return in the state where you won, even if you don't live there.

For example, if you live in California but had gambling winnings in Mississippi, you might be required to file a nonresident tax return with Mississippi. California may allow you to deduct part or all of the taxes you paid to Mississippi when you file your state income tax return. Check with your tax adviser to find out what the laws and regulations are in your state.

If you gamble and win in other countries, you'll have to declare those winnings on your federal tax return, and you may have to file a nonresident tax return in the country where you won. Each country has its own rules and tax treaties with the United States; be sure to ask what the requirements are when you're at an overseas casino.

Comps as Taxable Income

Those free trips to the buffet, discounted hotel rooms, and match play coupons—all the incentives casinos shower upon you to keep you on the gaming floor or to motivate you to return—are considered gambling winnings and are therefore taxable. The casino should be able to give you a listing of the comps you received and their dollar value, but you may have to ask for it. The good news is that, with proper record keeping, you can apply your gambling losses against both your cash winnings and your comps.

Tabulating Wins and Losses

There are several good reasons for keeping a simple diary or log of your gambling wins and losses. First, you'll need such a document if you've claimed winnings and losses and subsequently get audited by the IRS. Second, a diary helps you keep track of the money you're spending on gambling. Third, a good diary can show you where your betting strategy or playing skill needs improvement.

A gambling diary doesn't have to be complicated. Many players use a small notebook to keep track of their wins and losses; others later transfer the information to a spreadsheet or other report on their home computers. Your gambling diary should include the following information:

- Date
- Time
- Name of casino

- Game
- Machine or table number
- Initial bankroll
- Cash out
- Net result (losses in parentheses)

Say you spend a weekend at the Borgata in Atlantic City, playing mainly blackjack and the slots, with a brief keno session one day. Here's what your gambling log for that trip might look like:

Date	Time	Casino	Game	Machine/ Table	Initial Bankroll	Cashed Out	Net
8/31	7–9:30 P.M.	Borgata	Blackjack	6	$400	$520	$120
8/31	10–11 P.M.	Borgata	Lucky 7s	1834	$50	$13	($37)
9/1	8–10 A.M.	Borgata	Throw the Dough	1022	$100	$112	$12
9/1	Noon–4 P.M.	Borgata	Blackjack	11	$200	$315	$115
9/1	7–8 P.M.	Borgata	Keno		$35	$18	($17)
9/2	10 A.M. –3 P.M.	Borgata	Blackjack	4	$500	$210	($290)

Some tax experts also recommend that your diary include the address or location of the casino or other gambling establishment, as well as the names of any people who accompanied you at a given session. In most cases, however, the name of the casino or gambling establishment should be sufficient.

In case of an audit, an accurate gambling log can be your saving grace. Tax courts have been unsympathetic toward gamblers who merely estimate their wins and losses without the proper supporting documentation. Also, because the requirements for filing W-2G forms are far from all-inclusive, tax authorities are almost automatically suspicious of anyone who claims only the gambling wins reported on W-2Gs.

Some players like to keep separate diaries for each type of game they play. This can be helpful in determining where you spend most of your gambling budget and which games you tend to win at more often. Since it's human nature to remember the wins and let the disappointing losses fade from memory, diaries also offer an objective look at your gambling habits and give you the information you need to decide whether the money you're investing is worth the recreation value you receive.

ESSENTIAL

If you use your player's club card faithfully, at the end of the year you can ask the casino(s) for a report detailing your activity throughout the year. Information contained in this kind of report varies from casino to casino, but usually it includes coins in/coins out, dates, times, machine numbers, etc. It's a good backup for your own records.

Online Gambling Records

Several states have outlawed Internet gambling and several other states are considering outlawing it. Many credit card companies, under pressure from the federal government, have prohibited customers from using their cards to set up online gambling accounts. Nevertheless, gambling on the Internet is quite prolific, and, as previously noted, the IRS considers all gambling income—whether technically legal or not—as taxable. If you engage in online gambling and elect to declare online winnings and losses, you'll need to have documentation to support your claims.

Some online casinos offer logs to their players that track the players' transactions and play. These logs may be available on a weekly or monthly basis; if they are, you should print them out and keep them on file. Also, you can sometimes print so-called "screen shots" while you're logged into your online casino. These are snapshots of your activity as shown on your computer screen and can be useful as supporting documentation.

Nongambling Expenses

Unless you're a professional gambler, chances are your nongambling expenses are not allowable expenses on your income tax return.

However, to help with budgeting, it's useful to add a nongambling expense category to your gambling diary. This is where you record such items as tokes for dealers and tips for waiters and waitresses, hotel room cost, valet parking, show tickets—basically everything you spend that is not a wager.

You also can—and should—record the value of any comps you receive, such as a free or discounted hotel room, meal vouchers, and so on. Comps add value to your gambling experience, and it's nice to see what you're getting in return for the money you drop at the tables or the slot machines. If you have to include them as gambling winnings, you'll avoid an unpleasant surprise at tax time by keeping track of your comps as you go.

Chapter 20

E The Psychology
of Gambling

According to the American Gaming Association, more than 51 million people visit casinos each year. What keeps them coming back? For some, it may be the profit motive. But for most of us, the thrill in gambling comes from a combination of the fast pace of the games and the rush we get when we find ourselves on a winning streak. Understanding the psychology of gambling can enhance your enjoyment of your sessions and help you identify potential problems before they get out of hand.

Discipline

Every successful gambler needs discipline. For our purposes here, successful isn't necessarily the same as winning. A successful gambler is one who takes the time to gain the knowledge he or she needs to play the games, who understands the house edge and how it works, who can create a gambling budget and stick with it, and who enjoys the gambling session. All of these things take a great deal of discipline, whether you're winning or losing.

Know Your Game

The first element of discipline is understanding the game or games you want to play. If your game is blackjack, that means learning and applying basic strategy. If you prefer craps, it means understanding your betting options and knowing how to hedge your bets. If you'd rather play the slots, it means knowing the payout rates for specific machines and the pros and cons of playing maximum coins.

Recent research on the physiological effects of gambling indicates a moderate amount can be beneficial for both the heart and the brain. Low excitement levels are healthy stimulants for the cardiovascular system, and playing games—especially problem-solving games—helps keep the brain healthy and active in older adults.

Anybody can walk onto a gaming floor, toss a chip on the table, and trust to chance that it will come up a winner. You can play your hunches at blackjack. You can stay at a cold slot machine because you have a feeling it's due to hit big. You can buy only bingo cards with the "lucky" number 7 and hope that tonight's your night. But if you don't know the rules, procedures, and best betting options, the odds are stacked against you from the start.

Fortunately, there are several avenues for learning about the games you want to play, aside from the book you're reading now. Some casinos offer free classes in blackjack, poker, craps, and other table games to help the novice get started. The Internet also is a good source of information; there are scores of sites that not only explain the various games but allow you to play, usually for free. Likewise, home computer programs can be excellent learning devices, especially for more complicated games like poker and craps. Learning the ins and outs of your game can be daunting, especially in the beginning. But experience really is the best teacher, and in the long run your discipline will pay off in greater knowledge and fewer losses.

Stop, Look, Listen

Simply watching for a few hands or rounds before joining in is a good way to get a feel for the pace and flow of the game, and no one minds if you watch, as long as it doesn't interfere with play. This also is a good way to test your knowledge. When you're watching blackjack, for example, you can compare what the players do with your knowledge of basic strategy, identify players' mistakes, and figure out what you would do with that particular hand. The same applies to virtually any table game. You can pick up a lot just as a spectator.

Don't discount the dealer as an educational resource. Part of his job is to make you feel welcome and comfortable, and he should be happy to answer any questions you might have. However, remember to be courteous to the dealer and to other players. Choose an empty or nearly empty table if you anticipate needing a lot of help from the dealer, and try to find one where the pace of the game is on the slow side.

Understand the House Edge

The house edge is what keeps the casino in business, and it is not an easy thing to overcome. The wise and disciplined gambler knows what the house edge is on the games she plays and avoids the higher-risk bets. She also looks for opportunities that trim the house edge to 2 percent or less: playing basic strategy at blackjack, taking even-money bets on craps or a single-zero roulette wheel, and so on.

This is not to say that you shouldn't play keno or the money wheel—two games with some of the highest house edges in the casino—if you like. These games may appeal to you more than some of the other offerings; you might find them a relaxing respite from the frenetic pace of the craps pit or the blackjack table. By understanding how the house edge works and what the edge is on your game of choice, you can make informed gambling decisions that suit your style, your bankroll, and your tolerance for risk.

FACT

Because of the mathematics of the house edge, you're more likely to lose the longer you play. Giving yourself regular breaks from the action is not only a good mental strategy, it helps shave a little off that infamous house edge.

Creating and Sticking to a Budget

Once you really understand the house edge and how it works, it becomes obvious that you're more likely to lose than you are to win. If you do win, chances are your profit will be small. Disciplined gamblers learn to be content with small wins, because a bit of a profit is better than none, and it's much better than a loss. Establishing a budget before you set foot in the casino, with limits set both for losses and for how much of your winnings you're willing to risk, prevents you from chasing your losses when you lose and from being blinded by greed when you win.

Train yourself to think of your bankroll as investment money. In a savings account, your bankroll might earn you 2 or 3 percent interest. At the blackjack table, if you start with $100 and end up an hour later with $120, you've just earned 20 percent interest on your investment. Thinking in these terms can help you appreciate even the smallest wins.

Enjoying Yourself

Experts disagree over what motivates people who gamble. Psychologists and other professionals argue that players are driven by the profit motive, a chance to get big returns instantly on an investment. Other people who have spent their lives observing casino players, on the other hand, note that many, if not most, players continually make mistakes that put any potential profits out of reach. These observers argue that the true motivation must be something other than the smell of easy money. The real thrill must come from the action itself, the excitement of the surroundings, and the rush of adrenalin in a fast-paced game.

Any form of gambling is essentially a mental game. If you're tired, you won't enjoy it as much, and you're more likely to make mistakes. Disciplined gamblers get up from the table or slot machine when they feel fatigued; they take a break, get something to eat or drink, or just go outside for a breath or two of fresh air to recharge themselves.

Finally, your own emotions can overwhelm you in the midst of a hot or cold streak. It's tempting, after losing most of your bankroll in a session, to try to win it all back in one or two wagers. But it isn't an enjoyable sensation. If you've set your budget and stuck with it, the occasional losing streaks that all gamblers experience won't break your heart or your bank. You've still had the enjoyment of playing the game.

It's easy to lose track of your alcohol consumption when beverage servers are always at your elbow, but overindulgence dulls the mind and blurs judgment. If you're drinking too much, it will interfere with your enjoyment of the experience of gambling.

On the other hand, if you're on a roll, winning hand after hand or throw after throw, it's easy to get caught up in the moment and forget all those well-laid plans you made earlier. If you're winning, by all means, keep playing and enjoy the ride; but when you begin to lose, as you inevitably will, stop. You've added the thrill of a winning streak to your experience, and that thrill will linger much longer when your wallet is fat with cash.

Winning Attitude

Vegas gambling pioneer Sam Boyd once summed up the difference between winning players and losing players: "The losers act like they are going to lose . . . while the winners act like they expect to win, talk like they are going to win, and bet like winners." He knew that attitude plays an important role in any gambling session. And he knew that winners approach their gambling from a unique perspective.

Here are some key differences in the attitudes of winning players and losing players:

- Winners want to win. Losers expect to lose.
- Winners accept small wins. Losers chase the big win.
- Winners set limits on how much they're willing to lose. Losers keep digging into their pockets, figuring their luck will change.
- Winners are alert and on their game. Losers rush ahead whether conditions are right or not.
- Winners believe in having fun but being careful with their hard-earned money. Losers look forward to the party atmosphere and regard their bankroll as "money to blow."

Think of a recreational sport, like softball or volleyball. The activity itself is fun, and the competition with other teams keeps it interesting. It doesn't really matter which team wins—you can enjoy yourself either way—but winning adds a little extra zest to the experience. Recreational gambling (as opposed to gambling professionally, when it becomes more of a business) has the same elements. The activity itself is enjoyable, and the competition—winning or losing against the house or other players— keeps it interesting. Expecting to win and being prepared to lose within reason are fundamental components of a winning attitude.

Self-Confidence

Self-confidence also is an essential part of a winning attitude. If you know your game, understand the odds, and have the discipline to stick to your established budget, you'll approach each gambling session with a great deal more self-confidence. And you'll be less likely to fall into the common errors so many players make.

When you know your game, you know the best way to play and the best way to bet. You know how to recognize when it's time to quit or take a break, and this knowledge gives you the self-confidence you need to walk away. You won't succumb to the tempting thought that your luck is due to change. Instead of believing in the illusion of control that many players have, you recognize which factors you actually have control over and which are beyond your control. And you won't relinquish the control you do have.

Acting on Your Knowledge

Winning players have enough self-confidence to give themselves permission to act on their knowledge and experience. They don't need others to reassure them that they're making the right decisions; they get that reassurance from inside, from the self-confidence they've built by learning about and playing their game. That doesn't mean winning players never make mistakes. It does mean that they learn from those mistakes and use that knowledge to avoid making the same mistakes again.

Of course, it takes time and discipline to acquire the knowledge that builds your self-confidence, which in turn gives you the internal permission you need to act on what you've learned. So, in a way, being aware of your limitations when first starting out also allows you to act on your knowledge. If you've read about craps but haven't actually played before, for example, you have enough knowledge to watch the action for a while before joining in and playing conservatively until you feel more comfortable with the game.

Remember, too, that your comfort level with a particular game is an intensely personal thing. Some people might need only a session or two to become comfortable and confident, while others may need more time and practice to feel truly confident. You are the only one who can judge your comfort level, so trust your gut when it comes to playing.

Luck Versus Skill

Every game of chance involves a certain amount of luck. In blackjack, for example, "the luck of the draw" influences your playing strategy; you can't control which cards you're dealt, but you play the hand differently if you hold a 5 and a 3 than you would if you held a 10 and a 9. On the other hand, some games involve no player skill at all. You can't influence the outcome of a spin of the roulette wheel or the numbers that come up in a keno race. All you can do is place your bet beforehand and wait for the result. Understanding the difference between these two types of games automatically puts you a step or two ahead of many gamblers.

ALERT!

> Don't think of your winnings as "the casino's money." Once you've won it, it's yours, and you should treat it the same way you treat your original bankroll. If you think of your winnings as your own money, it's easier to stick with your predetermined budget—and easier to go home a winner.

The Gambler's Fallacy

"The gambler's fallacy" is the notion that something is more likely to happen if it hasn't happened for a long time. Roulette players who subscribe to this idea will play red, for example, on the grounds that black has come up on the last seven spins and therefore red is "due" to come up. Likewise, craps players will bet on 12 thinking that every roll brings that number closer to appearing if it hasn't shown up all evening.

This is a fallacy, because in true games of chance like roulette, craps, keno, and bingo, the outcome of one round bears no relationship to the outcome of the next round. Each spin of the roulette wheel and each throw of the craps dice is an independent event, not influenced by anything that came before. Occasionally, you may encounter patterns, runs, or streaks in games of chance, but they are just as random as the game itself. The wise gambler recognizes this and bases his bets on his knowledge of the game and the odds, not on any misleading "pattern" in the play.

Winning and Losing Streaks

Even when you play the best strategy and make the most advantageous bets, you'll run into occasional streaks. Winning streaks are terrific, but they are bound to end sooner or later; that's the way the luck element works. Many players fail to recognize when a winning streak is beginning to fizzle, and they end up handing back everything they've won—and even then some—and go home losers after all. The flip side is when a player continues to fight against a losing streak, determined to "win it all back."

Winning players have the knowledge, confidence, and discipline to realize that streaks occasionally happen. They take advantage of winning streaks, but they have the self-control to quit when they meet their win goals, or when they begin to lose. And they have the patience to ride out losing streaks by adhering to their predetermined budgets.

Recognizing Problems

As many as 70 percent of American adults gamble in one form or another, and almost all of them gamble responsibly. But for a small portion of the population, gambling presents serious problems, and the effects can be as devastating as any addiction to alcohol or drugs. Fortunately, there are some typical warning signs that may signal a tendency toward problem gambling, and there are numerous avenues to get professional help if you're worried about your gambling habits.

Pathological Gambling

Pathological gambling has been a recognized behavior disorder since 1980, when it was listed in the American Psychiatric Association's *Diagnostic and Statistical Manual of Mental Disorders*. People who suffer from this disorder typically see a progression from what might be called "normal" gambling behavior to an increasing preoccupation with gambling, such as continually reliving prior gambling experiences or planning ways to finance the next gambling outing. The majority of pathological gamblers are men, and they usually start gambling in their teens; women tend to begin gambling later in life and may be drawn to it as an escape from other problems.

Warning Signs

Most problem and pathological gamblers seek the rush from the action rather than profit. Over time, it may take more gambling sessions and bigger stakes to achieve the same feeling of excitement, much like an alcoholic needs more drinks to achieve the same level of intoxication. In addition, most problem and pathological gamblers will habitually chase their losses, trying to make up for yesterday's loss with a big win today.

As the disorder progresses, the problem or pathological gambler may lie to family members, coworkers, friends, and others to cover up his or her gambling. He or she may try to hide the amount of money used for gambling by taking cash advances on a credit card instead of making withdrawals from a checking or savings account. He or she may try to borrow money on the pretext of some emergency—car repairs, say, or to pay off a past-due bill—and use it to gamble.

The urge may become so irresistible that the person skips work or misses family functions in order to gamble. The person may become irritable or depressed if he or she tries to cut back on gambling or stop completely. In desperate cases, the pathological gambler may resort to forgery or embezzlement to finance his or her habit.

In general, the problem or pathological gambler is not interested in games of chance, such as lotteries, keno, or roulette. The rush comes in large measure from "outsmarting" the house, so the games of choice are those that involve some level of skill, like blackjack, poker, or video poker. Horseracing and sports betting also involve pitting your wits and knowledge against the handicappers, so these kinds of wagers also can be attractive to the compulsive or pathological gambler.

Questions to Consider

Gamblers Anonymous, a twelve-step, self-help support group similar to Alcoholics Anonymous, has developed a list of questions to help players assess their gambling habits and determine the degree, if any, of addiction. If you're concerned about your gambling or the gambling habits of someone close to you, here are some important points to consider:

Have you ever lost time from work because of gambling?

Have you ever felt remorse or guilt after gambling?

Have you ever sold anything to raise money for gambling?

Have your gambling habits been the subject of arguments with family or friends?

Have you ever used "scared money"—that is, money earmarked for other expenses such as rent or groceries—to gamble?

Have you ever gambled to forget other problems?

Have you ever lost sleep thinking about or worrying about gambling?

If you answer yes to any of these questions, you might want to seek a professional evaluation of your gambling habits and risk for developing a gambling disorder.

Where to Go for Help

Most states have a center or council for problem gamblers that provides evaluation and counseling services. A complete list of these organizations is included in Appendix B of this book. Most states also have a public education and awareness program to encourage people who might have gambling problems to seek help. And Gamblers Anonymous has more than 300 chapters nationwide, as well as a Web site *(www.gamblers anonymous.org)*.

Self-Exclusion Programs

If you want to avoid even the temptation of gambling, you can have yourself declared persona non grata. Most gambling establishments offer some form of voluntary self-exclusion program. When you sign up for self-exclusion, the casino takes your name off its mailing list, ends any check-cashing or other credit privileges you might have, and removes you from its player's club. Usually, if you show up at the casino after joining the self-exclusion program, security personnel will escort you off the property; in some cases, you might even face arrest on trespassing charges.

Only a handful of states have implemented mandatory self-exclusion programs, and these programs usually are administered by the same agency that regulates gambling in the state. These programs have strict privacy standards, and casinos or other gambling establishments can be fined for violating terms of the self-exclusion program. In some states, once you sign up for the program, you are barred for life from any gambling outlet in that state.

Hotlines and Counseling Services

The National Center on Problem Gambling offers a toll-free, twenty-four-hour hotline (800-522-4700). In addition, most casinos have brochures and posters listing statewide hotlines and places that offer counseling and intervention services. Some statewide hotlines are offered only during normal business hours (9 A.M. to 5 P.M., Monday through Friday); others are offered twenty-four hours a day, seven days a week.

Hotline and counseling services are always confidential; in many cases, they are offered free of charge. Some groups, like Gamblers Anonymous, use a meeting format to help problem gamblers cope with and overcome their addiction. Hotlines and other organizations usually offer one-on-one counseling sessions.

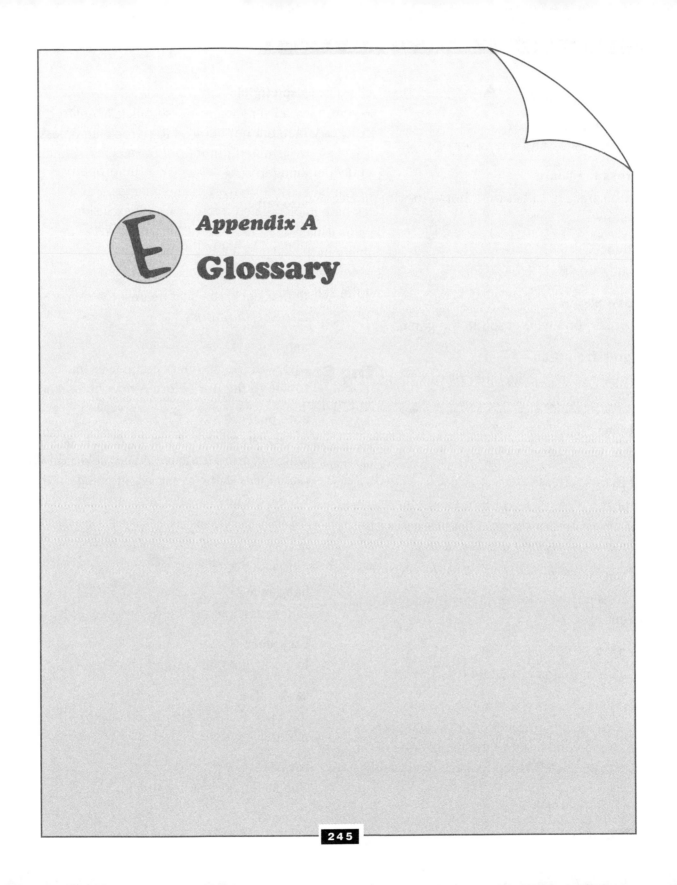

Appendix A

Glossary

A

aces up
A pair of aces and any other pair.

across the board
In horseracing, to bet on a horse to win, place, or show.

action
Money wagered.

active player
In poker, one who is still in the game.

aggressive action
A wager to intimidate other players into folding; an unusually high wager.

all blue
A flush in spades or clubs.

all in
In poker, a player who has wagered all of his or her chips; in sportsbook, a bet that cannot be refunded unless the event is canceled.

all out
In horseracing, a horse that is putting forth all its effort.

all pink
A flush in hearts or diamonds.

allowances
In horseracing, a reduction in weight because of course conditions or the experience of the jockey; also used when females race against males.

also eligible
In horseracing, a horse officially entered for a race but not allowed to participate unless a predetermined number of starters are scratched; an alternate.

also-ran
In horseracing, a horse that finishes a race but doesn't win any money.

anchor seat
In blackjack, the seat nearest the dealer's right; also see *third base.*

ante
In poker, the amount each player must contribute to the pot before a new hand starts.

ante post
In sportsbook, a bet placed on a future event, which is nonrefundable if your selection doesn't participate in the event, e.g., betting on the Chicago Cubs to win Game 1 of the World Series.

B

baby race
In horseracing, a race for two-year-olds.

back door
In poker, making a hand you weren't trying for.

back raise
In poker, to raise after another player has raised.

backside
The stable area at horseracing tracks.

backstretch
In horseracing, the straight portion of the far side of the track.

bad beat
A hard loss, especially in sports.

banker
In card games, the dealer or player who keeps track of the action of other players.

bankroll
The amount of money a player has set aside for gambling.

basic strategy
In blackjack, a widely accepted method of playing and betting according to which cards are showing.

beard
A person who places bets on behalf of another person; also see *runner*.

bearing in/bearing out
In horseracing, veering off a straight course.

bet
A wager.

betting limits
The minimum and maximum amounts you can bet at one time.

big blind
In poker, the largest blind.

bingo marker
An ink or crayon marker used to mark bingo numbers on a game card; also see *dauber*.

black
In roulette, a bet that any black number will win; also the common color for $100 chips.

blank
In poker, a card that adds little or no value to a player's hand.

blanket finish
In horseracing, when horses finish the race so close together that they could be covered by a blanket.

blind bet
In poker, a bet that a player is required to make because of his or her position at the table.

blind game
Any card game that requires blind bets.

blinders
A device attached to a harness to limit a horse's field of vision; also called "blinkers."

blowout
A win by an exceptionally large margin; in horseracing, a final workout a day or two days before a race.

bluff
In poker, to bet or raise on a weak hand in hopes of driving other players to fold.

board
In poker, community cards in the center of the table; in horseracing, a display indicating odds, betting pools, and other information.

boat
In poker, another term for a full house.

bolt
In horseracing, a sudden deviation from a straight course.

book
An organization or establishment that sets odds and accepts bets on the outcomes of various sporting events.

bookie
Slang for bookmaker; a person or group that sets the lines and books bets in sports or racing.

box
In sports betting, a combination bet in which all possible numbers are covered.

breakage
Leftover cents in pari-mutuel pools when payouts are rounded to the nearest nickel or dime.

break-even point
The point at which your winnings match or closely match the total amount of money you wagered.

break maiden
In horseracing, the first win of a career for a horse or jockey.

breaking hand
In blackjack, a hand that will go over 21 with one additional card; also see *stiff*.

breeding fund
A bonus prize fund in some states for state-bred horses that win races.

breeze
In horseracing, a light workout for a horse.

bring-in
In the first round of betting in seven-card stud, a mandatory bet made by the player with the lowest up-card.

Brood mare
In horseracing, a female Thoroughbred used for breeding.

buck
Slang for a $100 bet; also see *dollar bet*.

bug
In poker, the joker, especially when it can be used only as an ace; in horseracing, an apprentice rider.

bullet work
In horseracing, a horse's best time for the distance at a specific track on a given day.

bull ring
In horseracing, a short track, usually less than a mile.

bump
To raise, especially in poker.

burn card
A card that is taken off the top of the deck and temporarily removed from play after shuffling, before the cards are dealt.

busted
To lose one's bankroll; in blackjack, a hand over 21.

button
A plastic disk used to denote which player is acting as dealer for the hand; also see *dealer button*.

buy

In sports betting, an additional price a bettor pays to receive a) at least half a point in his favor on a point-spread game, b) fewer points with the favorite, or c) more points with the underdog.

buy-in

The amount required to enter a game.

c

call

In poker, matching the current bet; in bingo and keno, drawing numbers for the game.

caller

In poker, the player who has called a bet; in bingo, the person who announces the drawn numbers.

cap or capped

In pot-limit games, the point in the betting round at which players can no longer raise.

card counting

A technique for keeping track of dealt cards and adjusting your betting accordingly.

carousel

A ring or group of slot machines or VLTs.

cashier's cage

The area in the casino where players redeem chips, tickets, etc., for cash.

casino rate

Special hotel rate for preferred players.

catch

In keno, to match a number on your card with one that has been drawn.

chalk

In sports betting, the team favored to win.

chalk player

A bettor who always or usually bets on the favored team.

chase

To continue gambling in hopes of winning back losses; in poker, to play a hand that is unlikely to beat another player's.

check

Another term for *chip;* in poker, to stay in the game but not bet; in horseracing, when a jockey pulls up his horse.

check-raise

An option in poker where the player waives his or her right to bet until another player bets, then raises the other player's bet by an equal amount or more.

chip tray

A tray with compartments for each denomination of chip.

chips

Tokens of various denominations used in lieu of cash.

chute

In horseracing, an extension of the backstretch or homestretch.

circle game

In sports betting, a game in which betting is significantly curtailed because of concerns about injuries, weather, or other factors.

closer

In horseracing, a horse that gives its strongest performance in the later stages of the race.

clubhouse turn

In horseracing, the turn closest to the clubhouse.

coin size

The number of coins wagered, usually 1 to 5 on a typical slot machine/VLT.

coins per spin

The minimum and maximum number of coins you can wager per spin.

cold

A slot machine that isn't hitting, or a player on a losing streak.

color up

Exchanging small denomination chips for larger denomination chips.

colt

A male horse less than five years old.

column bet

In roulette, a bet on one of three columns of a dozen nonconsecutive numbers.

combination way ticket

In keno, an option that offers several ways to win.

community card(s)

Up-cards in the middle of the table that can be used by any player to complete a hand.

comps

Complimentary gifts or services; used by casinos to reward good players and high rollers.

condition race

In horseracing, a race limited to certain classes of horses, e.g., two-year-olds, etc.

copy

In Pai Gow poker, a tie hand between dealer and player.

corner bet

In roulette, a four-number bet.

cover

In sports betting, to win by more than the point spread.

credit button

In slot machines and VLTs, a button that allows the player to bank winnings in the form of credits until he or she is done playing.

croupier

French for "dealer," commonly used at baccarat and roulette tables.

cuppy

In horseracing, a track surface that breaks away under the horse's hoof.

cushion

In horseracing, the surface of the track; a layer of the track.

cut
Dividing a card deck into two stacks and reversing their order.

cut card
A plastic card used to cut a deck of cards.

D

daily double
In horseracing, a bet on the winners in two consecutive races on the same day.

dauber
An ink or crayon marker used to mark bingo numbers on a game card; also see *bingo marker*.

dead heat
In horseracing, a tie at the finish line between two or more horses.

dead track
In horseracing, a track surface that lacks bounce or resilience.

dealer button
A plastic disk used to identify the player acting as dealer; also see *button*.

designated dealer
The player who acts as dealer during a hand.

deuce
In card games, a 2.

dime bet
Slang for a $1,000 bet.

dime line
A money line in which the bookie's commission is 10 percent.

discard
To take cards from your hand in order to make room for replacements; any card thrown away; also see *muck*.

discard tray
Tray to the dealer's right where discarded or already played cards are stacked.

distaff
In horseracing, a term for female horses; a distaff race is for fillies and/or mares.

distanced
In horseracing, a long lead; horses that are distanced finish well behind the leader.

dog
An underdog; a team not favored to win.

dog player
A bettor who always or usually bets on the underdog.

dollar bet
Slang for a $100 bet; also see *buck*.

double-down
An option in blackjack that allows the player to double his or her bet but restricts the player to only one more card.

double-zero
The compartment marked 00 on a roulette wheel; the name for a roulette wheel containing the number 00.

dozens bet

In roulette, a bet on a set of twelve consecutive numbers.

draw

To take additional card(s); a form of poker in which draw cards replace dealt cards; in blackjack, additional cards dealt in an attempt to reach 21; in sports, a tie.

drop box

Repository for cash, chips, and markers at a gaming table.

drop down

In horseracing, a horse facing a lower class of competitors than in previous races.

E

early position

In poker, a seat where you have to take action before most of the other players at the table.

eased

In horseracing, an assessment that a jockey is deliberately slowing a horse down to prevent injury.

edge

Advantage.

eighth

In horseracing, one-eighth of a mile, or 220 yards; also see *furlong*.

even (bet)

In roulette, a bet that an even number will win.

even money

A bet that pays the same amount wagered and returns the original wager; 1:1 odds.

exacta

In horseracing, a wager in which the bettor must predict the first two finishers in the correct order; also called a "perfecta."

exotic bet

In sports betting, a wager other than a straight bet or parlay.

expectancy

A mathematical formula showing whether a player can expect to win or lose a particular game.

exposure

The amount of money a house risks losing, especially in sports betting.

extended

In horseracing, being forced to run at top speed.

F

face card
A king, queen, or jack.

false favorite

In horseracing, a horse heavily favored by bettors, even though other competitors appear to have better form.

family pot
In poker, a pot that everyone at the table decides to enter.

fast track
In horseracing, ideal track conditions; a dry, even track surface.

field
In horseracing, all horses in a given race; in sports, all individual competitors in an event.

field horse
In horseracing, two or more horses entered as a single betting unit because there isn't enough room on the board to list all entrants; also called a "mutual field."

fifth street
In seven-card stud, the third round of betting, so called because the players have five cards; in Texas Hold'em, the fifth card onboard.

figure
The amount of money owed by or to a bookie.

fill
Refilling an empty coin hopper on a slot machine.

filly
A female horse no more than four years old.

firing
Betting large amounts of money, especially in sports betting.

firm track
In horseracing, a turf track with ideal conditions; the equivalent of a fast dirt track.

first base
In blackjack, the first seat at the table, immediately to the dealer's left.

fishing
In poker, a player who should fold but is looking for a good card.

fixed limit
Any game where betting is capped or limited, especially in poker.

fixed odds
Odds that are unchangeable at the time the bet is made.

flashed card
A partially exposed card.

flat top
A fixed jackpot on a slot machine.

flatten out
In horseracing, when a horse drops its head to almost a straight line with its back, usually taken as an indication of exhaustion.

flea
A bettor who expects something for nothing, e.g., a comp for a nominal bet.

flop
In Texas Hold'em and other community card games, three face-up cards in the middle of the table.

flush
A poker hand consisting of five cards of one suit, not necessarily consecutive.

foal
A newly born male or female horse; the term applies until the foal is weaned.

fold
In poker, dropping out of the hand and surrendering money already wagered.

forced bet
A wager required to begin action in a game, especially certain versions of poker.

forced bring-in
In the first round of betting in seven-card stud, a mandatory bet made by the player with the lowest up-card.

form
The performance expected of a horse or sports team based on how it looks on paper.

foul
In Pai Gow poker, a losing hand in which the two- and five-card hands are set wrong.

four of a kind
A poker hand consisting of four cards of the same value.

fourth street
In seven-card stud, the second round of betting, so called because the players have four cards; in Texas Hold'em, the third round of betting.

fresh or freshened
In horseracing, a rested horse.

front money
Money deposited with a casino to establish credit.

front runner
In horseracing, a horse that leads or attempts to lead the field.

full house
A poker hand consisting of three of a kind and a pair.

furlong
One-eighth of a mile, or 220 yards; also see *eighth*.

future bet
Wagers made and accepted far in advance of a race or sporting event.

G

gait
The pace at which a horse moves, i.e., trot, canter, gallop, etc.

gate
In sporting events, the amount of admission fees collected; in horseracing, the starting mechanism.

gelding
A castrated male horse.

good bottom
In horseracing, a track that is wet or muddy on top but firm underneath.

good track
In horseracing, an average track condition, neither fast nor slow.

graduate
In horseracing, winning in one class and moving up to the next class.

green
Slang for currency; also the common color used for $25 chips.

green numbers
0 and 00 on a roulette wheel.

gross win
Total winnings before subtracting expenses and/or losses.

H

half
In horseracing, half a mile.

hand
An individual player's cards; a round of play in a card game; in horseracing, a unit of 4 inches used to measure a horse's height.

handicapper
A person who studies sports or horses and predicts the outcomes of games or races.

handle
In racing, the amount of money wagered in the pari-mutuel pool; may be used to describe individual events, a day's racing, or a year's action.

hard hand
In blackjack, a hand without an ace, or where the ace cannot be counted as 11 without going over 21.

head
In horseracing, a unit of distance between horses; one horse may lead another by the length of its head.

heads up
In poker, play involving only two players.

heavy
In horseracing, a track that is slower than a muddy track.

hedge bet, hedging
Wagering on both sides of a bet to minimize losses or guarantee a nominal win.

high bet
In roulette, a bet that a number higher than 18 will win.

high roller
A bettor who wagers large amounts of money.

hit
In blackjack, dealing another card to a player; on slot machines, a winning spin.

hit rate
Ratio of winning spins to nonwinning spins on slot machines or at roulette; also the ratio of winning hands to nonwinning hands in blackjack.

hold
Also called "house edge"; the amount of each bet the house keeps, usually between 3 percent and 15 percent depending on the game; also see *house advantage*.

holding your own
Breaking even, or winning small amounts.

hole card
Face-down card.

home-field advantage
A theoretical edge for a home team because of familiarity with the venue, support from fans, and the effects of travel on the other team.

hook
In sports betting, a half-point in the point spread.

hooked
Losing by half a point.

hoops
Slang for basketball.

hopper
A container inside slot machines that holds coins or tokens.

hot
A slot machine that is hitting, or a player on a winning streak.

hot game
In sports betting, a game that generates heavy action on one side.

hot tip
Inside information, usually considered something the oddsmakers are not aware of.

house advantage
Also called "house edge"; the amount of each bet the casino keeps instead of paying out in winnings; also see *hold*.

I

in the money
In horseracing, a horse that finishes first, second, or third.

inside bet
In roulette, a bet on any of the numbered pockets of the wheel.

inside straight
A poker hand consisting of four consecutively or almost consecutively numbered cards where the straight can be completed only one way.

insurance
In blackjack, a side bet allowed when a dealer has an ace showing; the player bets that the dealer's hole card is a 10 or a face card. Generally considered a "sucker bet."

J

jackpot
The highest prize on a slot machine or in bingo or keno.

joker
A playing card sometimes used in poker as a wild card.

juice
A bookmaker's commission; also see *vigorish*.

juvenile
In horseracing, a two-year-old horse.

K

keno
A game similar to lotto, in which players try to predict which numbers will be drawn.

keno board
An electronic display of numbers drawn in a keno game.

keno lounge
The main area of a casino where keno is played.

keno runner

A casino employee who takes keno tickets and bets from players in other areas of the casino to the keno lounge and delivers winnings.

kicker

In poker, a high card that doesn't contribute to a straight, flush, or full house.

L

late double

In horseracing, a second daily double offered later in the racing program.

late position

In poker, a seat where you can't take action until after most of the other players at the table.

laying the points

Betting on the favorite; also called "laying the price."

layoff bet

A bet between bookmakers to balance the action and reduce exposure.

layout

The table game surface, marked with information about the game and spaces for making bets.

length

In horseracing, the length of a horse, usually about 8 feet; used to describe the distance between horses in a race.

limit

The maximum wager allowed; in sports betting, the maximum bet accepted before odds or points change.

line

Listed odds for a game in sports betting.

line bet

In roulette, a bet on any six consecutive numbers; also see *six-number bet*.

load up

Playing the maximum number of coins or credits on one slot machine or VLT spin.

lock

A sure thing; a sure winner.

lock-up

A chip or marker that holds a player's seat.

longshot

An underdog with unusually large odds against it.

loose

A slot machine that is hitting frequently; in poker, playing more hands than usual.

low bet

In roulette, a bet that a number lower than 19 will win; does not include 0 or 00.

M

maiden

In horseracing, a horse or jockey who has not yet won a race.

mare

A female horse at least five years old; a female horse of any age that has been bred.

marker

A check written at a gaming table by a player who has established credit with the casino.

max bet

The highest bet allowed on a specific game.

mini-baccarat

A version of baccarat with fewer players but the same rules.

minus pool

In pari-mutuel betting, a pool created when so many bettors wager on a horse that there isn't enough money to pay all bets after taxes and commission are deducted.

misdeal

A mistake in dealing that forces a reshuffling of the cards and dealing of a new hand.

money line

Odds expressed in currency, usually the amount you have to bet to win $100 or the amount you win if you bet $100.

morning glory

In horseracing, a horse that performs well in morning workouts but doesn't live up to form in races.

morning line

In horseracing, preliminary odds quoted before betting action determines precise odds.

muck

Discarded cards; also see *discard*.

muddy track

In horseracing, a dirt track condition that extends beyond the surface.

mudder

In horseracing, a horse that runs well on muddy tracks.

N

natural

In blackjack, a hand that totals 21 in two cards; in baccarat, a hand that totals 8 or 9 in two cards.

neighbors

In roulette, the numbers on either side of the winning number.

net win

Total winnings after subtracting losses and expenses.

neutral site

In sports, a venue where neither team has a home-field advantage.

nickel

Slang for $500 bet.

no limit

A game in which bets and raises are not capped.

nose

In horseracing, the smallest margin a horse can win by.

number pool

Range of numbers from which players select, usually between 1 and 80 in keno.

O

odd (bet)
In roulette, a bet that an odd number will win.

odds
Probability ratio, usually expressed as "to," as in 35 to 1, 100 to 8, etc.

oddsmaker
The person who establishes the odds for a given event.

odds-on favorite
In horse and sports betting, a competitor so heavily favored by bettors that the odds are less than 1:1.

off the board
In sports betting, a game on which no wagers are accepted.

off track
In horseracing, a wet racing surface.

official line
The odds line bookmakers use to book bets.

on the board
In horseracing, finishing a race in the top four.

on the nose
In horseracing, betting on one horse to win only (not place or show).

one-armed bandit
A slang term for slot machine, referring to the handle on the side of the machine.

opener
In poker, the player who makes the first bet.

outside bet
In roulette, any bet outside the numbered boxes on the layout.

over and under
In sports betting, a wager that the total score will be higher or lower than the total predicted by the sportsbook.

overlay
A wager that favors the bettor rather than the house.

P

pair
In card games, any two cards of the same value.

parlay
Also called "press"; to leave winnings from the previous bet on top of the current bet; in sports betting, a wager on multiple teams in which all teams must win in order for the bettor to win.

pari-mutuel
A wagering pool in which all winning bets are combined, commission and taxes are deducted, and the remainder is split among the winning bettors.

pass
To not bet; fold.

past post
A bet placed after a race or other event has begun.

pat hand

In blackjack, a hand with a value of 17 to 21; in draw poker, a hand that does not need any other cards.

pay table

A chart listing all possible winning combinations on a slot machine and the payout rate for each combination.

pay line

A horizontal line on slot machines where the proper symbols must fall in order for the player to win.

payoff

A return on a wager; winnings.

payout percentage

The long-term average rate at which money is paid out to players as winnings.

photo finish

In horseracing, a finish so close that the winner must be determined by the camera at the finish line.

pick

In sports betting, a game where there is no favorite.

pit

The arrangement of table games where the center is restricted to certain casino employees.

pit boss

A casino employee in charge of supervising the games.

place

In horseracing, second place.

place bet

In horseracing, a wager that a horse will finish first or second.

play the board

In community card games, using all community cards to build your hand.

pocket

In horseracing, a horse that is racing with other horses in front and alongside it is said to be in the pocket.

point spread

The number of points given by the favorite to the underdog for wagering purposes.

pole

In horseracing, markers around the track that measure the distance from the finish line.

post

In horseracing, the starting point or position in the starting gate; also called "post position."

post time

A scheduled starting time for a race or sporting event.

pot

In poker, the accumulated wagers in a hand.

price

Odds; point spread.

probability
A mathematical calculation of the likelihood of any given outcome.

progressive jackpot
A portion of each bet on any of a series of linked slot machines that is added to the jackpot for the highest winning combination.

proposition bet
In poker, a side bet between players, not related to the outcome of the hand; in craps, a one-roll wager on a specific number or group of numbers; in sports betting, a side bet on a specific aspect of a game, such as how many field goals or touchdowns will be made.

protecting cards, protecting hand
Placing a chip or other item on top of your cards so they won't be mistaken for discards or a folded hand.

puppy
An underdog; a team not favored to win; also see *dog*.

purse
Prize money, especially in horseracing and boxing.

push
A tie. In blackjack and three-card poker, a tie between the dealer and the player; the player doesn't win any money but keeps his or her bet; also see *standoff*. In sports betting, when neither team wins, wagers are returned to bettors.

Q

quads
Four of a kind.

qualifier
In poker, the lowest hand eligible to win part of the pot.

quinella
In horseracing, a wager in which the bettor picks the top two finishers in either order.

R

rabbit
In horseracing, a horse that is entered to ensure a fast pace but is not expected to win.

rack
A tray for organizing, transporting, and counting chips, tokens, coins, etc.

rags
Cards not worth playing, or cards that do not improve anyone's hand.

rail runner
In horseracing, a horse that prefers to run next to the rail on the inside of the track.

raise
In poker, to increase the current bet.

rake
In poker rooms, the fee the casino charges for each hand, usually taken from the pot.

random number generator (RNG)
A computer program that generates random whole numbers, which in turn correspond to various reel positions on slot machines.

rank
The value of a hand of cards.

red
In roulette, a bet that a red number will win; the common color for $5 chips.

reels
The spinning wheels on a slot machine that display various symbols and produce winnings in the proper combination.

reraise
To increase another player's raise.

RFB
Acronym for room, food, and beverage, the most common comps offered to players.

river
The final card dealt in stud or Texas Hold'em.

round robin
In sports betting, a form of parlay betting in which various team combinations are used to make the wager.

route
In horseracing, a race distance of a mile or more.

router
In horseracing, a horse that performs well in distance races.

royal flush
The highest poker hand, consisting of an ace-high straight flush.

run
A series of the same result, such as five consecutive even numbers in roulette or three consecutive "heads" in a coin toss.

run-down
In sports betting, an updated line.

runner
A person who places bets on behalf of another person; also see *beard*.

S

scoop
To win both the high and low halves in a split-pot game.

scratch
To withdraw or cancel a bet; in horseracing, a horse taken out of the race before post time.

session
A period of play at any casino game.

set
In Pai Gow poker, separating seven cards into hands of two cards and five cards.

seventh street
In seven-card stud, the final round of betting, so called because the players have seven cards.

shoe
The box out of which the dealer takes cards.

short stack
A player who has fewer than the average number of chips on the table.

show
In horseracing, to finish in third place.

show bet
In horseracing, to bet on a horse to finish in first, second, or third place.

showdown
In poker, revealing cards after the last round of betting to determine the winner.

side pot
In poker, a new pot formed "on the side" when one or more players are all in for the original pot.

single bet
In roulette, a bet on one specific number; also see *straight bet*.

singleton
In poker, a card that is not part of a pair.

six-number bet
In roulette, a bet on any six consecutive numbers; also see *line bet*.

sixth street
In seven-card stud, the fourth round of betting, so called because the players have six cards.

slots
Machines that accept coins, tickets, or personal account cards and offer a variety of games; in roulette, the compartments on the wheel.

small blind
A forced bet, usually half the amount of the big blind, in some versions of poker.

smart money
Bets placed by knowledgeable handicappers.

soft hand
In blackjack, a hand with an ace, so called because the ace can be counted as 1 or as 11.

sophomore
In horseracing, a three-year-old horse.

split bet
In roulette, a bet on any two adjacent numbers on the layout.

split pairs
In blackjack, a player who has been dealt two cards of the same denomination has the option of splitting the pair and playing each as an individual hand; this requires an additional bet.

split pot
In high-low poker games, players with the highest and lowest hands split the pot; also used when two or more players tie for high hand.

spot
The number or numbers selected on a keno ticket.

square
A novice or unsophisticated bettor.

stack
The chips in front of a player.

stake
In horseracing, a race in which owners must pay a fee to run their horses.

stakes horse
In horseracing, a horse capable of being competitive in stakes races.

stand
Playing a hand as it is; declining additional cards (in blackjack) or replacement cards (in poker).

standoff
In blackjack, a tie between the dealer and the player; the player doesn't win any money but keeps his or her bet; also see *push*.

steal
In poker, winning by bluffing.

stiff
In blackjack, a hand that will go over 21 with one additional card; also see *breaking hand*.

(The) Store
Bookmaker.

straight
A poker hand consisting of five consecutively numbered cards.

straight bet
In roulette, a bet on one specific number; also see *single bet*. In sports betting, a bet on a single team for the point spread offered.

straight flush
A poker hand consisting of five consecutively numbered cards of the same suit.

straight keno
A basic keno game.

street bet
In roulette, a bet on any three consecutive numbers.

stretch
In horseracing, the final straight portion of the track before the finish line; also called the "homestretch."

stretch runner
In horseracing, a horse that finishes races fast.

string raise
A bet in which the player goes back to his stack more than once without announcing his intent to raise (prohibited in most card rooms).

stud
A variation of poker; in horseracing, a male horse used for breeding.

sucker bet
A wager with poor odds for the player.

surrender
In blackjack, the player gives up half of his or her bet when the dealer shows an ace; in roulette, the player gives up half of his or her wager on an even-money bet when the ball lands on 0 or 00.

symbols
Graphics, pictures, numbers, or other images used on reels in slot machines; also can refer to images on VLTs.

T

table stakes
The amount of money a player has on the table; a game in which players cannot purchase more chips in the middle of a hand.

tapped out
Broke, busted.

Texas Hold'em
A variation of poker.

third base
In blackjack, the last seat at the table, immediately to the dealer's right.

third street
In seven-card stud, the first round of betting, so called because the players have three cards.

three of a kind
Three cards of the same value.

tight
In slots, a machine that isn't hitting; in poker, playing fewer hands than usual.

toke
Tip or gratuity for dealers.

top prize
The maximum payout on a nonprogressive machine.

top-line bet
In roulette, a bet on the first five numbers 0, 00, 1, 2, and 3.

toss-up
A bet where the odds are too close to call.

totalizator
In horseracing, a machine that tracks wagers, shows odds, and displays payoffs.

touts, tout service
A person or business that sells opinions on sports betting or horseraces; handicapper.

track bias
In horseracing, a track condition that favors a specific running style or post position.

trey
In card games, a three.

trifecta
In horseracing, a wager choosing the first three finishers in order.

Triple Crown
In horseracing, the Kentucky Derby, Preakness Stakes, and Belmont Stakes races.

triple sharp
Unusually smart or savvy.

trips
In poker, three of a kind.

true odds
A mathematical probability, not counting the house edge.

turf course
In horseracing, a grass track.

turn
In poker, the fourth community card dealt.

twenty-one (21)
Another name for blackjack.

two pair
Poker hand consisting of two sets of pairs and a singleton.

U

underlay
Betting odds that favor the house.

under wraps
In horseracing, a horse under strict restraint during a workout or race.

up-card
Face-up card.

V

vigorish
Also called "vig"; the house's hold or take; also see *juice*.

VLT
Acronym for video lottery terminal; often used to refer to any electronic video gaming machine.

W

walkover
In horseracing, a race in which all but one horse is scratched before starting; the remaining horse gallops the required distance to be declared the winner formally.

way ticket
In keno, an option that offers more than one way to win.

wheel checks
The special colored, unmarked chips that are used to differentiate among different players' bets at roulette.

white
The common color for $1 chips.

wild card
A card, often a joker or a deuce, that can substitute for any other card to complete a hand.

winner-take-all
A structure in which only one prize is awarded.

winning hand
In video poker, the button that allows the player to draw new cards.

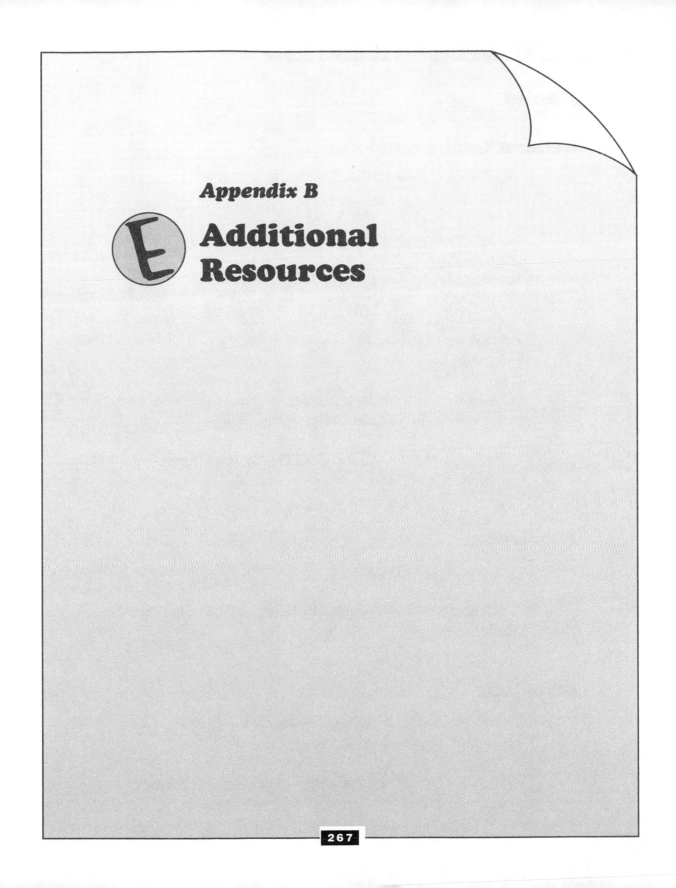

Appendix B

E Additional Resources

Books

General Casino Gambling

American Casino Guide, 2004, by Steve Bourie, et al. Casino Vacations, 2003.

The Casino Answer Book: How to Overcome the House Advantage When You Play Blackjack, Video Poker and Roulette, by John Grochowski. Chicago: Bonus Books, 1998.

Casino Gambling: A Winner's Guide to Blackjack, Craps, Roulette, Baccarat, and Casino Poker, by Jerry Patterson et al. New York: Perigee Books, 2000.

Guerrilla Gambling: How to Beat the Casinos at Their Own Games, by Frank Scoblete. Chicago: Bonus Books, 1993.

Unofficial Guide to Casino Gambling, by Basil Nestor. New York: John Wiley & Sons, 1998.

Baccarat

Baccarat Battle Book, by Frank Scoblete. Chicago: Bonus Books, 1999.

Winning Baccarat Strategies, by Henry J. Tamburin. Greensboro, NC: Research Services Unlimited, 1983.

Blackjack

Beat the Dealer: A Winning Strategy for the Game of Twenty-One, by Edward O. Thorp. New York: Vintage Press, 1966.

Beginner to Pro, by Stephen Mead. Las Vegas, NV: Mead Publishing Company Inc., 2002.

Blackjack Bluebook II: The Simplest Winning Strategies Ever Published, by Fred Renzey. Elk Grove Village, IL: Blackjack Mentor, 2003.

Blackjack for Blood: The Card-Counters' Bible, and Complete Winning Guide, by Bryce Carlson. Las Vegas, NV: Pi Yee Press, 2000.

Blackjack's Hidden Secrets: Win Without Counting, by George Pappadopoulos. Somers Point, NJ: ME-n-U Marketers, LLC, 1999.

Gregorian Strategy for Multiple Deck Blackjack, by Gregory Mannarino. New York: Lyle Stuart Hardcover/Kensington Publishing Corp., 2003.

Knock-Out Blackjack: The Easiest Card-Counting System Ever Devised, by Olaf Vancura and Ken Fuchs. Las Vegas, NV: Huntington Press, 1998.

Million Dollar Blackjack, by Ken Uston. Los Angeles: Gambling Times, 1992.

Playing Blackjack as a Business, by Lawrence Revere. New York: Lyle Stuart Hardcover/Kensington Publishing Corp., 1977.

Professional Blackjack, by Stanford Wong. Las Vegas, NV: Pi Yee Press, 1994.

Theory of Blackjack, 6th edition, by Peter A. Griffin. Las Vegas, NV: Huntington Press, 1999.

Gambling Times Guide to Blackjack, by Stanley Roberts. Los Angeles: Gambling Times, 1984.

Winning Casino Blackjack for the Non-Counter, by Avery Cardoza. New York: Cardoza Publishing, 1992.

Craps

Craps Strategy: How to Play to Win at Casino Craps, by Michael Benson. Guilford, CT: The Lyons Press, 2001.

Craps: Take the Money and Run, by Henry J. Tamburin. Greensboro, NC: Research Services Unlimited, 1995.

Forever Craps! by Frank Scoblete. Chicago: Bonus Books, 2000.

Get the Edge at Craps: How to Control the Dice, by Frank Scoblete. Chicago: Bonus Books, 2002.

John Patrick's Advanced Craps: The Sophisticated Player's Guide to Winning, by John Patrick. New York: Lyle Stuart Hardcover/Kensington Publishing Corp., 1995.

Winning Casino Craps, by Edwin Silberstang. New York: Random House Puzzles & Games, 1980.

Horseracing

Ainslie's Complete Guide to Thoroughbred Racing, by Tom Ainslie. New York: Fireside, 1988.

Ainslie's New Complete Guide to Harness Racing, by Tom Ainslie. New York: Simon & Schuster, 1986.

The Best of Thoroughbred Handicapping: Leading Ideas & Methods, by James Quinn. New York: Daily Racing Form, 2004.

Betting Thoroughbreds: A Professional's Guide for the Horseplayer, by Steve Davidowitz and Andrew Beyer. New York: Plume/New American Library, 1997.

Gambling Times Guide to Harness Racing, by Igor Kusyshyn, Al Stanley, and Sam Dragich. Las Vegas, NV: Gambling Times, Las Vegas, 1984.

Harness Overlays: Beat the Favorite, by Bill Heller. Chicago: Bonus Books, 1993.

How to Win at the Races: Education of a Horseplayer, by Sam Lewin. North Hollywood: Wilshire Book Co., 1979.

Off the Charts: Turning Result Charts into Profitable Selections at the Track, by Nick Borg. New York: Daily Racing Form, 2003.

Picking Winners: A Horseplayer's Guide, by Andrew Beyer. New York: Mariner Books, 1994.

Speed to Spare: Beyer Speed Figures Uncovered, by Joe Cardello and Andrew Beyer. New York: Daily Racing Form, 2003.

Success at the Harness Races, by Barry Meadow. North Hollywood: Wilshire Book Co., 1979.

Internet Gambling

BeatWebCasinos.com: A Shrewd Player's Guide to Internet Gambling, by Bill Haywood. Las Vegas, NV: RGE Publishing, 2000.

Insider's Guide to Internet Gambling: Your Sourcebook for Safe and Profitable Gambling, by John G. Brokopp. Chicago: Bonus Books, 2001.

John Patrick's Internet Gambling: The Complete Guide to Playing and Winning, by John Patrick. New York: Citadel Trade/Kensington Publishing Corp., 2002.

Poker

Hold'em Poker for Advanced Players, by David Sklansky and Mason Malmuth. Pittsburgh: Two Plus Two Publishing, 1999.

Internet Texas Hold'em: Winning Strategies from an Internet Pro, by Matthew Hilger. Matthew Hilger, 2003.

Play Poker Like the Pros, by Phil Hellmuth Jr. New York: HarperResource, 2003.

Poker on the Internet, by Andrew Kinsman. West Sussex, UK: D&B Publishing, 2003.

The Theory of Poker, by David Sklansky. Pittsburgh: Two Plus Two Publishing, 1999.

Winning Low Limit Hold'em, by Lee Jones. Pittsburgh: ConJelCo, 2000.

Roulette

Gamble to Win: Roulette, by R. D. Ellison. New York: Kensington Publishing Corp., 2002.

Get the Edge at Roulette: How to Predict Where the Ball Will Land! by Christopher Pawlicki. Chicago: Bonus Books, 2001.

Roulette Secrets Revealed, by John C. Steele. Aikon Informations, 2001.

Spin Roulette Gold: Secrets of Beating the Wheel, by Frank Scoblete. Chicago: Bonus Books, 1997.

Slots

All Slots Made Easier #2 (More Winning Strategies & More Bonus Video Slots), by Gayle Mitchell. Las Vegas, NV: Casino Players Workshop & Seminars, 2000.

Powerful Profits from Slots, by Victor H. Royer. New York: Lyle Stuart Hardcover/Kensington Publishing Corp., 2003.

Secrets of Modern Slot Playing, by Larry Mak. Naples, FL: L&M Publications, 2003.

Slot Machine Strategy: Winning Methods for Hitting the Jackpot, by MacIntyre Symms. Guilford, CT: The Lyons Press, 2001.

Slot Smarts: Winning Strategies at the Slot Machines, by Claude Halcombe. New York: Lyle Stuart Hardcover/Kensington Publishing Corp., 1996.

Sports Betting

The Basics of Winning Sports Betting, by Avery Cardoza. New York: Cardoza Publishing, 2002.

Book on Bookies: An Inside Look at a Successful Sports Gambling Operation, by James Jeffries and Charles Oliver. Boulder, CO: Paladin Press, 2000.

How Professional Gamblers Beat the Pro Football Pointspread, by J. R. Miller. Readyville, TN: Flying M Group, 1997.

Insights into Sports Betting, 2nd edition, by Bob McCune. Readyville, TN: Flying M Group, 1999.

Sharp Sports Betting, by Stanford Wong. Las Vegas, NV: Pi Yee Press, 2001.

Magazines

Blackjack Confidential

www.blackjacktime.com

Magazine aimed at tournament blackjack players, with news, strategies and tips, and updated tournament listings.

Card Player

www.cardplayer.com

Biweekly magazine covering poker, blackjack, Pai Gow poker, and other card games; includes news, features, strategies, and book and software reviews.

Casino Player

www.casinoplayer.com

Monthly consumer magazine with news, strategies and tips, and dining, entertainment, and tournament listings.

Casino World

www.casinoworld.co.uk

Ten-month magazine covering casino gaming around the world.

Gambling Magazine

www.gamblingmagazine.com

Offers a wealth of information about all forms of gambling, including news, gaming guides, reviews, rules, and tips.

Gambling Times

www.gamblingtimes.com

Covers casino gambling, Internet gambling, horse and sports betting, and travel to gambling destinations.

GamingToday

✍ *www.gamingtoday.com*

Weekly magazine covering all aspects of casino gambling, horseracing, and sportsbook.

Indian Gaming Magazine

✍ *www.igmagazine.com*

Covers all aspects of American Indian gaming.

Las Vegas Insider

✍ *www.lasvegasinsider.com*

Monthly magazine aimed at the Vegas visitor, covering gambling, entertainment, and travel; also features specials and coupons for Vegas casinos.

Official Sportsbook Guide

✍ *www.sportsbook-guide.com*

Offers betting tips and strategies, reviews of online sportsbooks and how to choose a sportsbook, and an FAQ section for the novice sports bettor.

PokerPages

✍ *www.pokerpages.com*

Extensive Web site devoted to news and information about poker; includes downloadable software, tournament information, and tips and strategies.

Poker Player

✍ *www.gamblingtimes.com/poker_player*

Biweekly poker newspaper with news, expert columnists, tournament listings, and a wide variety of worldwide poker information.

Strictly Slots

✍ *www.strictlyslots.com*

Monthly magazine focusing on slots and video poker, with news, features, and reviews.

Software Titles

Baccarat Buster, Mesa Verde Software

Blackjack Master Course for Windows, Ne Plus Ultra

Blackjack Trainer, Conjelco

Casino Vérité Blackjack, QFIT

Masque Blackjack, Masque Publishing

Statistical Blackjack Analyzer, Conjelco

Craps Sim II Interactive, Conjelco

Craps Sim Pro Professional Version Simulator, Conjelco

Video Slots, Masque Publishing

Slot Software, Masque Publishing

Slot Software II, Masque Publishing

Harness Racing Handicapper, Educated Guess

Harness Horse Handicapping, PDS Sports

Gambling-Related Web Sites

6 Best Online Casinos

www.6-best-online-casinos.com

Provides rules and tips for online gambling games; rates and reviews online casinos based on payout rates, quality and quantity of games, customer service, and policies. Also includes tips on choosing an online casino and a gambling dictionary.

Betting to Win

www.bettingtowin.co.uk

Provides newsletter, hints, and tips about online gambling, as well as strategies and rules for online games; reviews and recommends online casinos for payout rates and promptness, bonuses, and customer service. Also notes which casino sites offer downloadable software, free play, and other options.

The Crapshooter

www.thecrapshooter.com

News, strategies, and tips for playing craps in casinos and online.

Daily Racing Form

www.drf.com

Horseracing entries, race results, charts, and past performances for all North American tracks; live odds for all racetracks; free handicapping software.

Free Casino Games

www.your-free-casino-games.com

Free downloads and demo versions of popular casino games.

Gamblers Bookstore

www.gamblersbook.com

Online bookstore devoted to gambling books, software, videos, and DVDs.

Gambling Smart

www.gamblingsmart.com

News and information site, with tips, strategies, and links to free and pay gambling sites.

Gaming Day

www.gamingday.com

Rules, strategies, and general information about casino games, as well as links to several online gambling sites.

Greedyhog Gambling

www.greedyhog-gambling.com

Offers news about online gambling, tips and rules for playing, and keeps track of payouts and bonuses for online casinos.

Il Dado

www.ildado.com

General gambling information site, with directories of land-based casinos, bingo halls, horse and dog racetracks, as well as rules and strategies for most casino games.

Ion Thunder

www.ionthunder.com

Free games with chat capabilities. Games include bingo, lottery, poker, slots, solitaire, and puzzles.

Online Casino News

www.onlinecasinonews.com

Daily news updates on the casino industry, including land-based and online gambling sites. Reviews, tips, and strategies for playing.

Winner Online

www.winneronline.com

Free e-newsletter, rules and tips for casino games, reviews of online casinos and software.

Wizard of Odds

www.wizardofodds.com

Provides mathematical evaluations of casino games, reviews of casino software, rules, advice, and strategies for games.

Regulatory Agencies and Trade Organizations

American Gaming Association

Washington, D.C.

www.americangaming.org

American Horse Council

Washington, D.C.

www.horsecouncil.org

Association of Racing Commissioners International, Inc.

Lexington, KY

www.arci.com

e-Commerce and Online Gaming Regulation Assurance

London, UK

www.ecogra.org

Harness Tracks of America, Inc.

Tucson, AZ

www.harnesstracks.com

Interactive Gaming Council

Vancouver, British Columbia

http://igcouncil.org

International Association of Gaming Regulators

Reno, NV

✍ *www.iagr.org*

International Internet & Wireless Gaming Association

Larchmont, NY

✍ *www.mmsionline.com/iiwga*

Internet Gaming Commission

✍ *www.internetcommission.com*

The Jockey Club

New York, NY

✍ *www.jockeyclub.com*

National Indian Gaming Association

Washington, D.C.

✍ *www.indiangaming.org*

National Indian Gaming Commission

Washington, D.C.

✍ *www.nigc.gov*

National Thoroughbred Racing Association, Inc.

Lexington, KY

✍ *www.ntra.com*

Nevada State Gaming Control Board

Carson City, NV

✍ *http://gaming.state.nv.us*

New Jersey Casino Control Commission

Atlantic City, NJ

✍ *www.state.nj.us/casinos*

North American Association of State and Provincial Lotteries

Cleveland, OH

✎ *www.naspl.org*

North American Gaming Regulators Association

Lincoln, NE

✎ *www.nagra.org*

North American Pari-Mutuel Regulators Association

Meridian, ID

✎ *www.napraonline.com*

Securities and Exchange Commission

Washington, D.C.

✎ *www.sec.gov*

United States Trotting Association

Columbus, OH

✎ *www.ustrotting.com*

Problem-Gambling Organizations

Gamblers Anonymous

Los Angeles, CA

✎ *www.gamblersanonymous.org*

National Center for Responsible Gambling

Kansas City, MO

✎ *www.ncrg.org*

National Council on Problem Gambling, Inc.

Columbia, MD

✎ *www.ncpgambling.org*

National Council on Problem Gambling, State Affiliates

Arizona Council on Compulsive Gambling, Inc.

Phoenix, AZ

✍ www.azccg.org

✆ (800) 777-7207

California Council on Problem Gambling, Inc.

Palm Springs, CA

✍ www.calproblemgambling.org

✆ (800) 522-4700 (in-state only)

Colorado Council on Compulsive Gambling

Lakewood, CO

✆ (800) 522-4700

Connecticut Council on Problem Gambling

Guilford, CT

✍ www.ccpg.org

✆ (888) 789-7777

Delaware Council on Gambling Problems, Inc.

Wilmington, DE

✆ (888) 850-8888 (in-state only)

Florida Council on Compulsive Gambling, Inc.

Longwood, FL

✆ (800) 426-7711

Georgia Council on Compulsive Gambling

Atlanta, GA

✆ (770) 242-8781

Iowa Problem Gambling Council, Inc.

Des Moines, IA

✆ (800) 238-7633 (in-state only)

Illinois Council on Problem and Compulsive Gambling, Inc.

Evanston, IL

✆ (800) 522-4700

Indiana Council on Problem Gambling

Ft. Wayne, IN

✆ (800) 994-8448 (in-state only)

Kentucky Council on Compulsive Gambling

Crestwood, KY

✆ (800) 426-2537 (in-state only)

Louisiana Association on Compulsive Gambling

Shreveport, LA

✆ (800) 749-2673 (in-state only)

Massachusetts Council on Compulsive Gambling, Inc.

Boston, MA

✆ (800) 426-1234

Maryland Council on Compulsive Gambling, Inc.

Baltimore, MD

✆ (800) 522-4700

Michigan Council on Problem Gambling

Detroit, MI

✆ (800) 270-7117 (in-state only)

Minnesota Affiliate: North American Training Institute

Duluth, MN

✐ *www.nati.org*

✆ (218) 722-1503

Missouri Council on Problem Gambling Concerns, Inc.

Kansas City, MO
☎ (800) BETS OFF (238-7633)

Mississippi Council on Problem and Compulsive Gambling

Jackson, MS
✎ www.msgambler.org
☎ (888) 777-9696

Council on Compulsive and Problem Gambling of North Dakota, Inc.

Bismarck, ND
☎ (800) 472-2911 (in-state only)

Nebraska Council on Compulsive Gambling

Bellevue, NE
☎ (800) 560-2126 (in-state only)

Council on Compulsive Gambling of New Jersey

Trenton, NJ
✎ www.800gambler.org
☎ (800) 426-2537

New Hampshire Council on Problem Gambling, Inc.

West Chesterfield, NH
☎ (603) 256-6262

Nevada Council on Problem Gambling, Inc.

Las Vegas, NV
☎ (800) 522-4700

New York Council on Problem Gambling, Inc.

Albany, NY
☎ (800) 427-1611 (in-state only)

Ohio Council on Problem Gambling

Brecksville, OH
📞 (888) 869-9600 (in-state only)

Oregon Problem Gambling Program

Salem, OR
📞 (800) 233-8479 (in-state only)

Council on Problem Gambling of Pennsylvania

Audubon, PA
📞 (800) 848-1880 (in-state only)

Rhode Island Council on Problem Gambling, Inc.

Providence, RI
📞 (877) 9-GAMBLE (942-6253) (in-state only)

South Carolina Council on Problem Gambling, Inc.

Columbia, SC
📞 (803) 748-1313

South Dakota Council on Problem Gambling, Inc.

Sioux Falls, SD
📞 (888) 781-4357

Texas Council on Problem and Compulsive Gambling, Inc.

Richardson, TX
📞 (800) 742-0443

Washington State Council on Problem Gambling, Inc.

Seattle, WA
www.wscpg.org
📞 (800) 547-6133 (in-state only)

Wisconsin Council on Problem Gambling

Green Bay, WI
📞 (800) 426-2535 (in-state only)

Appendix C

E Types of Gaming Establishments

American Indian casinos—ranging from high-stakes bingo and pull-tabs to full-service casinos, usually modeled after resorts in Las Vegas or Atlantic City; unlike commercial casinos, profits benefit the tribe and its members.

Bingo halls—sometimes attached to full-fledged casinos, sometimes stand-alone establishments that offer a variety of bingo games with jack-pots typically in the thousands of dollars. Many churches and fire departments run low-stakes bingo nights as fundraisers. High-stakes bingo halls are run by American Indian tribes.

Commercial casinos—operated by private or public companies, usually offering a full range of traditional casino games and other amenities like lodging, dining, and live entertainment. Land-based commercial casinos can be found in Nevada and New Jersey; in other states, gambling companies like Harrah's and Park Place Entertainment have partnered with American Indian tribes to run land-based casinos.

Cruise ships—commercial casinos that leave port for a few hours or a few days, offering the same games and services found at land-based casinos.

Electronic gambling outlets—often bars or restaurants licensed by the state that offer versions of keno, video poker, or other games. These games are usually linked to the state lottery system.

Internet casinos—any of hundreds of sites offering everything from bingo to poker; almost always licensed overseas because of a ban in the United States.

Lottery agents—retail establishments, most commonly convenience stores and supermarkets, that sell a variety of state-sponsored lottery products, including scratch-off tickets and tickets for numbers drawings.

Off-track betting (OTB) parlors—not attached to a racetrack, but accepts wagers on simulcast races from a variety of tracks.

Pari-mutuel establishments—typically horse and dog racetracks and jai alai frontons.

Racinos—gambling halls, usually limited to traditional slot machines or video lottery terminals, attached to horse or dog racetracks; part of the proceeds usually goes toward race purses and part goes to the state government.

Riverboat casinos—sometimes permanently docked and sometimes offering cruises, usually offering all traditional casino games.

Gaming Establishments by State

Alabama
American Indian casinos and high-stakes bingo; dog racing.

Alaska
American Indian bingo/pull-tabs.

Arizona
American Indian casinos and high-stakes bingo; greyhound racing; horseracing.

Arkansas
dog racing; horseracing.

California
American Indian casinos; card rooms; gambling cruise ships; horseracing.

Colorado

American Indian and commercial casinos; dog racing; horseracing.

Connecticut

American Indian casinos; dog racing.

Delaware

horseracing/racinos.

Florida

American Indian casinos and high-stakes bingo; gambling cruise ships; dog racing; jai alai; horseracing.

Georgia

gambling cruise ships.

Idaho

American Indian casinos and high-stakes bingo; horseracing/racinos.

Illinois

riverboat casinos; horseracing.

Indiana

riverboat casinos; horseracing.

Iowa

American Indian casinos and high-stakes bingo; riverboat casinos; dog racing; horseracing/racinos.

Kansas

American Indian casinos; dog racing; horseracing.

Kentucky

horseracing.

Louisiana

riverboat casinos; horseracing/racinos.

Maine

gambling cruise ships; horseracing.

Maryland

horseracing.

Massachusetts

gambling cruise ships; dog racing; horseracing.

Michigan

American Indian casinos and high-stakes bingo; horseracing.

Minnesota

American Indian casinos and high-stakes bingo; horseracing/racinos.

Mississippi

American Indian casinos and high-stakes bingo; riverboat casinos.

Missouri

riverboat casinos.

Montana

American Indian casinos and high-stakes bingo; horseracing.

Nebraska

American Indian casinos and high-stakes bingo; horseracing.

Nevada

commercial casinos; horseracing.

New Hampshire

dog racing; horseracing.

New Jersey

commercial casinos; horseracing.

New Mexico

American Indian casinos and high-stakes bingo; horseracing/racinos.

New York

American Indian casinos and high-stakes bingo; gambling cruise ships; horseracing/racinos.

North Carolina

American Indian casinos and high-stakes bingo.

North Dakota

American Indian casinos and high-stakes bingo; horseracing.

Ohio

horseracing.

Oklahoma

American Indian casinos and high-stakes bingo; horseracing/racinos.

Oregon

American Indian casinos and high-stakes bingo; dog racing; horseracing.

Pennsylvania

horseracing.

Rhode Island

jai alai; dog racing.

South Carolina

American Indian casinos; gambling cruise ships.

South Dakota

American Indian casinos and high-stakes bingo; horseracing.

Texas

American Indian casinos; gambling cruise ships; dog racing; horseracing/racinos.

Virginia

horseracing.

Washington

American Indian casinos, card rooms and high-stakes bingo; gambling cruise ships; horseracing.

West Virginia

dog racing; horseracing/racinos.

Wisconsin

American Indian casinos and high-stakes bingo; dog racing.

Wyoming

American Indian high-stakes bingo; horseracing/racinos.

Index

THE EVERYTHING SERIES!

BUSINESS & PERSONAL FINANCE

Everything® Budgeting Book
Everything® Business Planning Book
Everything® Coaching and Mentoring Book
Everything® Fundraising Book
Everything® Get Out of Debt Book
Everything® Grant Writing Book
Everything® Home-Based Business Book
Everything® Homebuying Book, 2nd Ed.
Everything® Homeselling Book, 2nd Ed.
Everything® Investing Book, 2nd Ed.
Everything® Landlording Book
Everything® Leadership Book
Everything® Managing People Book
Everything® Negotiating Book
Everything® Online Business Book
Everything® Personal Finance Book
Everything® Personal Finance in Your 20s
    and 30s Book
Everything® Project Management Book
Everything® Real Estate Investing Book
Everything® Robert's Rules Book, $7.95
Everything® Selling Book
Everything® Start Your Own Business Book
Everything® Wills & Estate Planning Book

COOKING

Everything® Barbecue Cookbook
Everything® Bartender's Book, $9.95
Everything® Chinese Cookbook
Everything® Cocktail Parties and Drinks
    Book
Everything® College Cookbook
Everything® Cookbook
Everything® Cooking for Two Cookbook
Everything® Diabetes Cookbook
Everything® Easy Gourmet Cookbook
Everything® Fondue Cookbook
Everything® Gluten-Free Cookbook

Everything® Grilling Cookbook
Everything® Healthy Meals in Minutes
    Cookbook
Everything® Holiday Cookbook
Everything® Indian Cookbook
Everything® Italian Cookbook
Everything® Low-Carb Cookbook
Everything® Low-Fat High-Flavor Cookbook
Everything® Low-Salt Cookbook
Everything® Meals for a Month Cookbook
Everything® Mediterranean Cookbook
Everything® Mexican Cookbook
Everything® One-Pot Cookbook
Everything® Pasta Cookbook
Everything® Quick Meals Cookbook
Everything® Slow Cooker Cookbook
Everything® Slow Cooking for a Crowd
    Cookbook
Everything® Soup Cookbook
Everything® Thai Cookbook
Everything® Vegetarian Cookbook
Everything® Wine Book, 2nd Ed.

CRAFT SERIES

Everything® Crafts—Baby Scrapbooking
Everything® Crafts—Bead Your Own Jewelry
Everything® Crafts—Create Your Own
    Greeting Cards
Everything® Crafts—Easy Projects
Everything® Crafts—Polymer Clay for
    Beginners
Everything® Crafts—Rubber Stamping
    Made Easy
Everything® Crafts—Wedding Decorations
    and Keepsakes

HEALTH

Everything® Alzheimer's Book
Everything® Diabetes Book
Everything® Health Guide to Controlling
    Anxiety

Everything® Hypnosis Book
Everything® Low Cholesterol Book
Everything® Massage Book
Everything® Menopause Book
Everything® Nutrition Book
Everything® Reflexology Book
Everything® Stress Management Book

HISTORY

Everything® American Government Book
Everything® American History Book
Everything® Civil War Book
Everything® Irish History & Heritage Book
Everything® Middle East Book

HOBBIES & GAMES

Everything® Blackjack Strategy Book
Everything® Brain Strain Book, $9.95
Everything® Bridge Book
Everything® Candlemaking Book
Everything® Card Games Book
Everything® Card Tricks Book, $9.95
Everything® Cartooning Book
Everything® Casino Gambling Book, 2nd Ed.
Everything® Chess Basics Book
Everything® Craps Strategy Book
Everything® Crossword and Puzzle Book
Everything® Crossword Challenge Book
Everything® Cryptograms Book, $9.95
Everything® Digital Photography Book
Everything® Drawing Book
Everything® Easy Crosswords Book
Everything® Family Tree Book, 2nd Ed.
Everything® Games Book, 2nd Ed.
Everything® Knitting Book
Everything® Knots Book
Everything® Photography Book
Everything® Poker Strategy Book
Everything® Pool & Billiards Book
Everything® Quilting Book
Everything® Scrapbooking Book

All Everything® books are priced at $12.95 or $14.95, unless otherwise stated. Prices subject to change without notice.

Everything® Sewing Book
Everything® Test Your IQ Book, $9.95
Everything® Travel Crosswords Book, $9.95
Everything® Woodworking Book
Everything® Word Games Challenge Book
Everything® Word Search Book

HOME IMPROVEMENT

Everything® Feng Shui Book
Everything® Feng Shui Decluttering Book,
    $9.95
Everything® Fix-It Book
Everything® Homebuilding Book
Everything® Lawn Care Book
Everything® Organize Your Home Book

EVERYTHING® *KIDS'* BOOKS

All titles are $6.95
Everything® Kids' Animal Puzzle & Activity
    Book
Everything® Kids' Baseball Book, 3rd Ed.
Everything® Kids' Bible Trivia Book
Everything® Kids' Bugs Book
Everything® Kids' Christmas Puzzle
    & Activity Book
Everything® Kids' Cookbook
Everything® Kids' Crazy Puzzles Book
Everything® Kids' Dinosaurs Book
Everything® Kids' Gross Jokes Book
Everything® Kids' Gross Puzzle and
    Activity Book
Everything® Kids' Halloween Puzzle
    & Activity Book
Everything® Kids' Hidden Pictures Book
Everything® Kids' Joke Book
Everything® Kids' Knock Knock Book
Everything® Kids' Math Puzzles Book
Everything® Kids' Mazes Book
Everything® Kids' Money Book
Everything® Kids' Nature Book
Everything® Kids' Puzzle Book
Everything® Kids' Riddles & Brain Teasers Book
Everything® Kids' Science Experiments Book
Everything® Kids' Sharks Book
Everything® Kids' Soccer Book
Everything® Kids' Travel Activity Book

KIDS' STORY BOOKS

Everything® Fairy Tales Book

LANGUAGE

Everything® Conversational Japanese Book
    (with CD), $19.95
Everything® French Phrase Book, $9.95
Everything® French Verb Book, $9.95
Everything® Inglés Book
Everything® Learning French Book
Everything® Learning German Book
Everything® Learning Italian Book
Everything® Learning Latin Book
Everything® Learning Spanish Book
Everything® Sign Language Book
Everything® Spanish Grammar Book
Everything® Spanish Practice Book
    (with CD), $19.95
Everything® Spanish Phrase Book, $9.95
Everything® Spanish Verb Book, $9.95

MUSIC

Everything® Drums Book (with CD), $19.95
Everything® Guitar Book
Everything® Home Recording Book
Everything® Playing Piano and Keyboards
    Book
Everything® Reading Music Book (with CD),
    $19.95
Everything® Rock & Blues Guitar Book
    (with CD), $19.95
Everything® Songwriting Book

NEW AGE

Everything® Astrology Book, 2nd Ed.
Everything® Dreams Book, 2nd Ed.
Everything® Ghost Book
Everything® Love Signs Book, $9.95
Everything® Numerology Book
Everything® Paganism Book
Everything® Palmistry Book
Everything® Psychic Book
Everything® Reiki Book
Everything® Tarot Book
Everything® Wicca and Witchcraft Book

PARENTING

Everything® Baby Names Book
Everything® Baby Shower Book
Everything® Baby's First Food Book
Everything® Baby's First Year Book
Everything® Birthing Book
Everything® Breastfeeding Book
Everything® Father-to-Be Book
Everything® Father's First Year Book
Everything® Get Ready for Baby Book
Everything® Get Your Baby to Sleep Book,
    $9.95
Everything® Getting Pregnant Book
Everything® Homeschooling Book
Everything® Mother's First Year Book
Everything® Parent's Guide to Children
    and Divorce
Everything® Parent's Guide to Children
    with ADD/ADHD
Everything® Parent's Guide to Children
    with Asperger's Syndrome
Everything® Parent's Guide to Children
    with Autism
Everything® Parent's Guide to Children with
    Bipolar Disorder
Everything® Parent's Guide to Children
    with Dyslexia
Everything® Parent's Guide to Positive
    Discipline
Everything® Parent's Guide to Raising a
    Successful Child
Everything® Parent's Guide to Tantrums
Everything® Parent's Guide to the Overweight
    Child
Everything® Parent's Guide to the Strong-
    Willed Child
Everything® Parenting a Teenager Book
Everything® Potty Training Book, $9.95
Everything® Pregnancy Book, 2nd Ed.
Everything® Pregnancy Fitness Book
Everything® Pregnancy Nutrition Book
Everything® Pregnancy Organizer, $15.00
Everything® Toddler Book
Everything® Tween Book
Everything® Twins, Triplets, and More Book

All Everything® books are priced at $12.95 or $14.95, unless otherwise stated. Prices subject to change without notice.

PETS

Everything® Cat Book
Everything® Dachshund Book
Everything® Dog Book
Everything® Dog Health Book
Everything® Dog Training and Tricks Book
Everything® German Shepherd Book
Everything® Golden Retriever Book
Everything® Horse Book
Everything® Horseback Riding Book
Everything® Labrador Retriever Book
Everything® Poodle Book
Everything® Pug Book
Everything® Puppy Book
Everything® Rottweiler Book
Everything® Small Dogs Book
Everything® Tropical Fish Book
Everything® Yorkshire Terrier Book

REFERENCE

Everything® Car Care Book
Everything® Classical Mythology Book
Everything® Computer Book
Everything® Divorce Book
Everything® Einstein Book
Everything® Etiquette Book, 2nd Ed.
Everything® Inventions and Patents Book
Everything® Mafia Book
Everything® Philosophy Book
Everything® Psychology Book
Everything® Shakespeare Book

RELIGION

Everything® Angels Book
Everything® Bible Book
Everything® Buddhism Book
Everything® Catholicism Book
Everything® Christianity Book
Everything® Jewish History & Heritage Book
Everything® Judaism Book
Everything® Koran Book
Everything® Prayer Book
Everything® Saints Book

Everything® Torah Book
Everything® Understanding Islam Book
Everything® World's Religions Book
Everything® Zen Book

SCHOOL & CAREERS

Everything® Alternative Careers Book
Everything® College Survival Book, 2nd Ed.
Everything® Cover Letter Book, 2nd Ed.
Everything® Get-a-Job Book
Everything® Guide to Starting and Running a Restaurant
Everything® Job Interview Book
Everything® New Teacher Book
Everything® Online Job Search Book
Everything® Paying for College Book
Everything® Practice Interview Book
Everything® Resume Book, 2nd Ed.
Everything® Study Book

SELF-HELP

Everything® Dating Book, 2nd Ed.
Everything® Great Sex Book
Everything® Kama Sutra Book
Everything® Self-Esteem Book

SPORTS & FITNESS

Everything® Fishing Book
Everything® Golf Instruction Book
Everything® Pilates Book
Everything® Running Book
Everything® Total Fitness Book
Everything® Weight Training Book
Everything® Yoga Book

TRAVEL

Everything® Family Guide to Hawaii
Everything® Family Guide to Las Vegas, 2nd Ed.
Everything® Family Guide to New York City, 2nd Ed.
Everything® Family Guide to RV Travel & Campgrounds

Everything® Family Guide to the Walt Disney World Resort®, Universal Studios®, and Greater Orlando, 4th Ed.
Everything® Family Guide to Cruise Vacations
Everything® Family Guide to the Caribbean
Everything® Family Guide to Washington D.C., 2nd Ed.
Everything® Guide to New England
Everything® Travel Guide to the Disneyland Resort®, California Adventure®, Universal Studios®, and the Anaheim Area

WEDDINGS

Everything® Bachelorette Party Book, $9.95
Everything® Bridesmaid Book, $9.95
Everything® Elopement Book, $9.95
Everything® Father of the Bride Book, $9.95
Everything® Groom Book, $9.95
Everything® Mother of the Bride Book, $9.95
Everything® Outdoor Wedding Book
Everything® Wedding Book, 3rd Ed.
Everything® Wedding Checklist, $9.95
Everything® Wedding Etiquette Book, $9.95
Everything® Wedding Organizer, $15.00
Everything® Wedding Shower Book, $9.95
Everything® Wedding Vows Book, $9.95
Everything® Weddings on a Budget Book, $9.95

WRITING

Everything® Creative Writing Book
Everything® Get Published Book
Everything® Grammar and Style Book
Everything® Guide to Writing a Book Proposal
Everything® Guide to Writing a Novel
Everything® Guide to Writing Children's Books
Everything® Guide to Writing Research Papers
Everything® Screenwriting Book
Everything® Writing Poetry Book
Everything® Writing Well Book